The New Mexico Book of

Witches

The New Mexico Book of

Witches

John LeMay

Copyright © 2023 John LeMay. Published by Bicep Books, Roswell, New Mexico.

Front cover painting: Eanger Irving Couse (1866-1936) *Taos Pueblo, Moonlight* ca. 1935.
Back cover photo of the "Oldest House" by Donna Blake Birchell.

Printed in the United States of America

LeMay, John.
The New Mexico Book of Witches/John LeMay
ISBN 978-1-953221-24-7
New Mexico—Spanish Folklore

For the fine folks
of the Spooks, Creeps, & Assorted Devilry podcast.

Table of Contents

ACKNOWLEDGMENTS

This book stands not upon the shoulders of witches, but of giants. I speak of giants in the field of early day history, like Charles Lummis, Adolph Bandelier, Aurelio M. Espinosa, and many others who first collected the strange history of the Land of Enchantment. By the same token, I must express my gratitude to more modern historians, like Marc Simmons, whose *Witchcraft in the Southwest* was a huge influence on this book. *The Witches of Abiquiu* by Malcolm Ebright and Rick Hendricks was another big inspiration, along with the New Mexico state historian Robert Martinez's presentation on witchcraft in this state. Then there are authors like Nasario García, Ray John de Aragón, and Antonio R. Garcez, who collected many tales firsthand as well, which I quote from often in this book. I would also like to thank my good friend, co-author, and fellow historical adventurer, Donna Blake Birchell. Kathleen Dull, DCA at New Mexico History Museum, was also very helpful in obtaining many documents from the WPA New Mexico Collection from the Fray Angélico Chávez History Library in Santa Fe. Lastly, a big thank you to Tasha Olive for your proofreading skills!

Map of New Mexico Territory c.1857.

INTRODUCTION
New Mexico, the Land of Bewitchment

There are not now nearly as many witches in New Mexico as there were a few years ago, but there are enough —if popular belief is accepted.
—Charles F. Lummis, A New Mexico David

There was a time in New Mexico's past when witches seemed to hide behind every hacienda and lurk in every dark corner. That shadow seen slinking across the wall of an adobe courtyard? A witch on her nightly prowl, either in the form of a black cat or a mangy coyote. That stroke that poor Señor Garcia suffered last week? Well, it wasn't brought about by old age. He was bewitched, most likely by the old woman who lives alone on the outskirts of the village! And that fireball seen last night streaking over the mountains? It was probably a sorcerer on their way to a witches' sabbat in some haunted arroyo.

But aren't witches usually old women in pointy hats that cast spells and ride brooms? And they never turn into animals. That's a werewolf's business, isn't it? Not exactly, and certainly not in New Mexico. The idea of witches flying about on brooms, for instance, originated in an old illustration in Martin Le Franc's *Le Champions des Dames* in 1451. However, the woman riding the broom in the illustration wasn't exactly a witch. The woman was actually a member of the Waldensians, a subset of Christianity from the 12th century that the Catholic Church considered to be heretical. This was all due to the fact that women of that order could be priests and perform sacraments. As such, they were deemed witches. This illustration was later conjoined with an old pagan fertility rite wherein farmers would ride anything from pitchforks to poles to brooms as they danced in the moonlight. Somehow, this was supposed to make their crops grow. When they jumped into the air on whatever object they were riding, the hope was that the crop would also grow that high. Somehow the depiction of the Waldensians and this rite were conglomerated into the idea of witches riding broomsticks, which was cemented in our modern culture in the 1939 film adaptation of *The Wizard of Oz* and reemphasized in movies like *Hocus Pocus* (1993).

New Mexico witches don't have a great deal in common with either the Wicked Witch of the West or the Sanderson Sisters of *Hocus Pocus*, though. Just as New Mexico is very different from all the other 49 states in North America, so, too, are New Mexico's witches. As stated before, they don't ride brooms. Most of the time they ride fireballs in addition to pumpkins, gourds, and even eggs.[1] And unlike the European werewolf, they can transform into any animal they choose, from a tiny rat to an owl to a wolf. Finally, whereas most of the world has witches and warlocks, New Mexico has *brujas* and *brujos*, the latter masculine and the former feminine.

In their July 1, 1888 edition, the *Journal of American Folklore* ran a story not on past superstitions but on the current witchcraft beliefs of the territory of New Mexico:

Our witchology is full, detailed, and graphic. Every paisano in New Mexico can tell you their strange habits, their marvellous powers, and their baleful deeds. They never injure the dumb animals, but woe to the human being who incurs their displeasure! Few, indeed, are bold enough to brave their wrath. If a witch asks for food, wood, clothing, or anything else, none dare say her nay. Nor dare any one eat what a witch proffers; for, if he do, some animal, alive and gnawing, will form in his stomach. By night, dressed in strange animal shapes, they fly abroad to hold witch meetings in the mountains, or to wreak their evil wills. In a dark night you may see them flying through the sky like so many balls of fire, and there are comparatively few Mexicans in the territory who have not seen this weird sight.

12

Brujas, not to be confused with *curanderas* (folk healers), were capable of many strange things. In addition to shapeshifting into animals or objects, they could even turn men into women or vice versa. And, if not turning into an animal themselves, they might curse one of their victims by transforming them into a dog. Any ailment may have been brought on by a witch, no matter how great or small. But their powers extended far beyond sickness and shapeshifting. "People swore they had seen the brujas turn a picture upside down just by looking at it, or make a pot boil by pointing a finger at it, or throw a rose through a windowpane without breaking the glass," Jack Kutz wrote in *Mysteries & Miracles of New Mexico*.[2] Similarly, one of the interviewees in *Tales of Witchcraft and the Supernatural in the Pecos Valley* claimed she knew a brujo who could make his guitar play by itself while it was still hanging on the wall.

> ## Witch Scare Stirs Town; Hexer Held
>
> **Accused Man's Wife and Cousin Accuse Him of "Hexing" Them During Sleep**
>
> MORA, N. M., Jan. 1.—(P)—A witch scare inflamed this little Sangre de Cristo mountain hamlet.
>
> Sporadic fears of the Spanish-speaking folk have reached the courts and state police were ordered to investigate a weird story accusing Erelino Espinosa, knwon locally as "The Frog Man," of witchcraft.
>
> Crowds of mountain people thronged the courtyard while Espinosa was arraigned. He was held for preliminary hearing January 8 on charges of mayhem. Acquaintances quickly provided him $1,000 bond.
>
> Complaining witnesses, Espinosa's wife and her cousin, accused him of "hexing" them as they slept Christmas night.
>
> R. E. Cooper, assistant district attorney, recounted this story from the testimony:

Turn of the century folklorist Aurelio M. Espinosa laid it all out rather well in a 1910 piece for the *Journal of American Folklore* entitled "New-Mexican Spanish Folk-Lore":

A witch may have a person under the influence of some evil, illness, or even vice, at will. The unfortunate individual who is beset by witches is also pursued and molested by devils and other evil spirits who help the witches. The general name for any evil or harm caused by a witch is, in New Mexico, *maleficio* ("spell, enchantment, harm"), and the verb is *maleficiar* ("to do harm, to bewitch"). *Estar maleficiau* ("to be under the spell or influence of a witch") is the greatest of evils, and hard to overcome. A witch, however, may be compelled by physical torture to raise the spell or cease doing

13

harm; but this method is not advisable, since sooner or later the witch will again take revenge.[3]

Witchcraft in the Southwest was a very serious issue from southern Colorado and northern New Mexico all the way down to Old Mexico. In the rural Mexican state of Tlaxcala, hundreds of death certificates were submitted for infants citing their cause of death as "sucked by the witch"—drained of blood like a vampire. This occurred not in the days of the Old West or Colonial Spain, but the 20th century. In the mid-1950s and again in the early 1960s, the Mexican government investigated this epidemic of vampiric witchcraft until it mysteriously faded away. New Mexico wasn't quite as extreme as Mexico in that regard, but here, too, tales of witchcraft extended well into the 20th century. For instance, there is the story of two rural New Mexicans from the village of La Manga, Josefa and Maggie, who got into a fight. One night as Josefa was driving in her car on the highway, a cow suddenly trampled in front of her and she had a wreck. At the hospital, Josefa swore that Maggie was a witch who had turned herself into a cow to cause the accident. In 1943, former Santa Fe archivist Herbert O. Brayer was giving a talk at the Western Folklore conference in Denver, Colorado, and stunned his listeners when he revealed that "Just as recently as 1940 a grand jury indicted a man in Mora County (Northern New Mexico) on a charge of witchcraft because his wife claimed he turned into a frog and bit her. The trial judge changed the charge to 'disorderly conduct' but went ahead and tried the man on his wife's testimony that he had turned into a frog."[4] Brayer also let slip that drug stores in Santa Fe were currently doing "big business" selling love potions—mixtures of powdered milk, sugar, and coloring. Brayer's comments caused quite a stir, and while the so-called "frog man" was indeed taken to court, the claims of love potions for sale in Santa Fe were disdainfully contested by the druggists in a rebuttal article. Similarly, historian Wesley R. Hurt Jr. mentioned there being an old woman reputed to be a witch in Albuquerque's suburbs selling love potions that very same year. In neighboring Arizona, in 1953, a rancher was put on trial for shooting a woman dead who he suspected of being a witch who caused his wife to go blind.

Of course, by the 1950s, the heyday of the witches was long over, and the belief lingered in only certain portions of the Southwest. But one hundred years ago it was a different story. American historian and explorer Charles Lummis was astounded when he first came to New Mexico Territory and saw how superstitious it was. "I thought to have settled in New Mexico, U.S.A.; but it seemed that I had moved into another world and into the century before last," he remembered.[5] Lummis began collecting witch tales on his odyssey across the territory, and much of our information on 19th century New Mexico witchcraft comes from his writings. For instance, Lummis explained that to achieve the power of flight, witches needed to do only two things. First, they "rub a magical ointment onto whatever object they wish to ride, in the case of New Mexico those often being a pumpkin, gourd, or an egg."[6] After that, they say a special incantation in Spanish, that being, "Without God and without the Virgin Mary,"[7] and then "they rise into the air and sail away."[8] In his book *Mesa, Cañon and Pueblo*, he elaborated:

Mexican witches do not fly about on broomsticks, like those in whom our forefathers believed, but in an even more remarkable fashion. By day they are plain, commonplace people, but at night they take the shapes of dogs, cats, rats, or other animals, and sally forth to witch meetings in the mountains, or to prowl about the houses of those they dislike. So when the average Mexican sees a strange cat or dog about his home at night he feels a horror which seems out of place in a man who has proved his courage in bloody Indian wars and all the perils of the frontier.[9]

15

Lummis wasn't exaggerating, as witches were greatly feared amongst all native New Mexicans. In fact, just one look from a witch, called the *mal de ojo*, or evil eye, was enough to strike one ill. Infants especially were susceptible to the evil eye, so much so that it was considered impolite to stare too long at a baby for fear the parent might think you were casting a spell on it.[10] As in Europe, garlic hung around an infant's neck was used to ward off the evil eye. However, if one were looking for a more distinctly New Mexican herb, a portion of the wild gourd *calavacia* could be carried around by adults or infants alike to ward off witchcraft, as could a burnt portion of the *gachana*, which had to be carried in one's pocket.

When someone was bewitched, it was called *brujeria* and there were many ways in which a person could become bewitched. One of the most common ways to become bewitched was by ingesting food or drink from a witch prepared with herbal magic.[11] If you had been bewitched with food, according to one woman, you needed to "throw out the first spoonful, rub it with your right foot, and you are safe."[12] However, the more cautious would leave out food brought by an alleged witch for three days, after which it was said to turn into worms, while another folk custom claimed that only the first bite of bewitched food was harmful. Therefore, if one carved out a chunk of it and threw it away, the rest of the food might be safe to eat.

There were also many tales of bewitched people finding foreign objects in their bodies, often through means of something called "shooting sorcery" among the Native American population.[13] Though typically shooting sorcery involved cursed bone darts being shot into a victim, foreign objects could also magically materialize within a person's body. Anything from fruit to stones to quills to animals were allegedly removed from bewitched people via strange curing rituals. The files of the Federal Writer's Project contained an interview with an Albuquerque woman, Mrs. Rufujio Avilla, who recalled several instances of this. Once, when she went to visit a friend who was ill, she met a "brujo" from Isleta who had been called in to treat her friend via a magical ointment. Avilla claimed,

> He put a little of this ointment on the arm of the sick woman and started to rub the arm. It wasn't long before he pulled a stone out of her arm— a stone almost as big as a pearl. And it wasn't long after that the woman got well again. I was there and I saw this man do this.[14]

16

PIEDRA IMAN, THE LODESTONE

Due to their natural magnetic abilities, lodestones, made up of chunks of the mineral magnetite, were often regarded as magic talismans in the old world. This tradition made its way to New Mexico. Called the *Piedra Iman*, or magnetic stone, in New Mexico, it could be used by witches to increase their powers. Or, it could also be kept by non-witches as a form of protection against them. Cleofas M. Jaramillo wrote of this tradition in *Shadows of the Past*, where she said that in the Arroyo Hondo region graduates of witchcraft, which she called *ambularias*, were granted "unlimited powers" by possessing such a stone. Through the *Piedra Iman* they could be all-seeing and also transform into any shape they wished.[15] However, if a witch lost the stone or if it was stolen, they would lose their minds and disintegrate into a skeleton. As people in the old world believed the stone to be alive, they felt they had to feed it with needles, iron particles, and water every Friday (the day that witches were at their most powerful). This strange tradition dates back to Roman times, where the Romans believed the stone possessed life and needed to be fed.

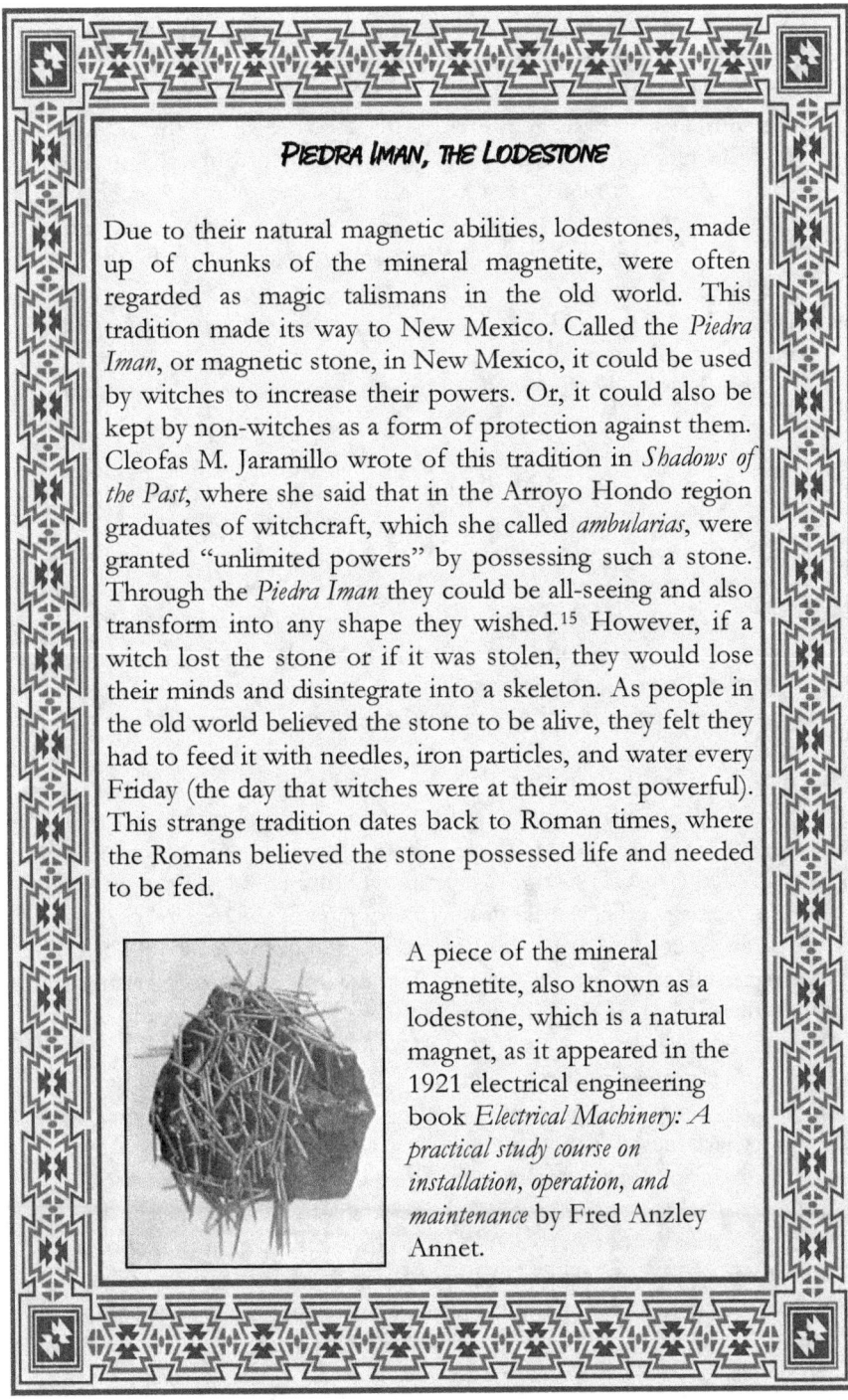

A piece of the mineral magnetite, also known as a lodestone, which is a natural magnet, as it appeared in the 1921 electrical engineering book *Electrical Machinery: A practical study course on installation, operation, and maintenance* by Fred Anzley Annet.

Avilla continued that on a second incident in 1905 she witnessed a curandero pull an apple from a sick woman's body, and she herself claimed to have used the ointment to remove several quills from an ailing Albuquerque woman. Later, Avilla used the ointment given to her by the curandero to remove a very small chick from a sick infant in San Jose. A similar story was related by a schoolteacher in Chimayo, Emilia A. Pacheco. She told of a Santa Cruz curandero named Juan Lujan who came to Chimayo to treat a bewitched boy. From his body, he removed several crickets. Stranger yet, a folktale uncovered by Aurelio M. Espinosa had an entire owl being removed from a woman's stomach.

In his 1910 article, "New-Mexican Spanish Folk-Lore," Espinosa recorded that

A certain woman suffered great pain in the stomach, and it was feared that she was *maleficiada*. Some living creature was felt to move about within her stomach; and her relatives became alarmed, and attributed the trouble to an old woman who was suspected of being a witch. She was purposely called in to visit the sick one as a *curandera* ("popular doctor"); and, fearing violence, she approached the *maleficiada* and instantly caused a large owl - the cause of her illness - to come out of her stomach.[16]

In addition to shooting sorcery, something akin to voodoo magic was also common wherein an effigy or doll of a person was created, often called *monos*. The targeted victim would then be pricked, often with a cactus needle, on the doll to cause pain in the desired part of the body. According to a source from La Manga, witches would bury the accursed items or dolls in holes. If the witch failed to disenchant their victims before they died, it was feared that person would stay bewitched forever.

Another strange form of bewitchment was the theft of the heart, mostly among the Pueblos. Not quite as dramatic as the heart-ripping dark magic of the Thugee in *Indiana Jones in the Temple of Doom*, in this case, an object is stolen from the victim which then represents the person's heart in some way. What exactly they steal isn't specified in any of the sources I've seen. Nor do the medicine men steal back the stolen object to heal the sick exactly. Instead, they steal an object representing the victim's heart from the witch, which is usually a single kernel of corn wrapped in the center of a bundle of rags. The kernel is given to the sick to swallow by the medicine man who

18

fought the witch to retrieve it, and thus their heart is returned to them.

But how did one tell who the witch might be? Naturally, there were many methods to test a witch, which we will get into later, but as for one simple observational skill, one way "of determining if a woman is a witch or not is to spy her while sleeping," wrote Aurelio Espinosa, "for all witches sleep with their eyes open."[17] It was also a unanimously accepted belief that most witches were lonely recluses who lived alone. If owls often congregated near their home, or if balls of fire were seen hovering about, then it was certainly the abode of a witch. Someone suffering a peculiar injury was also likely a witch. The most common witch-tale in all of New Mexico was that of someone shooting at a dog or owl in the night, only to find a suspected witch with a wound the next morning.

For instance, the Chimayo area had a midwife thought to be a witch for years due to the fact that she was often seen out late at night with another group of strange women. To locals, her witchy-nature was seemingly confirmed when she suddenly began wearing a white shawl bandaged around her head. Only the night before a man had shot at an owl hanging around his chicken coop. Supposedly, beneath the shawl was a hole in the old woman's head said to come from the shotgun blast when she was an owl.[18]

Similarly, in *Tales of Witchcraft and the Supernatural in the Pecos Valley*, Celia Benavídez told a story of how her husband and her uncle were coming home from work in a horse-drawn wagon when they stopped to sleep for the night near Tecolote. There they witnessed a fireball heading for the village and the uncle took out his rifle and shot at it. Upon striking the fireball, it disintegrated.[19] When they arrived in Tecolote, they heard news that last night a woman fell from her ladder and eventually died from her injuries. They assumed it must have been the witch, and the ladder story was just her excuse.

Similarly, sometimes it was difficult to tell if someone was suffering a routine illness, such as having caught the common cold, or if they were suffering a true case of bewitchment. One unique way to tell if someone had been bewitched was to go to one of New Mexico's hot springs. If the afflicted set foot into the water and all was normal, they had a simple illness. If they stepped into the springs and the water boiled, then they were bewitched. (Other stories said the springs would expel them if they so much as tried to dip a toe into them.)

Curiously, in New Mexico, afflictions caused by witchcraft were sometimes only suffered on Tuesdays and Fridays.[20] Fridays were the worst days of all. One shouldn't even speak of witches on Fridays, for on that day they could hear all that was said about them through supernatural means.[21] Nor did New Mexico witches observe traditional witch holidays including February 2nd, the eve of May 1st, August 1st, and October 31st. New Mexico witches seemed ready to gather at any time.

Common witch stories prevalent all the way from Bernalillo, New Mexico, to San Elizario, Texas, usually told of a person either willingly or accidentally observing a gathering of witches in the night. The commonalities in all accounts described a witches' sabbat occurring in some remote location, usually in a cave, arroyo, or sometimes in an old, abandoned building within the confines of certain villages. The ceremony would begin at sundown and last until sunrise with three distinct rituals: kissing a goat's tail, being kissed by a snake, and feasting on a corpse. One of the most popular tales had a young man, often from northern New Mexico, who was curious about mysterious goings on with his aunt and uncle. Specifically, he noticed they would ride off for parts unknown on certain nights. On one such night, he hid beneath their buggy and secretly accompanied them to their mysterious destination. The trip seemed almost supernatural as the wagon traveled at an unbelievable speed. The landscape in which he found himself also seemed foreign to New Mexico, as it was populated by cinnamon trees of all things.

The man's aunt and uncle stopped the buggy and dismounted it to head for a house concealed within the walls of a draw. The young man silently followed and peeked through the window. Inside the house, he saw a gathering of witches, and the proceedings weren't for the faint of heart. First, a large billy goat was brought into the room, with each witch kissing it on the tail (symbolic of the pagan custom of kissing the devil's hind quarters). Next came a huge snake that slithered into the room to grant knowledge either by the revelers kissing its tongue or the snake kissing theirs—the particulars deviated depending on who told the tale. Lastly, four men dressed in all black came into the room carrying a coffin.[22] They sat it on the floor, and in no time, the witches were upon it to feast on the corpse within. The man ran back to his aunt and uncle's buggy and waited for them to depart. However, according to variations of such stories, the man could have called out to God above and would have found himself magically transported away.[23] That was another common folktale, such as the story of a Bernalillo man who wished to become a witch. He knew a brujo from Mexico in his area, one who was said to have studied from something called *El Libro Negro*, or the Black

20

Book, to learn the dark arts. The brujo agreed to teach the Bernalillo man the art of witchcraft himself, and suddenly sprouted wings.[24] The brujo flew the man to a secret witch meeting with the same three ceremonies: the kissing of the goat's tail, the kissing of the serpent, and the feast upon the corpse. The man completed the first two rituals, but the third was too much for him, and he cried out to God to help him. Instantly, he found himself in the middle of the desert and began his two-day journey back home. A variation of this same story, only with a woman, was prevalent in San Elizario, Texas.

Another story told of a young man named Matias in the late 1890s. As he rode through the village of Arroyo Seco on horseback late one night, he spied a light emanating from a rundown old building along the main plaza. He approached the building out of curiosity and saw revelers dancing away the night through a broken window. Not understanding that this was a witches' sabbat, he went to the front door in hopes of joining in. When he did so, the room darkened and became quiet as if what he had seen earlier was an illusion. As a feeling of dread overcame him, he dashed back to his horse to ride away. Looking back, he saw that the lights had come back on and the dancing had resumed. It was then that he knew he had escaped a gathering of witches.

CAVE OF THE WITCHES

Even Adolph Bandelier wrote of witches during his travels. In a footnote in *Final Report of Investigations Among the Indians of the Southwestern United States, Carried on Mainly in the Years from 1880 to 1885* on page 514, he described a supposed witch cave in New Mexico:

Artificial caves are said to exist in some of the rocks in the hills visible from Cochiti. In the lower portions of the Canada is a low cliff famous in witchcraft stories. The people of Cochiti pretend that the wizards and witches meet there on certain nights, assembling at the cliff in the shape of owls, turkey-buzzards, and crows. At a signal the rock opens, displaying a brilliantly lighted cavity. Forthwith the animal shapes disappear, and the wicked sorcerers resume their human appearance and enter the cavern to carouse till daylight.

In addition to these initiation rituals, it was also sometimes thought that a person could be born a witch. In Ruth Laughlin Barker's "New Mexico Witch Tales," one informant stated, "It is unfortunate for a family to have a witch. Perhaps all the other children will be good, but one will show that she knows dark magic even when she is a child. Yes, it is hard for a family to have a witch."[25] This was also true of the Tlahuelpuchi, a bloodsucking witch from Tlaxcala, Mexico. Though it had all the traits of a vampire, the Tlahuelpuchi could not actually turn anyone into another Tlahuelpuchi. One was simply born that way or they weren't. More common, though, were those who voluntarily became witches through devilish indoctrinations. According to folklore, a witch in training would go to a hidden cave somewhere in the mountains where they would learn the dark arts. In the cave they would learn to cast spells, bewitch people, and how to turn into animals and objects alike. In terms of animals, it was said that they would learn to transform into doves, owls, and dogs in that order. One school was said to be overseen by the Devil himself within a cave near Peña Blanca, fifty miles north of Albuquerque. Supposedly, after the Devil had finished his works there, the cave vanished forever.

NEW MEXICO WITCHES AND BLACK CATS

New Mexican witches believed that a black cat possessed an invisible bone connected to the dark forces. A witch would boil a black cat in her cauldron until nothing remained but the bones. Then, she would inspect them one by one in a mirror. Whichever bone cast no reflection, much like a vampire, was the special "invisible" bone.

Of course, there were also many ways to protect oneself from a witch. Much like in the horror movies of old, holy water could be used to either immobilize or remove a witch's powers. Crosses were also used to ward off evil, but with Southwest flourishes. Pack mule drivers would make crosses out of cornmeal on each mule's shoulder, for instance, so that no one bewitched them on their journeys across the deserts and prairies. Crucifixes were placed above doorways, too. Crosses made of needles were particularly popular and were usually sat atop doorways with a broom hidden behind the door.[26] An alteration from the village of La Manga stated that a cross formed out of salt or pine was the best method. Yet another stated that the cross should be made out of two broom straws, rather than with needles. In either case, a witch could not pass through such an opening unless someone else or a dog preceded them, or until the needles were removed.[27] Speaking of dogs, there was also a strange custom that one bitten by a dog would sometimes be invulnerable to a witch's harm![28]

One way a witch may be confronted was to make a ring of salt around the suspected witch's home. One must also make the sign of the cross while throwing salt at an owl. A strange remedy for *suto*, or a state of terror brought on by a witch, was to take a bit of dust or earth from four corners of a graveyard. Then, you would place the dust on a piece of red flannel, then boil it along with your mother's wedding ring. When finished, the healer would make the sign of the cross over the water and then give it to the afflicted to drink.

Another witch repellent unique to New Mexico was revealed by Aurelio Espinosa in "New-Mexican Spanish Folk-Lore": "The cores of red peppers burned on Fridays will keep away the witches and their evil doings. Another preventive is to urinate in the direction of their homes."[29]

> Occasionally, New Mexico witches breathed fire. A humorous account from Albuquerque in the 1930s told of a mysterious apple thief. "One day, my father, he hid in the bushes by our apple trees to see who was stealing our apples," the man claimed. "He saw that old lady up in the apple tree, and just as he was going to jell at her, she turned around and fire came out of her mouth."[30]

As with vampires and werewolves, some considered a silver bullet to be able to kill a witch, though typically a bullet with a cross etched onto it worked best. According to Charles Lummis in *Some Strange Corners of Our Country*, a medicine man would kill a witch by shooting them with an arrow through their left side so that it protruded out the right. (No explanation was given as to why, that's just the way that it was.)[31]

If a fireball[32] was seen floating through the countryside, one needed only to draw a circle in the earthen road and the witch would eventually be drawn to it and become trapped. The ball of light would turn back into a human by morning, and the witch could not leave the circle until someone helped them out of it. Actually, that method may only have worked if you happened to be named Juan or Juana. You see, men by the name of John or Juan, or Juana in the case of a woman, had special anointing to deal with witches, as they were named after John the Baptist.[33] Some say that witches won't so much as enter a home where a Juan or a Juana lurks.

Lummis again explained it best in his book *A New Mexico David*:

Any one named Juan (John) can catch a witch by going through a curious rigmarole. He draws a large circle on the ground, seats himself inside it, turns his shirt wrong side out, and cries, "In the name of God I call thee, bruja," and straightway whatever witch is near must fall helpless inside his circle. Every one who lives here can tell you that a Juan has this power; but he seldom uses it, for he knows that if he does so all the witches in the country will fall upon him and beat him mercilessly to death.[34]

TWO JUANS ARE BETTER THAN JUAN

An amusing account comes from El Lano, located a little ways above Rancho de Taos, which was said to be a hotspot for witches to gather at night. Two young men named Juan laid in wait, each holding a stick and watching for the little fireballs they knew to be traveling witches. When they would see one, they would swiftly draw a circle in the earth with their stick, catching one witch after another. Soon a plethora of old women sat in the circles—some say a dozen or even more—waiting to be released. Juan and Juan identified each, taking their name, and then set them free. Talk about catch and release!

In another discourse by Lummis, he better specified that the circle had to be nine feet in circumference. Alternatively, Juan might also call out, "*Venga bruja!*" or, "Come witch!" (Obviously, there were many variations.) The source of Lummis's information predominantly came from a letter by a prominent New Mexico citizen, Amado Chaves, which detailed the ritual for Lummis in 1897:

> Have I ever told you how we used to catch witches in New Mexico when I was young? We would mark a large circle on the ground, as big as a room, and in the center set a man by the name of Juan with his shirt inside out. We did this on a dark night and invariably any witch who was near got into the circle and was caught. Sometime she would be in the shape of a fox, coyote, or black cat, but once inside the circle she became an old woman again.[35]

Aurelio Espinosa had his own variation on the circle ritual in that the Juan in question had to make "with his foot a circle around the witch."[36] Yet another variation on this ritual was to be performed in the specific instance that a witch had entered one's home in the form of an animal. In that case, Juan was to draw a circle near the doorway. Then he was to remove all his clothing, not just his shirt, and put it back on inside out before calling the witch. At that point, the invading animal would disappear, and the witch would be found dead in her home the next morning.

On the note of animal transformations, according to Stith Thompson's *Motif-Index of Folk-Literature*, witches could assume the forms of 13 different animals, including horses, cats, dogs, rabbits, wolves, foxes, bears, mice, hens, ducks, crows, flies, and toads. In New Mexico, there were seven known instances of the thirteen, but cats and owls were always the most common. Many New Mexican villages had a tradition where, if an owl was heard hooting outside the house or on the roof, a resident was to go outside and shout, "*Mañana vendrás por sal.*" ("Tomorrow you will come for salt.") Whoever arrived at the abode the next day to ask to borrow something, whether it be salt or not, was suspected of being the witch.

And, finally, as with exorcisms, witches could be rebuked in the name of Jesus Christ or the saints. As Lummis related in *A New Mexico David,*

25

The sign of the cross, or the spoken name of God or one of the saints, stops a witch at once. I know people here who assert that they were being carried on a witch's back, thousands of miles a minute, to some distant destination; but that when they became alarmed, and cried, "God save me!" they instantly fell hundreds of feet without being hurt and found themselves alone in a great wilderness.[37]

As stated earlier, witchcraft was still a serious issue in some parts of the state as late as the mid-20th century. In fact, cases of witchcraft in crimes are still reported today. As late as 2016, a Taos man was convicted of murdering a woman he thought had bewitched him.[38] Charles Lummis summed up his chapter, "Three Live Witches," in *A New Mexico David*, with the following, "School and church are gradually killing off these strange and childish superstitions, but they die hard, and it will be many a year before New Mexico will be bereft of her last reputed witch."[39] Over 100 years later, we are still waiting.

Section Notes

[1] Nasario García points out in *Brujerías: Stories of Witchcraft and the Supernatural in the American Southwest and Beyond* that balls of fire are also associated with witches in Nigeria.

[2] Kutz, *Mysteries & Miracles of New Mexico*, p.96.

[3] Espinosa, "New-Mexican Spanish Folk-Lore," *Journal of American Folklore* Vol. 23, No. 90 (Oct. - Dec., 1910), p.397.

[4] "MAN WHO 'TURNED INTO FROG' CITED IN REPORT ON NEW MEXICO WITCHCRAFT BELIEF," *Abilene Reporter News* (July 16, 1943), p. 25.

[5] Lummis, *Some Strange Corners of Our Country*, p.66.

[6] Ibid, p.72.

[7] In Jewish folklore, Lillith, the first witch, did just the opposite. She took flight by uttering the Ineffable Name of God, instead.

[8] Lummis, *Some Strange Corners of Our Country*, p.72.

[9] Lummis, *Mesa, Cañon and Pueblo*, p.350.

[10] To be clear, in Spanish folk belief, it was also possible for a non-witch to accidentally make an infant or any young person ill by staring at them lovingly too long. This rule never applied to the parents from what I can tell, but one young man claimed that a loving stare from his grandmother once made him ill accidentally.

[11] Page 171 of Nasario García's *Brujerías* recounts a Guadalupe family who would periodically find mysterious gifts of food left on their doorstop, notably eggs and suspiciously shiny apples. These "gifts" were always burned rather than eaten.

[12] Bright, "La Brujas," 5-5-7-44ocr. WPA New Mexico Collection, Fray Angélico Chávez History Library, Santa Fe, New Mexico, U.S.A.

[13] Though this often happened to the Spanish population, it may have derived from Apache and Navajo shooting sorcery, in which foreign objects could be shot into the body or magically materialize within them.

[14] Berg, "The Magic Ointmentm" 5-31-6. WPA New Mexico Collection, Fray Angélico Chávez History Library, Santa Fe, New Mexico, U.S.A.

[15] This included stationary objects in addition to animals.

[16] Espinosa, "New-Mexican Spanish Folk-Lore," p.398.

[17] Ibid, p.398.

[18] Usner, *Benigna's Chimayó*, p.57.

[19] It isn't said if any of the bullets were marked with crosses in this case.

[20] Wesley R. Hurt also notes Wednesday as another day a witch ailment may be in effect.

[21] Fridays seemed to be a day of note supernaturally speaking. An infant not cured of the Evil Eye by Friday was not likely to survive.

Sometimes, a Juan or Juana would be called in to spit on someone on Fridays only as a strange type of folk cure.

[22] Though this is always a staple of such tales, in the more fantastic ones the men are living skeletons.

[23] In addition to mentioning God, Christ, or the saints, simply mentioning the holy day of Sunday could also incite a reaction among the witches. This was only found in one folktale, though, about a hunchbacked man who encounters a gathering of witches. As they sing a song mentioning every day of the week but Sunday, the hunchback cries out, "And Sunday, too!" to their dismay.

[24] Perhaps not coincidentally, there is a sometimes-winged variety of witch in Mexico called the Tlahuelpuchi, which was responsible for Tlaxcala's infanticide problem in the mid-20th century.

[25] Barker, "New Mexico Witch Tales," *Tone the Bell Easy*, p. 66.

[26] Occasionally the needles were placed within the hairs of the broomstick.

[27] Yet another variation went that if a needle was used to make the cross and it was laid down flat, the witch could exit the house in a normal manner. If the needle was placed standing up, the witch had to leave through the eye of the needle.

[28] For instance, according to Isidora M. Flores in *Tales of Witchcraft and the Supernatural in the Pecos Valley* on page 43: "If a dog bit you, the witches wouldn't harm you."

[29] Espinosa, "New-Mexican Spanish Folk-Lore," p.399.

[30] Smith-Kromer, "Witchcraft in Ranchos de Albuquerque," WPA 5-5-31. New Mexico Collection, Fray Angélico Chávez History Library, Santa Fe, New Mexico, U.S.A.

[31] On the subject of killing a witch, and though I cannot find this anywhere else, and though it appears in fiction, the knowledgeable Rudolfo Anaya writes in *Bless Me, Ultima* that a witch cannot be buried in a coffin made of pine, pinon or cedar. They must be buried in a coffin weaved of cottonwood branches.

[32] The people of Cochiti Pueblo were also very specific in how they described the witch's fireball. According to them, they were six to twelve inches in diameter and had a black center under the red flames.

[33] Nasario García's notes on page 268 of *Brujerías* states that the names Juan and Juana are considered "magical in Latino communities" and that the specific names of "Juan Bautista, Juan José, and Juan de Dios were also viewed as imbued with special powers."

[34] Lummis, *A New Mexico David*, p.132.

[35] Letter of Amado Chaves to Charles F. Lummis (Santa Fe, December 5, 1897, Southwest Museum Collection, Los Angeles).

[36] Espinosa, "New-Mexican Spanish Folk-Lore," p.399.

[37] Lummis, *A New Mexico David*, p.132.

[38] The woman's burned remains had been found by two hikers on Christmas Day 2014 outside of Carson, NM. The man's cellmate said that he heard him talking about witches and drawing pictures of witch hunts. In this case, the murderer had also cut off the dead woman's hands for some reason, as they were found to be missing from her burned remains. This was yet another detail that the murderer had mentioned to his cellmate which was confirmed when the woman's mutilated body was found.

[39] Lummis, *A New Mexico David*, p.132.

Part I
THE SPANISH PERIOD

The Conquistadors considered the New World to be a land of witchcraft the minute they set foot upon the shores of Central America and observed the customs of the Aztecs in 1519. Though what would later be deemed New Mexico wasn't as bad as the heart-ripping domain of the Aztecs, the customs of the Indians they encountered there seemed like black magic to them as well. While many of the indigenous people's practices were a part of their normal belief system, the native peoples had what they considered witches among them as well. The Apache, for instance, believed in witches that could do great harm through shooting sorcery, while the Navajo spoke of the deadly, shapeshifting skinwalker. The Pueblo Indians, too, feared the deeds of witches, though often the Pueblo medicine men themselves were considered witches by the Spanish. Hearing such tales and observing strange rites, it didn't take long for the Church of New Spain to set up its own inquest in the New World, similar to the Spanish Inquisition, which began in 1478.

By the 1650s, things began to escalate between the Spanish and native peoples that occupied the pueblos. They reached their breaking point in 1675 when four Indians were hanged for witchcraft, another 47 were whipped, and many others were jailed. Among those to be whipped was a medicine man from San Juan Pueblo by the name of Popé. As it turned out, Popé would end up being a driving force in the Pueblo Revolt of 1680. For the next five years after his 1875 imprisonment, Popé began a campaign among the pueblo peoples, even going so far as to call himself *El Demonio*, an emissary of the Devil the Spaniards spoke of so often. Popé essentially became what the Spanish would call a *brujo*, presiding over diabolical rites beneath Taos Pueblo in an underground kiva. To go from one pueblo to the next, Popé was said to either ride or transform into a whirlwind. On August, Friday the 13th, Santa Fe was laid siege to by the united tribes. Years later, some would even claim that the Devil himself, in the form of a black giant, marched through Santa Fe during the attack. Just as the native peoples hoped, the Spanish were driven out of their kingdom, and it would take them nearly twenty years to reclaim what they had lost, with Diego de Vargas marching into Santa Fe unopposed in August of 1692. However, although the Spanish had returned, the witches remained…

MONTEZUMA, GRAND WIZARD OF THE SOUTHWEST

Coronación de Moctezuma II, en el folio.

The land of the Indian is truly the "home of Montezuma." Legend relates that the fires on the mountainsides, lighted one day in seven, are for the second coming of Montezuma. The Indian is always careful to be kind to a stranger, for at one time Montezuma returned in the guise of a beggar; and they turned him away.— Annie Laurie Snorf, Yucca Land: A Collection of the Folklore of New Mexico.

According to the historical record, Emperor Montezuma died sometime in late June of 1520 as Hernan Cortés and his conquistadors sieged Tenochtitlán. Reports of just how he died and on what exact day are disputed, but for certain his reign ended around this time. Some say he was stoned by his own subjects on June 29th, while Franciscan friar Bernardino de Sahagún claimed that Cortés' forces killed the emperor.

Even more mysterious than Montezuma's death was his birth. Most likely he was born in 1466 in Mexico. However, there is a strange tradition that Montezuma was really born somewhere in New Mexico. As J. Frank Dobie put it in *Coronado's Children*, "Various localities of New Mexico claim to be the birthplace of Montezuma and to be now the repository of his hidden treasures;

33

but the claim of Pecos village is most insistent, most famous."[1] While it is true that the Aztecs claimed they hailed from a land to the north and migrated south, this occurred long before Montezuma was born. It is assumed that the Indians heard tales of Montezuma from the Spanish and their servants and made a sort of folk hero out of him, which was later conjoined with the story of the sun god Poheyemo (also called Pose-yemu).[2]

The story went that Montezuma was born either at Pecos Pueblo or at the present-day location of Las Vegas, New Mexico, near the Hot Springs (though the former locale is the more widely accepted one). In short, the story went that Montezuma was a special figure who eventually took the main leadership position at Pecos Pueblo before departing on the wings of an eagle. But how could this be? "No mention is made of Montezuma in Spanish documents on the Southwest of an earlier date than 1664," wrote one of the first great historians of the Southwest, Adolph Bandelier.[3]

However, it wasn't just the Pecos Indians who told tales of Montezuma. So, too, did the Papago Indians of Arizona and northern Mexico. In their stories, Montezuma was even more of a god-man than as portrayed at Pecos, ascending to the sun and slaying monsters. In the *Journal of American Folklore*, it was recorded that the Papago feared Montezuma "because of his powerful magic, with which he could work them much harm."[4]

The Pecos Indians painted a more benevolent picture of Montezuma, conflating his legend with that of the sun god Poheyemo said to be born of a virgin in the pueblo of Pose Uingge (now a large prehistoric ruin near the hot springs twenty miles north of San Juan Pueblo).[5] Poheyemo kept to himself as a boy, scorning the other children to wander the wilderness where he conversed with animals and invisible spirits. When the pueblo *cacique*, or medicine man, passed on unexpectedly, lots were drawn to choose the successor. Poheyemo was chosen through this process, much to the chagrin of the older men. However, Poheyemo soon demonstrated special powers such as the ability to locate abundant game and call down rain from the heavens to water the crops. In no time, he was revered by all. However, the elders at his pueblo eventually angered him and so he traveled south to Pecos Pueblo. There he chose the new name of Montezuma for himself, and the once small pueblo grew into one of the largest settlements in the region. A vision from the Great Spirit instructed Montezuma to take for himself a wife, Malinche, the daughter of the *cacique* at Zuni Pueblo.[6]

For a time, the two ruled like a king and queen to the delight of their subjects. The Great Spirit sent Montezuma a great eagle for he and Malinche to ride upon.[7] Together they flew southward, with new pueblos springing in their wake until finally they arrived at the spot of Tenochtitlán in Mexico.[8] In his wake, Montezuma left the perennial lost treasure in addition to twelve virgins and a sacred flame burning somewhere either in a mountain cave or on a sun altar. If one found the flame, they might attain immortality and unlimited magical powers. Montezuma entrusted twelve virgin daughters of the pueblo leaders to keep the flame lit. If they did, one day he would return. However, one night one of the girls let the flame extinguish, thus explaining why Montezuma never returned.

Years later, pioneers in the 1800s would begin hearing the curious tales of the god-man Montezuma. In *A Visit to the Aboriginal Ruins in the Valley of the Rio Pecos*, Adolph Bandelier noted his own curiosity on the subject:

> What the Indians themselves say of this tale I have not as yet ascertained; but the people of the valley all assert that the people of the pueblo believe in it, that they even affirmed that Montezuma was born at Pecos; that he wore golden shoes, and left for Mexico, where, for the sake of these valuable brogans, he was ruthlessly slaughtered. They further say that, when he left Pecos, he commanded that the holy fire should be kept burning till his return, in testimony whereof the sacred embers were kept aglow till 1840, and then transferred to Jemez.[9]

"I cannot, therefore, attach to the Montezuma tale any historical importance whatever, not even a traditional value," Bandelier concluded in the same discourse.

"The Watch for Montezuma" by Paul Frenzeny and Jules Tavernier as it appeared in *Harper's Weekly* on May 22, 1875.

Pioneer Josiah Gregg likewise took note of Pecos and the legend of Montezuma. He was even astute enough to link Pecos to sun worship, though he was unaware of the myth of Poheyemo:

No other Pueblo appears to have adopted this extraordinary superstition like Pecos, however, they have all held Montezuma to be their perpetual sovereign. It would likewise appear that they all worship the sun; for it is asserted to be their regular practice to turn the face towards the east at sunrise.[10]

Gregg had firsthand knowledge of Pecos Pueblo, having observed even the sacred flame, or a recreation of it, he claimed.

Montezuma would appear with the sun, the deluded Indians were to be seen every clear morning upon the terraced roofs of their houses, attentively watching for the appearance of the 'king of light,' in hopes of seeing him 'cheek by jowl' with their immortal sovereign. I have myself descended into the famous *estujas*, or subterranean vaults, of which there were several in the village, and have beheld this consecrated fire, silently smouldering under a covering of ashes, in the basin of a small altar. Some say that they never lost hope in the final coming of Montezuma until, by some accident or other, or a lack of a sufficiency of warriors to watch it, the fire became extinguished; and that it was this catastrophe that induced them to abandon their villages, as I have before observed.[11]

In addition to the sacred flame, Montezuma also left a darker legacy behind in the form of a gigantic snake, sometimes known as Montezuma's serpent. For many years, tales persisted that the people of Pecos Pueblo kept a giant snake in a cave with a sacred fire, presumably linked to the eternal flame said to grant immortality. This giant rattlesnake was so big that the tribe's elderly were sometimes fed to it, and babies were occasionally given to it as a sacrifice.[12] In other cases, rather than a literal giant snake, Montezuma's serpent was a spectral creature that appeared to grant wisdom if one were to either kiss its tongue or place their head in its open mouth as a sign of their devotion. (This was possibly even tied into the witches' sabbat wherein the practitioners were required to kiss the serpent's tongue to gain wisdom.)

37

How did Montezuma become intertwined with serpents, though? It's possible that along with tales of Montezuma came the stories of the serpent god Quetzalcoatl, who himself departed Mexico on a raft of snakes, promising to return one day to the glory of his followers. The Pecos tales of Montezuma were also no doubt influenced by the teachings of the Catholics, as Montezuma's virgin birth was possibly modeled after the birth of Christ. And upon arriving in Mexico, Montezuma was also tempted by the "Evil One" to worship him, which he refused, similar to Christ's forty-day test in the wilderness where he rebuked the Devil's offers. The idea that Montezuma might one day return also mirrored Christ's promise to return to the Earth one day. Christ, Quetzalcoatl, and Poheyemo are odd bedfellows for certain, and the story of Montezuma represents an interesting milieu of Spaniard, Aztec, and Native American traditions. As to how Montezuma came to North America at all, the answer may lie in the Pueblo Revolt of 1680, to be covered later.

THE WITCH STONE OF TAOS

Taos Pueblo c.1936 by Arthur Rothstein. (Library of Congress)

One of the most famous spots in New Mexico for witches is Rancho de Taos, and it is also home to one of the earliest witch myths in the state. The legend stems from a 17th century friar, Fray Alonso de Benavides, who wrote a speculative history in 1634 relating to the people of Taos Pueblo. His theory tied in with tales from the Aztecs, stating that they had originated far to the north emerging from seven caves, emerging at a place called Aztlán before heading south to Mexico. Benavides speculated that the people split in two, with one half being led by the Devil himself to Mexico, while the other half was lured to present day Taos by a witch. A disgusting monster, she was said to have fangs along with clawed hands, feet, and heels, though otherwise she looked like an old woman. To separate the people from their brethren that had headed south and to mark their boundaries, the witch placed an iron boulder on her head and sank into the ground.

Fray Benavides claimed:

The boulder can be seen by everyone today. I have personally seen it several times. Stamped upon it are the marks of the infernal old woman's claws, feet, and hands, as well as the nails of her hands with which she appeared to have kneaded it as if it were of wax. Her very head with its tangled hair, upon which she had borne the globe, is there stamped. In the judgment of all those who see it, it is believed to weigh more than two hundred quintals, while others think that it weighs more. It is as wide as the largest wagon wheel and must be almost eight spans high. All those who travel back and forth from New Mexico see it. The horses used to shy at it and would not approach nearby, but one of our friars a few years ago exorcised it and said Mass over it, so that the horses lost their fear and today approach it without recoiling, even climbing over it.[13]

Another priest from the same period, Fray Geronimo de Zarate Salmeron, also wrote of it, though he never claimed to have seen it:

It is an ancient tradition among the Indians that a piece of virgin iron which is three leagues from Santa Barbara, half a league away from the road over which the carts that go to New Mexico pass, is a memorial to the coming of the Aztecs to settle this land They say that a demon in the form of an old Indian woman who was very wrinkled brought it on her back. Some feat for an old Indian woman![14]

Of course, no such stone can be seen today, leaving one to wonder if it disappeared or simply never existed to begin with.

CORONADO, THE SEVEN CITIES OF GOLD, AND THE TRICKSTER

Coronado sets out to the north,
oil painting by Frederic Remington, c. 1900

Often forgotten about in the pantheon of New Mexico sorcerers was "the Turk," in fact a Pecos Indian whom the Spaniards called "the Turk" simply because he looked like one. He was discovered by Francisco de Coronado's expedition in 1540 just when hope was beginning to wane that the fabled Seven Cities of Gold resided somewhere in the New World. Historians will recall that Zuni Pueblo, mistaken for Cibola, had been a bust despite the claims of Fray Marcos de Niza and Esteban. But then, at Pecos Pueblo (at the time called Cicuye), was discovered the man called the Turk. He told the Spaniards of a rich land called Quivira to the east.

Though they should have by now been skeptical, they believed the Turk. However, this is because during the Turk's confinement, he demonstrated supernatural powers. Paul Horgan explained in *Conquistadors in North American History* that,

How could the Turk know all such things? He was a man of marvels, and on one occasion he was a man of holy terror, for without ever leaving his cell or talking with anyone else, he told the guard who kept watch on him how many Spaniards had been killed in battle against a certain Indian town in the third week of February, 1541. The guard understood where such powers came from when one day he saw, he swore under oath that he saw, the Turk talking to the

40

Devil who was enclosed in a jug filled with water. The books of learned chroniclers at home were full of creatures like the Turk, who must be dealt with carefully, but whose knowledge must not be dismissed.[15]

It speaks volumes as to the Spaniards' true nature that they didn't execute the Turk for communing with the Devil at once. Apparently, if the Devil could tell them the way to one of the Seven Cities, then it was okay. (It's also worth noting a similarity of sorts between the magic of the Turk, who communed with the Devil via a jug of water, and an accused witch named María De Zamora from the same time period, who summoned the Devil via a basin of water.)

Under the guidance of the Turk, the army set out for Quivira on April 23, 1541. As it turned out, the devious Turk was leading them on a wild goose chase that concluded at Quivira in what is today near Salina, Kansas. It was Zuni Pueblo all over again, as the village before them was comprised of simple grass huts. The Turk confessed that it had all been a ruse from Cicuye to lead the Spaniards away and hope that they died of starvation along the way. But why was the Turk willing to sacrifice himself for this cause? Perhaps he believed the Devil might protect him, or maybe he was happy to play the role of the Trickster to the greedy Spaniards. In any case, he was executed via strangulation before Coronado departed to return to New Mexico.

THE TRIAL OF MARÍA DE ZAMORA

One of the first major witch trials to be held in New Mexico was that of María de Zamora in the early 1600s. Zamora was a native of Mexico, and her husband Bartolomé de Montoya was a soldier who had come to the New World directly from Spain. Both were living in a little village named San Gabriel when 33-year-old Maria was accused of witchcraft in late 1606. Her accuser was none other than her son-in-law, Diego Robledo, a conquistador who had accompanied Vicente de Zaldívar to explore the buffalo plains in 1598.[16] Robledo had recently married Zamora's thirteen-year-old daughter, Lucía, whose loyalties were more so with her new husband than with her mother, apparently.

Upon marrying Lucía, Diego claimed to have learned from his young wife that her mother had given her strange powders with which to poison him. Specifically, she was to administer it

41

...by sprinkling it in his shoes and on his back. And after this the said wife produced some small leaves of a plant and said that her mother had given her those leaves so that she might put them in the water when he was drinking, and they would block the flow of his urine and cause a bellyache, and he would die of this...[17]

Diego brought these claims and more to Padre Francisco de Escobar. The friar listened as Diego listed a litany of wild accusations from Lucía, among them that María had a secret chamber in her home where she conducted devilish rituals. Inside she would chant in a strange language Lucía did not recognize—perhaps an unusual dialect from Mexico if it wasn't indeed some occult tongue.[18]

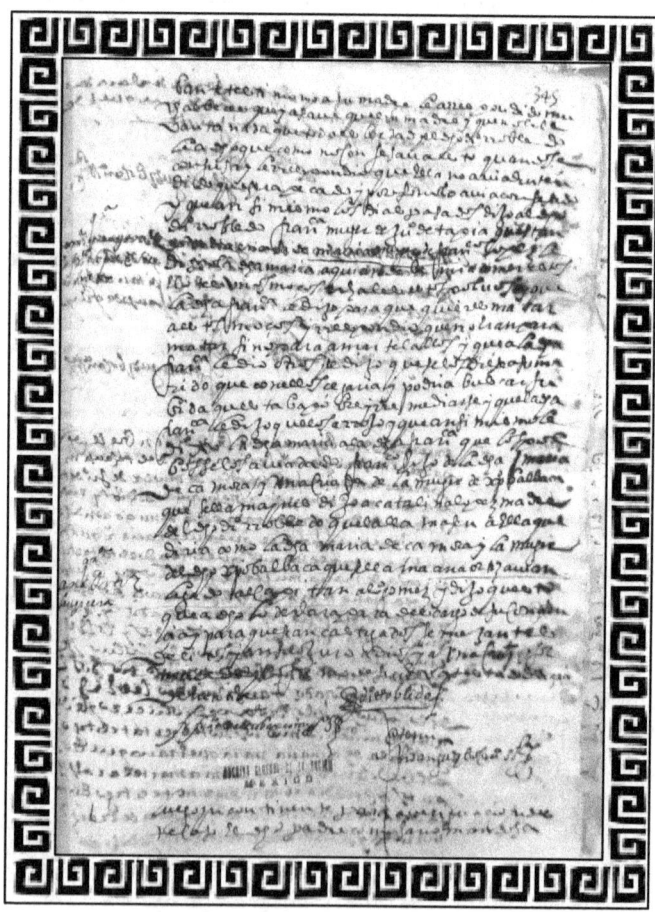

Original court document from Mexico.

42

María would take a basin of water and place near it two beans and two corn kernels. She would then either walk or crawl around the basin whilst conducting her strange chants. Eventually, the beans and corn would jump into the basin under their own power. A pounding would come from one of the walls, and a bit later, a creature alternately described as either a small goat, a pig, or a combination of the two, would emerge from the basin. María would then mount and ride the strange beast around the room. According to Lucía's testimony, in addition to the pig/billy goat creature, once a "woolly little black dog" appeared from the bowl—had María summoned a small hellhound?

However, rather than paraphrasing it, here it is straight from the court records of the time via Lucía's testimony:

> And about a year ago she has also three times seen the said her mother, while her father was at the mill, take an earthenware pot with water, and on the rim of this pot she placed two beans and two grains of maize facing each other, and the said her mother crawled around the pot saying some words that did not seem to this witness to be in the Spanish language, and the last word that this witness heard was "la chobera." And at this word the grains of maize jumped into the water, as did the beans one after another, and the maize fell away from the pot, and then an animal appeared that to this witness seemed something like a year-old billy goat, sort of like yellow, she could not quite say what color, with a twisted tail lifted up over a haunch like a pig's tail, and it got into the water and this witness's mother mounted it and sat astride the said animal. And at this point this witness left so that the said her mother would not see her.[19]

On another occasion about a year and a half ago, while her father was away at the mill, Lucia also claimed that

> ...her mother went into a room, and after she closed the door this witness saw her mother through the cracks in the door of the room that is the pantry—because the door is damaged—, and she had a burning tallow candle and some embers in an earthenware pot, and she was half naked with only a cloth around her waist, and this witness saw that she was anointing all her joints—her hands and elbows and shoulders and knees and toes—and the ointment was kind of

yellow. After applying this ointment she anointed herself on the same joints with another that was black; and she knows that these were their colors because she had seen that the said her mother kept them in some little gourds inside a basket with cotton hanging in the same room. And this witness saw that after she had anointed herself she rose a little from the ground and the flame from the green candle froze and said her mother disappeared and then the candle went out, and this witness was afraid and went to where her brothers and sisters were sleeping. And she did not see her again until the next day in the morning when this witness got up.[20]

Likewise, Diego gave testimony that Lucía had told him his mother went into the special chamber to summon demons. María would close her fist and rap on the wall five times. She would hold up her hand and offer her finger to the Devil. Diego, too, then went on to relate tales of the creature materializing in the room that María would take to riding. (According to New Mexico state historian Robert D. Martinez, these strange rituals could have been made up by Lucía based upon a similar witch folktale told in Spain.[21])

In addition to her own witchery, it was also said that María herself had quarrels with other witches. Lucía recalled an incident once where Maria believed that a witch was out to kill her son Juan as a baby.

And this witness has heard the said her mother say that a witch tried to kill Juan, this witness's brother, when he was a child, and that the next night she placed a broom with the bristles down at the foot of the bed, and at the head a pair of scissors and a man's dirty pants, and that way no witch would come in.[22]

Speaking of other witches, María wasn't the only one on trial. Also in the mix were two more women accused of love magic. The first was Ana Ortiz, blamed for making a Captain Alonso Gómez impotent. The other was María López, who attempted to make two men fall in love. According to the testimony of Francisca Robledo, María López spread some red powder over a meal of corn to be given to Francisco de Nieles and Pedro Lucero, which would make them lust after one another.

María's methods of warding off the witches are interesting, as we have here what appears to be the first written record in New Mexico of a woman trying to ward off a witch via a broom, which would eventually become common practice. As for the dirty pants and scissors, this goes back to Mexico, where a pair of scissors was considered to be the best repellant to ward off the Tlahuelpuchi. A vampiric witch that suckled the blood of infants in the night, the Tlahuelpuchi was said to abhor any type of metal, scissors chief among them for some reason. As such, scissors would often be placed under the crib of an infant. The meaning of the dirty pants is a bit harder to pin down, but, for whatever reason, the Tlahuelpuchi could be warded off by way of taking off one's pants, turning one leg inside out, and flinging them at the witch. Since María was herself from Mexico, one might surmise she heard tales of the Tlahuelpuchi or something similar.

During the trial in January of 1607, which was more of a preliminary hearing, no witnesses could corroborate Lucía's wild stories, nor did María de Zamora's servants, who were stoically silent through the proceedings. María, naturally, denied all charges except for possessing peyote, although she claimed she never used it herself. Regarding talk of witchcraft in their home, she said she was merely relating tales she had heard about such things but did not practice them herself. And as for warding off a witch from Juan's room, what harm was there in that? When Lucía escorted Frey Escobar to her parent's home to see the chamber, said chamber was lacking the elaborate door that Lucía had described, though there was a chamber at least. Frey Escobar recommended that the trial be brought to the Inquisition in Mexico City and that Governor Juan de Oñate be informed about it as well. María and her husband were eventually banned from San Gabriel, while Diego and Lucía were forbidden to leave New Mexico after the trial. However, in the end, neither Ana Ortiz nor either of the Marías were called in front of the Inquisition in Mexico City as planned. If they were punished in any way is unknown.

45

That said, at the end of the year on New Year's Eve in Santa Fe, Father Escobar preached a sermon warning that anyone practicing witchcraft would be excommunicated from the Church.

FIRST WITCHES OF SANTA FE

One of the first witches of the Santa Fe area was a half-Mexican and half-Indian woman, Beatriz de los Angeles, along with Juana de la Cruz, Beatriz's half-Spaniard daughter whom she had with her late husband, Juan de la Cruz of Catalunya. Initially, in the 1620s, Beatriz was considered to be a curandera or healer only. She and her daughter lived on an *estancia* in the Tano pueblos southeast of Santa Fe, and Beatriz often made calls to do healings. In 1628, she traveled to Senecú to help Doña María Granillo get well from a serious ailment. Allegedly, she saved Granillo's life by playing a game of *patoles* with her whilst reciting a number of spells.

The game of Patolli or patoles being played by a group of Pueblo Indians c.1890. (Library of Congress)

Beatriz must have made some enemies, for accusations against her and her daughter were brought to Father Esteban de Perea, an official of the Inquisition in Santa Fe, by 1626. However, nothing much came of the charges. In 1631, the case was reopened by Freya Stefan de Maria when it was reported that two of Beatriz's Indian servants died when she tested out one of her potions on them. Though that incident may or may not have been an accident, Beatriz intentionally poisoned several victims in Santa Fe, among them one of her lovers, Diego Bellido, with a bowl of bewitched corn gruel after he beat her. (Some say he beat her when Beatriz gave birth to his child which ended up being stillborn.) Before he died, Bellido made the accusation that Beatrice had bewitched him.[23]

Similarly, when a royal officer named Hernando Marquez slept with her daughter, Juana, Beatriz hexed him and he died. Actually, stories about Juana were even wilder than those concerning her mother. She could fly, for instance, by hiding herself within an egg. She could cast the evil eye in such a manner as to cause death, and she had poisoned her husband with enchanted milk for being unfaithful.[24]

By November of 1631, about fifty people had testified that Beatriz and Juana were witches. Since no proof of any of these stories could be presented to him, Freya Stefan considered them to be gossip from town busybodies who perhaps had their own agendas against the women. As such, no charges were filed against the two by the Church.

An accused witch brought before the Inquisition.

THE WITCH OF NAMBÉ

What is possibly a related tale and a variation of Juana de la Cruz is the story of the Nambé witch Juana Chavez. Nambé is only a little ways north of Santa Fe, and supposedly Juana Chavez operated during Spanish colonial rule, so they could possibly be one and the same. Tales of Juana Chavez are even more far-out than those of Juana de la Cruz. Chavez was so powerful locals whispered she could strike down her victims with lightning. By chanting, use of voodoo dolls, or simply striking her fist into the palm of her hand, she could cause death in a matter of days. Eventually the villagers of Nambé had enough and stormed her home in a scene similar to an old Universal horror film. The villagers found Chavez in her abode and locked her inside. Then, they set fire to the place, burning her alive within. In the burned remains, they found strange looking dolls hidden within the home's foundation. The villagers assumed Juana had hidden them there and decided to burn them as well. They set up a pyre of the wicked-looking dolls, but when it came time to light them, they came to life and ran away. All night long, the villagers chased down the cursed dolls and torched them one by one. Although the bit about the dolls is just fanciful folklore at its best, the story probably is an embellished version of the execution of a real Nambé witch sometime during the colonial period.[25]

LUIS DI RIVERA'S DEAL WITH THE DEVIL

One of New Mexico's oldest witchcraft tales not stemming from the Spanish coming into conflict with the indigenous peoples is that of cowboy Luis di Rivera. An illiterate immigrant from Spain, Rivera came to Chihuahua, Mexico, at a young age as a stock herder. At

48

fourteen, the impressionable young man fell victim to the charms of magic in the New World when an Indian taught him how to enchant women via special herbs. However, the charms of the herbal magic failed, and so he threw away the herbs and ceased contact with the Indian. Soon after, Rivera met an unnamed African slave along the trail. This enigmatic man was charmed in the sense that he had what appeared to be the supernatural ability to round up cattle with ease— he could even catch a mustang on foot! Whether or not Rivera ever witnessed these deeds is unknown, but the man claimed that he could impart these abilities to Rivera through the Devil.

Intrigued, Rivera began conversing with the slave, who put him on a path towards arts much darker than herbal magic. The unnamed slave taught Rivera that he had sold his soul to the Devil some time ago. As proof, he lifted up his bare foot and showed him a tattoo of the Devil on the sole of his foot. Then there was the mysterious book he carried with him in which the slave had painted crude depictions of demons. The slave offered to sell the book to Rivera, for which he paid a peso and a half. Then the man instructed Rivera to draw blood from his nose and use it to sign his name in the book, thus selling his soul. The ignorant Rivera did so, and the slave went on his way. However, Rivera soon began to regret his decision.

Within only one week, the reality that he was going to hell one day became too much for him, and so he tore up the book and began to repent. However, Rivera had invited the Devil into his life, and his tormented soul received no rest. In 1628, Rivera signed on as a muleteer for a wagon train to transport a herd of mules into New Mexico to the north. Rivera hoped perhaps this new land would give him peace. It didn't. The journey was beset with bad luck, and the straw that broke the camel's back was a mule and cattle stampede that occurred in the Santa Bárbara Valley. After this, the other trail drivers began to suspect that an emissary of the Devil was among their number. Rivera finally broke down and confessed to a friar in the wagon train, Fray Esteban Perea,[26] that he had sold his soul some time ago. Though Rivera could have been executed on the spot by angry cowboys, the friar saw to it that he was taken to Santa Fe. There he was brought before a representative of the Inquisition, Father Benavides, who convinced him to return to Mexico City to stand trial with the ecclesiastical court and beg for mercy. There Rivera did just that at the feet of the church representatives. When they learned that Rivera made this pact with the Devil at the tender, impressionable age of fourteen, they gave him leniency. They reasoned that Rivera, at that age and being uneducated, still believed and aligned himself with God and only sought the Devil's help but did not wish to fully turn away from God. Whether it was the truth or not, Rivera claimed that even when he was in possession of the book, he still prayed to God. (Rivera, it should be noted, had once served an officer of the Inquisition and had some knowledge of how the Inquisition worked. Therefore, the argument was made that Rivera may have known exactly what to say under the circumstances to save his skin.) As such, they let Rivera off with a mild penance— mild meaning that he wasn't jailed for life or burned at the stake. Instead, he was simply sentenced to a two-month confinement at a Jesuit convent and had to fast every Friday for an entire year. He was also permanently banned from Durango, Mexico. Under the circumstances, and compared to others, it was a rare instance of mercy from the Inquisition.

Insignia of the Inquisition.

FREY BENAVIDES AND THE DEMON

For three years between 1626 and 1629, Fray Alonso Benavides, mentioned in the previous entry as the friar who sent Luis di Rivera back to Mexico, served as the first official of the New Mexico Inquisition. Throughout that time he naturally encountered many witches, sorcerers, and the Demon, or the Devil. Benavides's written record of his interactions with the native peoples is worth reprinting, notably the Indians observations of the Penitente brotherhood:

I cannot refrain from telling here a saying of the Demon, by the mouth of an Indian wizard convinced of the word of God. . . . And it befell that seeing himself convinced, and that under my reasoning all the pueblo had determined to be Christian, the wizard was much angered and said at the top of his voice: "You Spaniards and Christians, how crazy you are! And you live like crazy folks! You want to teach us that we be also!" I asked him wherein we were crazy. And he must have seen some procession of penance during Holy Week in some pueblo of Christians, and so he said: "You Christians are so crazy that you go all together, flogging yourselves like crazy people in the streets, shedding [your own] blood. And thus you must wish that this pueblo be also crazy!" And with this, greatly angered and yelling, he went forth from the pueblo, saying that he did not wish to be crazy. Over which matter all were left laughing, and I much more, since I recognized and was persuaded that it was the Demon, who went fleeing, confounded by the virtue of the divine word.

Another relevant portion of his writings related that

These are the populations which we have, in this region,

51

converted and baptized, in what we call New Mexico... All of which must have close to eighty thousand souls. All these folk and nations were in their gentilism divided into two factions, warriors and sorcerers. The warriors tried, in opposition to the sorcerers, to bring all the people under their dominion and authority; and the sorcerers, with the same opposition, persuaded all that they made the rain fall and the earth yield good crops, and other things at which the warriors sneered. Wherefore there were between them continuous civil wars, so great that they killed each other and laid waste whole pueblos, wherein the Demon had his usual crop. Their religion, though it was not formal idolatry, was nearly so, since they made offerings for whatsoever action. As, at the time when they were going out to fight their enemies, they offered up flour and other things to die scalps of those they had slain of the hostile nation. If they were going to hunt, they offered up flour to heads of deer, jackrabbits, cottontail rabbits, and other dead animals. If to fish, they made offerings to the river. The women who wished that the men should desire them, went out into the country fat and well, and set up a stone or some small pole on some hill, and there offered flour to it; and for eight days, or as many as they could, did not eat, except something to disturb their stomachs and provoke vomiting; and they flogged themselves cruelly. And when they could endure no more, and from fat had made themselves lean and of the mien of the Demon, they returned very confident that the first man that they might see them would desire them, and would give them *mantas* [cotton]—which is their chief end. But this adoration of these poles and stones is in nowise reverential; for it makes no odds to them that they trample upon them nor spit upon them, but as a ceremonial they put them thus. . . . And in this manner the Demon kept them deceived with a thousand superstitions...

NECROMANCER OF THE JORNADA DEL MUERTO

One of the most notorious stretches of desert in the Southwest is New Mexico's aptly named Jornada del Muerto, or Journey of the Dead. And though one would think the route was christened as such for its many collective victims over the years, one in particular was chosen for the name. Sometimes called a "German necromancer" or a sorcerer, it is thought that Bernard Gruber was simply a European trader who got drunk in the wrong place at the wrong time. Even though today it's assumed he was merely playing a joke, Gruber's activities on Christmas Morning of 1667 at Quarai have since branded him a brujo.

Quarai Pueblo postcard.

Also called El Alemán, or "The German" in Spanish, Gruber was a trader who traveled up from Sonora into New Mexico. It's unknown when Gruber came to North America from Germany, but it is thought that through his trading activities as a merchant, he eventually became a man of means. His mules were packed with everything from weapons to tools to fine clothing accessories such as stockings and gloves. Supposedly he had a small entourage he traveled with consisting of a few Indian women and a young Apache boy, Atanacia, while other sources state he usually traveled in a large pack train. As stated before, on Christmas Day he found himself at a Tiwa pueblo known as Quarai, where he and two Indian acquaintances attended mass at Nuestra Señora de la Purísima Concepción de Cuarac.

It is unknown why he did so, but at some point that morning, Gruber shared with his two companions an esoteric rite from his home country said to bring about invulnerability on the first day of the feast of the Nativity. It was done by writing a special incantation on a piece of paper and then eating it. At Gruber's trial sometime later, a witness stated that Gruber told them, "If a person eats one of these writings, he becomes so strong that for the space of twenty-four hours after having eaten the said paper, he cannot be injured by any sword or bullet whatsoever." Another witness at the trial stated that Gruber had given him one of the special papers and that if he ate it that "neither the arrows of the Apaches, nor bullets, nor swords, would wound him. He said it was customary in his nation, Germany, to use this paper when they went to war. This Bernardo tried out the paper on an Indian boy of Las Salinas, who, although they struck him with a knife, was not wounded."

But we're getting ahead of ourselves in quoting from the trial. Back on Christmas Day with his two friends,[27] Gruber wrote an odd sequence of letters—+A.B.N.A.+A.D.N.A.+—interspaced with crosses between each sequence of letters with the instructions that if ingested, the swallowers would be invincible for a full 24 hours. The two companions, rather than eating them, climbed into the choir loft and shared this exciting new information with some of the singers. One of the ones who took the bait was José Nieto, a 19-year-old Tano Indian adopted by Captain José Nieto. Wanting to impress some elderly members of the pueblo, José took the paper before them, told them of its powers, and then ate it. After that, to demonstrate his invulnerability, he took out an awl and pretended to pierce himself without drawing blood in front of his amazed onlookers. The boy then went home to do the same in front of his family. Young José swiftly admitted that he did not believe in the German's strange magic and it was all a prank. Or was it? Conversely, when Paul Horgan, a seasoned historian, related this tale in *Great River: The Rio Grande in North American History*, he acted as though the boy might really have been invulnerable, writing that

> ...the young man pricked himself with an awl but without any effect. At another time... he stabbed himself with a dagger and a knife, but without making wounds. It was astounding and frightening.[28]

Likewise, in *The Witches of Abiquiú*, which gives a cursory history of the case, nothing is mentioned of Nieto faking the stabbing. Instead, it's implied that all witnesses, along with Nieto himself, were convinced of his invulnerability. So, perhaps some historians simply inferred that Nieto was faking it. In any case, it might well all have been fun and games if not for one thing: Gruber chose the time of the Mexican Inquisition to perpetrate his magical prank.

Since Gruber was surely intelligent enough to know this, scholars have since speculated that Gruber must have been drunk and careless when he created the papers. (Others have suggested Gruber was overconfident.) As for his two complicit companions, at least one ate his paper and decided to test the magic himself against Gruber. The friend drew his sword in front of Gruber to test the matter, and Gruber, in turn, drew his own sword to do the same. At that point the friend became frightened and let the matter drop. The matter was not dropped, however, by the José Nieto family, who reported Gruber's heretic actions to local authorities. Gruber was then ordered to stay in the village pending an investigation. When questioned as to why his little papers no longer worked a few days later, Gruber explained the incantation only worked on Christmas Day. Never mind that he should have been telling people it was all a joke instead of doubling down on his sorcerer ways.

Abó Pueblo Postcard.

On April 29, 1668, Gruber was finally arrested by Captain Nieto, his adopted son, and others under the authority of Fray Juan de Paz, an agent of the Holy Office of the Inquisition. Gruber still didn't seem to grasp the urgency of the situation and wasn't terribly concerned with his predicament. He felt he would be exonerated and go back on his merry way. Furthermore, according to F. Stanley in his booklet *The Abo (New Mexico) Story*, it's possible that Gruber was set up:

> Gruber insisted that [the accusations] was the concoction of the governor who had an eagle eye on his worldly goods. Perhaps he was right. No sooner was he imprisoned than he was notified he was poorer that the poorest Indian in the land.[29]

Abó Pueblo Postcard.

Whatever the case, Gruber was imprisoned in a small room guarded by two men at Abó, part of the Salinas Pueblo Missions. A thorough inventory of Gruber's belongings were made as he was shackled in Abó for a month. Among his possessions, no sorcerous items were found. Despite this, Gruber was still transported to Mexico City, to the estancia of Captain Francisco de Ortega to face the Holy Tribunal. Usually, the trials were held swiftly, but not for Gruber. Times were hard due to drought, food shortages, and raids by the Apache.[30] As such, he was kept in prison for two years. But, as luck would have it, Gruber's jailer was none other than one of his old customers, and one who owed him money at that. At the promise that Gruber would wave his debt, the jailer agreed to help Gruber escape. The first step of the plan was to fake an illness so as to rid Gruber of his restrictive shackles, which he did by refusing to eat for three days straight and complaining of a pain in his side. It worked, and the shackles came off, enabling step one of the plan. Also aiding in the escape was Gruber's Apache helper, the boy named Atanacia. He visited him often, secretly smuggling him supplies needed to escape and also gradually loosening the heavy wooden bars of his enclosure.

At midnight on June 22, 1670, Atanacia snuck to the prison with several horses. For several hours, he and Gruber worked to dislodge the wooden posts keeping him confined. At 3 AM, coincidentally the witching hour, Gruber finally escaped. Gruber and his companion then rode swiftly up the Camino Real de Tierra Adentro, little knowing that Gruber's final destination would be the Dead Man's Route to eventually bare his name. The 90-mile stretch of desert before them was especially dry during this period in history, and it wasn't long before the duo ran out of water. Atanacia, in addition to being younger, also had the benefit of not having been jailed for the past two years. Gruber was in a greatly weakened state and decided to stay at a place known as the Point of Rocks. However, in Atanacia's absence, Gruber became restless. Remembering some tall cottonwoods the duo had passed earlier on their journey, Gruber decided to seek them out, as the trees were indicative of a water source. When Atanacia returned to the Point of Rocks, he found his old employer gone and never saw him again.

Seal of the Inquisition.

On July 30, 1670, Gruber's remains were found by some fellow traders and friends, among them Francsico Betancur, who spotted a dead horse tied to one of the trees. Also there was Captain Andres de Peralta, who helped to eventually find Gruber's body. After stumbling upon a coat and some trousers he recognized as the German's, he found his remains. In a report, he explained, "I examined [the clothes], and as it seemed that they belonged to Bernardo Gruber, the fugitive, I made a search which did not result in vain, for I found at once all of his hair and the remnants of the clothing which he had worn. I and my companions searched carefully for the bones, and found in very widely separated places the skull, three ribs, two long bones, and two other little bones which had been gnawed by animals. It is supposed that Indians traveling with the German killed him." Although the last bit about Gruber's companion killing him has recently been contested by historians, Gruber's remains were for certain taken to El Paso del Norte and buried outside the mission of La Conversion de los Mansos Y Sumas. As for the spot of his demise, it was named Aleman, after his nickname of "The German," and is located within the confines of what is today Spaceport USA.

Was Gruber really a sorcerer? The practice of writing a spell or incantation on a piece of paper and then ingesting it was indeed an occult practice in Europe from whence he came. What prompted his ill-fated joke? Did he really believe it, or was he out to fool the gullible natives of the area? Whatever the case, the desert that now bears his name got the last laugh.

THE WIZARD OF NAMBÉ AND THE HOLY WATER

Kiva at Nambé.

Of all the villages and pueblos in New Mexico, Nambé is one of the ones most associated with witchcraft. In the 1670s, a priest

58

whose name has since been lost came to the village. He was on a mission to cleanse it of all paganism and went about destroying every relic he could find from the kivas. He even had Táhwi, the *cacique*, or head priest, arrested and taken to Santa Fe in fetters to stand trial as a witch. The reason for this, he said, was that whenever he tried to say Mass, sharp pains would pierce his back. Furthermore, Táhwi had bewitched his brethren so badly that they wouldn't come to church. Nor could the priest sleep at night. Táhwi was tortured in Santa Fe when he at first denied accusations of bewitching anyone. However, under torture he did confess to stealing holy water from the church to see what magic he could work with it.

Some time ago, under an earlier, gentler priest, Táhwi had watched his methods with intense interest. In fact, this priest was so different from the other that Táhwi went to church often to learn his ways. What fascinated him the most was the special water, or holy water, that the priest used to guarantee his parishioners safe passage into the next life with. Táhwi wondered what kind of magic it might work in his own hands, and so when the opportunity arose, he stole some for himself.

In his home, Táhwi experimented with the water. In *Indian Stories from the Pueblos*, author Frank Applegate related that

First he placed his finger in it to test it, but since nothing happened except that his finger was wet when he took it out, he tried rubbing some of it on himself to see the effect of that, but he felt no different, beyond a slight feeling of dampness, than he had felt before trying the experiment. Then he tasted the holy water, but it only seemed to him like the river water. He was a little puzzled at the lack of results from his experiments, but was not yet discouraged. He next called to his wife, who was grinding corn in another room, and ordered her to come in where he was. Then imitating the padre's tone of voice and words as best he could, he sprinkled his wife liberally with the holy water. This time, he got a quick and strong reaction coupled with a very good scolding. His wife told him that he had better not fool with the white priest's sacred water when he did not know its powers, or he might use it wrongly and bewitch someone.[31]

After his wife had planted the idea in his head, Táhwi took his wife to the river where he bathed her with sacred amole root, just in case

59

he accidentally put a curse on her in misusing the water. Frank Applegate continued that Táhwi

> ...sprinkled her well with sacred corn meal of his own blessing and told her that she was now all right again; but after that he left holy water alone and let the padre attend to ceremonies in the church, while he himself attended to performing Indian ceremonies to cure the sick, keep witches from the pueblo, lay ghosts, bring rain, make the corn grow, make game easy to catch, and a thousand and one other things that a successful cacique must do if his people are to prosper and be happy.[32]

Nambé Pueblo.

Unfortunately for Táhwi, the nice "smiling priest" was eventually replaced by the more forceful, fanatical priest who had Táhwi arrested. In Santa Fe, the old man was jailed, and when he denied bewitching the priest and parishioners of Nambé, they tied his hands behind his back and strung him up by his thumbs until he confessed what was admittedly the innocent story of stealing the Holy Water. Instead of seeing this as Táhwi having an interest in the Catholic religion, they used this as a means to his end. Táhwi, along with another cacique from San Idelfonso arrested under similar charges, was hanged from the gallows until dead. Little did the Spaniards know, but they were sowing some of the first seeds of the Pueblo Revolt soon to erupt.[33]

As for the angry priest, Marc Simmons noted in *Witchcraft in the Southwest* that "he may have suffered retribution if he was the Fray Tomas listed in the Spanish documents as the priest slain at Nambé on August 10, 1680."[34] This seems like a possibility since F. Stanley noted in *The Nambé New Mexico Story* that Fray Tomas de Torres had been in New Mexico for about three years and was originally a native of Teposotlan.

POPÉ AND THE PUEBLO REVOLT

Taos Pueblo, New Mexico   *Photo by Dick Kent*

It was [Popé's] distinction that great powers had been revealed to him. He was able to say that Montezuma, their ancient war god, in his other-kingdom of Po-he-yemu, was gathering all his forces to lead the Indian people in revolt against the Spaniards. Popé was in direct communication with him through three spirits of the underworld who regularly came to him in the kiva and told him what to do. He could tell their names. They were Caudi, Tilini and Tleume.—Paul Horgan, The Great River[35]

After the death of Táhwi sometime in the 1670s, he was succeeded at Nambé by Ahóa, who did well to practice the old ways in secret. One day, while meditating in his home, a strange figure appeared before him. "The stranger had a large nose and a mouth that looked as though it had never smiled, and when he looked at Ahóa, the cacique felt as though he could keep no thought hidden from this man," recorded Frank Applegate in *Indian Stories from the Pueblos.*[36]

61

This enigmatic figure was none other than Popé, an embittered survivor of the 1675 witch purge. That year, tensions that had been simmering for years between the Spaniards and the Indians finally reached a breaking point when 47 medicine men[37] were arrested and brought to Santa Fe under the orders of Governor Juan Francisco Treviño at the behest of Church officials. Among the charges leveled at the men were sorcery, communion with the Devil, and more specifically, the deaths of several missionaries and the bewitchment of a church inspector, Father Andres Durán. Most of those arrested were either jailed, whipped, or enslaved after being found guilty, but three were hung,

Statue of Popé by Cliff Fragua (2005) representing New Mexico in the National Statuary Hall in Washington D.C.

and a fourth committed suicide by hanging himself. After the deaths of the four medicine men,[38] a united procession of Tewa Indians from various pueblos along the Rio Grande marched to Santa Fe. There they confronted the governor, demanding the release of the medicine men still living by offering commodities like chicken eggs, tobacco, and beans as ransom. The governor buckled under the pressure and released the prisoners, showing the Puebloans that they had power in numbers. Among the released medicine men who had been whipped was one known as Popé from San Juan Pueblo.

For those thinking that Popé will end up being the hero of the story, this is not so. Like so many conflicts, in truth, there was no clear-cut hero or villain in what would become the Pueblo Revolt of 1680, as Popé would ultimately make himself as much a dictator as the Spaniards had been.[39] Bound and determined to take revenge upon his tormenters after his 1675 ordeal, Popé turned to the very Devil himself for guidance in thwarting the Spaniards. As the old saying went, the enemy of my enemy is my friend.

62

"The revolt was boldly and brilliantly conceived," wrote J. Manuel Espinoza in *The Pueblo Indian Revolt of 1696 and the Franciscan Missions in New Mexico*.[40] Using a unique combination of Aztec and Christian beliefs against the Spanish, Popé either really did commune with devilish figures or was clever enough to choose ones that the Indians would revere and the Spanish would fear. Popé told his followers that at the kiva at Taos, the god Poheyemo came up from the underworld to commune with him in person. Espinoza wrote, "The word was spread that the 'representative' of Poheyemo was very tall and black, with frightful eyes that were large and yellow. The stratagem was to leave it unclear whether or not Popé was Poheyemo's chosen representative or the earthly embodiment of Poheyemo himself."[41] In addition to Poheyemo, before Popé had also appeared "three devils in the form of Indians, most horrifying in appearance, shooting flames of fire from all the senses and extremities of their bodies, named Caudi, Tilimi and Tleume."[42]

Taos Pueblo by F.A. Nims, Cunningham & Co. (1880-1889).
(Library of Congress)

In essence, while Popé claimed to commune with the Devil and his demons, more often than not, the names given to said demons were often linked to Aztec belief. Case in point, the aforementioned Caudi, Tilimi, and Tleume were thought to be versions of the Aztec gods of Fire and Water. Later, when the rebellion was in progress, and it was not yet known that Popé was the mastermind, a captured Indian told the Spaniards that their orders had come from an "Indian

63

who lives a very long way from this kingdom, toward the north, from which region Montezuma came, and who is the lieutenant of Po he yemu; and that this person ordered all the Indians to take part in the treason and rebellion." Governor Antonio de Otermín felt that the Indians were beguiling his men with fairy tales and reportedly had the prisoners executed soon after.

South Taos Pueblo and Kiva (Adam Clark Vroman, 1899).

After his 1675 whipping, Popé, now based out of Taos Pueblo, spent the next five years going about various pueblos planting the seeds of rebellion, one of which was Nambé, where we began our story. Popé told Ahóa that he had come from Taos with a plan to drive away the Spaniards and instructed Ahóa to assemble those who could be trusted. Later, fifty members of Nambé assembled within an old round kiva. Sitting in the darkness, it was said that Popé made a supernatural entrance when a "little light came in through the square opening in the center of the roof, where the ladder entered." *Indian Stories from the Pueblos* related that "The stranger stood just at the foot of the ladder, looking upon those seated about the room. As he looked at them, his eyes seemed to give off sparks of fire."[43]

When the stranger announced himself as Popé, everyone in attendance already knew who he was. They had heard tales of how he traveled to and fro in a whirlwind and was a great medicine man. However, Popé was now more than a mere medicine man; he claimed to commune with the enemy of the Spanish God himself, the Devil. Popé essentially used the recent droughts to claim that the old gods had turned their backs on them when they embraced the Spanish. Similar to the Biblical story of Nimrod and the tower of Babel, Popé esteemed to defeat God, proclaiming, according to *Indian Stories from the Pueblos*:

It is true that the Spanish God has always before been too strong for us, but this time it will be different. I have been making powerful ceremonies, and I have been able to raise up two great devil spirits to help us. On the appointed morning these two devil spirits will kill the white God, Jesus his son and Mary the mother of Jesus, who will then be unable to help the Spaniards, and we will then kill them all.[44]

Popé explained that very soon one early morning as the sun rose, they would storm Santa Fe, drive out the Spanish, and reclaim their land. In the absence of the Spaniards, the old gods would return, and so would the much-needed rains. Popé then took a small bag of sacred corn meal from beneath his blanket and made a large circle of corn meal at the foot of the kiva's ladder. Next, he withdrew a "strange-looking material from a little bag be carried, and placing it on the ground in the center of the magic circle, set fire to it."[45] After this, "A dense, pungent, thick smoke curled upward and out of the opening in the roof."[46]

Popé then invoked the spirits to come and show the men of Nambé their power and that "on the appointed day you will kill the Spanish white God and his son Jesus and the mother of Jesus, so that they cannot help the Spaniards, and then that you will also help us to kill all the Spaniards."[47]

With his invocation, Popé threw something into the fire which gave a vile odor, likely sulfur. As the smoke began to clear, at the foot of the ladder appeared "two tall, strange and grotesque-looking figures, their heads crowned with owl feathers, the insignia among the Indians of evil and witchcraft."[48] At the sight of the strange beings, the men of Nambé were nearly frightened to death and felt as though "something were crawling under their scalps."

As promised, Popé asked the two spectral figures if they would help to which they affirmed they would. Popé threw the unknown substance into the fire once more and the figures disappeared in another large waft of smoke. The terrified men of Nambé agreed to participate in the revolt.

Eventually, Friday the 13th of August 1680 was chosen as the day of uprising. To communicate the plan, runners were sent to the pueblos carrying knotted ropes to serve as a countdown to the insurrection. However, on August 9, two Tesuque runners, Nicholas Catua and Pedro Omtua, were captured on their way to one of the pueblos. Under torture they confessed to the date of August 13th. The Indians learned of this and so moved up the insurrection to the 10th. That morning, the Indians set free the horses of the Spaniards so they could not flee and then sealed off the roads leading into Santa Fe. Village by village they began their siege and by the 13th had reached Santa Fe. The city fell within a week, the Spaniards fled, and in the end 400 were dead, including 21 out of 33 Franciscan missionaries. The Spanish made their way to the safety of El Paso, where they eventually concluded that the Indians only carried out this magnificent feat with the aid of the Devil, just as Popé had pledged.

Popé, along with his two lieutenants, Alonso Catiti of Santo Domingo and Luis Tupatu of Picurís, traveled from village to village to reset things to the way they were before the Spaniards came. This comprised of tearing down the churches and removing all religious iconography from the land. In addition to this, any baptized Indians were to cleanse themselves in the river with yucca root soap. Popé even went so far as to insist that anyone married under the Spanish custom had to renounce their vows and take their mates by way of the old ways. He also forbade the planting of crops introduced by the Spanish.

Despite Popé's claims, the old gods didn't return to bring the rain and the droughts persisted. The raids by the Navajo and Apache, who had not taken part in the revolt, not only continued but became worse without the Spaniards there. Popé only lasted as the new leader of the Puebloans for nary a year before he dropped out of the history books, never to be seen again. Many have since theorized that he died in 1688, a little before the Spanish reconquest of 1692.

Recently a statue was erected of Popé in Washington D.C. However, despite a desire among some to make him out to be a hero, New Mexican historian Ray John De Aragón sheds a different light on Popé that others are reluctant to acknowledge. In *New Mexico Native Lore*, Aragón wrote, "This has been a taboo subject among New Mexico historians, a subject many steer away from."[49] Aragón explained atrocities committed by Popé against his own people who refused to renounce Catholicism. Even worse was his treatment of Spanish families left behind, namely the killing, rape, enslavement and a few instances of ritual sacrifice of young Spanish girls. Among those abused and captured were Aragón's ancestor, Juana de Arzate. Family tradition held that the five-year-old girl watched as Popé's men raped her mother, then beheaded her and her father. The girl remained a slave until the Spanish reconquest of 1692. While the greedy Spanish were no angels, neither were Popé and some of his followers.

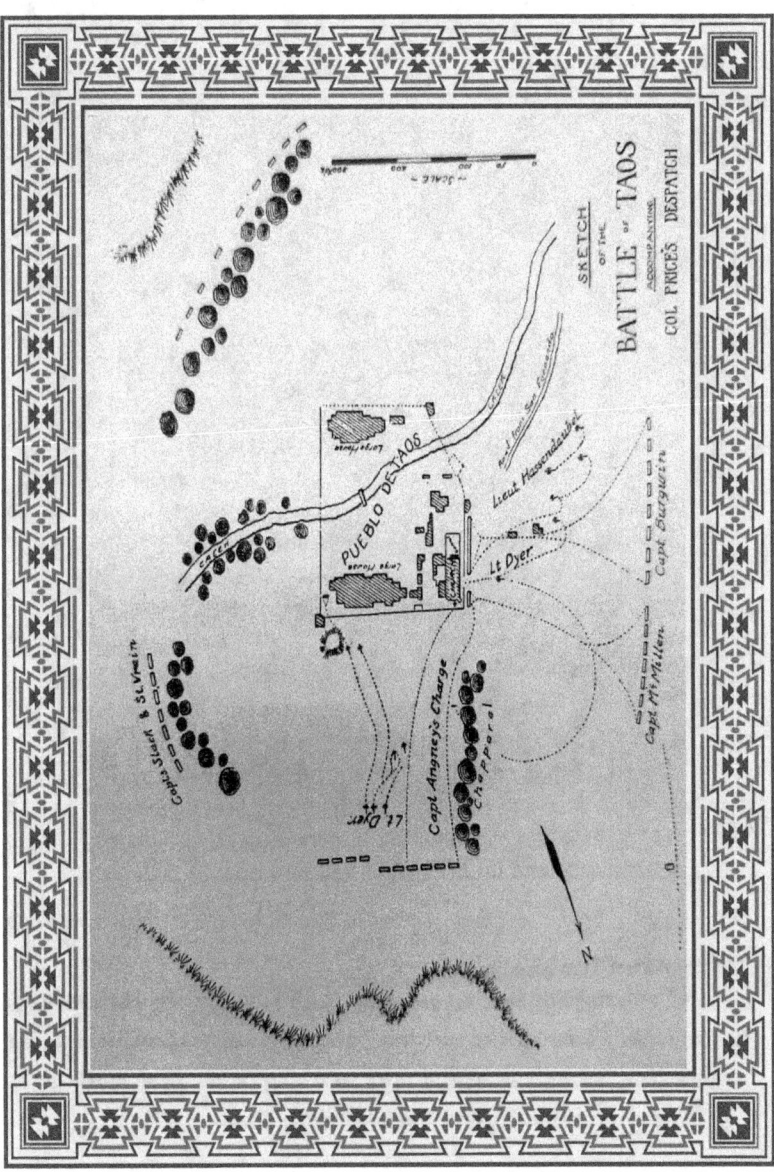

This painting by an unknown artist in the mid-1800s showcases the story of "The Virgin of the Macana," a statue that miraculously survived the siege of Santa Fe during the Pueblo Revolt. Take note of the top right corner of the painting, which shows the Devil hanging a man from a tree, which will come into play in the next section. (History Collections New Mexico History Museum 2012.32.1.)

BLACK DEVIL OF TAOS PUEBLO

"This giant, who lived unseen like a god in a kiva at Taos, guiding Popé and giving him power, planned the revolt."—Paul Horgan, Conquistadors in North American History[50]

Although Popé is often given all the credit for masterminding the Pueblo Revolt, many modern historians think that he not only had help in plotting the uprising, but that he quite possibly wasn't the mastermind at all. As stated before, reports that Popé communed with various spirits, including the Devil, leading up to the revolt were initially brushed off as superstition. However, one of these "spirits" stood out and was said to be a flesh and blood god incarnate in the form of a "black giant with yellow eyes." Nor was this man an emissary of the Devil, but of Montezuma, the long-dead Aztec ruler of Mexico. Why Montezuma? As covered in an earlier entry, at an unknown point in history, Montezuma had grown to become a mythical figure among the Pueblo Indians of northern New Mexico, so much so that they claimed Montezuma was born at Pecos Pueblo and flew south to Mexico on the wings of an eagle. Some have speculated that the Indians heard tales of Montezuma from either the Spaniards or their servants and then based a legend around him. As it turns out, the myth of Montezuma may have been born during the Pueblo Revolt.

To better explain, let us return to the mythical sounding "black giant" with "yellow eyes" who served as Montezuma's emissary to Popé. Though the golden-eyed giant might sound like a spectral figure that materialized from the supernatural, there is good evidence that he was a flesh and blood man who lived at Taos Pueblo. As it is, this "giant" is thought to have simply been a mulatto from New Spain by the name of Diego Naranjo, who was said to be adept at sorcery. He was living in San Felipe, New Mexico, by the year 1626 where he served at a Spanish hacienda and married an Indian woman from a nearby pueblo. A bit later, he was found participating in what some called an orgy and others called a kachina dance at the Alameda parish church in 1632.

Catholic scholar Fray Angelico Chavez later put forth the theory that Naranjo was impersonating Poheyemo, the sun god. In an article on the subject, Chavez explained how two captured Tesuque Pueblo youths told of the giant prior to the rebellion. The two messengers were captured on August 9th just two days before the uprising was set to commence. Eventually they described an "Indian

lieutenant of Po he yemu" that "was very tall, black, and had very large yellow eyes, and that everyone feared him greatly."[51] The Spanish leaders brushed it off as fable and ignorant superstition, little knowing that the revolt would succeed. Around the same time, other Indian captives alluded to the mysterious figures behind the imminent revolt, stating that they "had a mandate of an Indian who lives a very long way from this kingdom, toward the north, from which region Montezuma came, and who is the lieutenant of Po he yemu; and that this person ordered all the Indians to take part in the treason and rebellion...."[52]

As we all know, the rebellion commenced and was a success, and it may all have been thanks to the mysterious man known as Diego Naranjo posing as Poheyemo. But who was he? Experts aren't entirely sure, but they believe he descended from a very dark-skinned mulatto from Puebla, New Spain, by the name of Mateo. He was freed at the age of 20 by his master, Mateo Montero, and he agreed to settle in New Mexico. Mateo next served a soldier named Alonso Martin Naranjo and then married an Indian woman. They were reported to have three children by the names of Diego, Pedro, and Domingo. As it turns out, Pedro was encountered by the Spaniards on a return survey mission to New Mexico in 1681 after the revolt. Then 80 years old, he identified himself as Pedro Naranjo when he was arrested at Isleta. It was said that he was "a great sorcerer who had come down from the upper pueblos to teach his superstitions."[53] It was Pedro who first told of how Popé communed with three spirits by the names of Caudi, Tilini, and Tleume. According to Pedro, these three spirits claimed that they were on their way to a mythical place called Lake Copala, which was near where the Aztecs emerged from the underworld in their creation myth. That an Indian man would know of Aztec mythology had always been eyebrow-raising for historians. Therefore, it makes sense that if the Naranjo brothers were the sons of Spanish slaves, they would be fairly well-versed in the history of the Aztecs. It is thought that Diego and Pedro used this lore to their advantage to

70

frighten the Spaniards and, in the process, passed off the Aztec legends to the Indians, who began to revere Montezuma. As related earlier, the myth of Poheyemo is itself similar to the Pecos Pueblo myth of Montezuma. Through Naranjo's influence, was this when the story of Montezuma somehow conflated with Poheyemo? It seems to be a possibility.

Fray Chavez wrote an entire discourse on Naranjo and ended it with a pueblo folktale about Poheyemo that he speculated could have been composed by Naranjo himself shortly before the revolt. In it, Poheyemo and God have a contest which Poheyemo wins. One could interpret this as representing Popé's bold claims that they would extinguish the Holy Trinity of the Catholic Church. The story ended in a similar manner to Montezuma's departure from Pecos Pueblo:

> Before [Poheyemo] left he told the Indians that there wouldn't be any more war between the Indians and anyone. If there were he would come back. He would gather all the Indians in one place and separate the good people from the witches. Then the earth will crack. Then everything will be new again—"when a mule has a baby."[54]

Though I am uncertain as to the meaning of "when a mule has a baby," I am fairly confident that reference to the earth cracking was another allusion to the beliefs of the Aztecs. Specifically, the Aztecs believed that the world had been created and recreated four different times, as did many Native American cultures. According to the Aztecs, the Fourth World was destroyed in a flood, but the Fifth World would be destroyed in an earthquake, and this would be the final cycle. The exact meaning of the story aside, it seems possible that this tale was a form of pre-rebellion propaganda infused with more Aztec flourishes created by the Naranjos.

Furthermore, Diego Naranjo may not have remained in the shadows as much as we were led to believe. Remember the two demons decked out in owl feathers from Nambé? If they were flesh and blood men in on a ruse with Popé, and considering that they were described as being quite tall, perhaps they were, in fact, the Naranjo brothers, but this is just my own speculation. It's also possible that Naranjo actually fought in the revolt. Could the "myth" of "the Devil" marching through Santa Fe in the form of a "black giant" have been based upon Naranjo's imposing figure cutting a swath of violence through the siege?

71

Statue of the Virgin.

Fray Chavez thinks so due to a folktale, which he believes to have at least some basis in truth, concerning a statue of the Virgin. The motivations of the story are a tad confusing, but it goes that one of the Indian Chieftains entered the home of a Christian amid the revolt and singled out a statue of the Virgin. He removed a crown from its head and then decapitated the statue with a sharpened macana, out of which blood flowed from the wound. Said chieftain then went insane and ran about the battlefield, being of little use to anyone. Then, the Devil, though he should have been happy with the deed, took the chieftain and executed him by hanging him from a tree. In a footnote for his article devoted to a statue of the Virgin, Chavez speculated that Naranjo was the devil in the account,

"But who was this Indian? And why should Diego Naranjo (or the devil) punish him for such a devilishly laudable deed? Unless this Indian, having once been a pious Christian, repented of his crime and upbraided the rebel chiefs afterward. These killed him, and Naranjo hung up his corpse from a mountain poplar of the Santa Fe stream as an example to others... 55

It may also be possible that Naranjo appeared in accounts of New Mexico witchcraft before the Pueblo Revolt. In an earlier section dealing with Luis di Rivera's deal with the Devil, you might recall the Spanish-owned mulatto slave who sold Luis di Rivera a cursed book in 1628. Could that magic-practicing mulatto have been Diego Naranjo? Considering that Naranjo was in Mexico and New Mexico alike during this time frame, it's possible.

In any case, some have wondered if Naranjo, acting as Poheyemo's human emissary, had ideas of becoming the new leader of New Mexico once the Spanish fled. As Fray Angelico Chavez put it, "Either to enjoy personal power, or to avenge himself on the Europeans who for so long, and sometimes most cruelly, had lorded

72

it over the primitive colored races, or for both reasons, he most cleverly employed the myth of Pohe-yemo to unite the ever-dissident Pueblo Indians for a successful blow."[56]

Whatever the case, the ultimate fate of both Naranjo brothers is unknown, and if either had ideas of ruling New Mexico after the Spanish fled, these dreams never came to fruition.

THE WITCHES IN THE OLDEST HOUSE

Woodcut Engraving of the Oldest House in Santa Fe.

One of the better-known Santa Fe folktales is that of the witches in the oldest house and the accompanying headless horseman. How much truth the tale contains is hard to say, but the oldest house still exists and today stands across the street from the San Miguel Chapel. Located along a narrow one-way street, the varying legends of the oldest house are many. One links it to the Montezuma myth, going that an unnamed Indian chief lived there "who ruled over Montezuma's northern empire."[57] While it's unknown if the house for certain is pre-conquest, it is constructed of puddled adobe, an ancient method wherein a layer of grass-hewn mud was poured between blocks. The walls are measured at three feet thick at the bottom, tapering to fifteen inches at the top.

Regardless of the exact date, most Santa Fe residents attest that at some point in the 19th century, the house was occupied by two powerful witches. Though usually unnamed, most say they were at least part Indian. Their services were sought by everyone, albeit under the cover of night. It was said that everyone from the poorest

73

to the richest upper-crust citizens sought the witches' aid, usually in the form of love potions and other herbal magic.

On one occasion, two young men consulted the witches at different times for the hand of the same girl. In Jack Kutz's version of the tale, for instance, each young man consulted a different witch at separate times, hence the confusion. The young man who lost the girl's hand angrily returned to the witches to demand back his gold coins. They refused and he struck one of the old women out of anger. One of the women grabbed a big hunting knife and swung at the young Spaniard's head. He was decapitated, and his head rolled down the street on its way to El Palacio to seek justice against the witches. This is where the ghost aspect of the tale came in, as ever since the man's headless ghost riding a horse can be seen galloping along College Street. Other times, the head will roll by on its own.

Though typically the tale is recounted as I just did above, with no names or firm dates, author Jane Ann Turzillo heard a more detailed account from artist Bobbie Garcia in Santa Fe in 2018.[58] According to Garcia, the tale took place shortly after the Pueblo Revolt in 1692. The headless horseman was a young soldier by the name of Juan Espinoza, while the beautiful object of his desire was Catalina Monroy. According to Garica, Catalina was a flirt with many suitors, among them Juan's best friend, Pedro Pino. Making matters worse, Pedro was tall, dark, and handsome, while Juan was short and on the pudgy side. Eventually, when Juan learned that Catalina was betrothed to Pedro, he consulted the witches of the oldest house, in this case identified as Doña Filomena and Doña Lugarda. To Juan's amazement, the women knew his name before he even introduced himself. He made his request of them, and they began to mix a potion. However, having Catalina drink the potion was not enough. First, for reasons unknown, Juan needed to slaughter a pig and then eat its heart raw, then take the tea to Catalina. However, Juan never proceeded onto the grotesque first step and simply took Catalina the potion. In the end, the tea did nothing but make Catalina ill for a time, but not enough to call off the wedding to Pedro, who she still loved. It was then that the angry suitor destined to become the headless horseman stormed back to the witches. When the two women asked him if he ate the pig's heart first, he lied and said he did. But the two old witches knew he was lying and called him on it. Juan went to attack the old women with his sword, but they were too quick for him. One whacked him over the head with her cane. He tumbled to the ground, losing his sword, which the other witch then picked up and beheaded him with. Then, Juan's head rolled down De Vargas Street, leaving a bloody trail in its wake. The witches then took his rotting corpse and propped it up in a chair outside their home as a warning to anyone who might cross them again.

FRAY JUAN ÁLVAREZ AND THE WITCHES

Some of our first accounts of witchcraft post-reconquest come from the investigations of Fray Juan Álvarez, who was stationed by the Church in Santa Fe in the early 1700s. He was one of three Franciscan commissaries in New Mexico appointed by the tribunal of The Holy Office in 1698. By 1706, Fray Álvarez had gathered a plethora of witchcraft accusations, which prompted a full-scale investigation, or witch hunt, if you will.

The bulk of the accusations concerned love magic, with many testimonies given against Marfa de Ancissu, the mulatto wife of Agustin de la Cruz of Zacatecas. One account told how she instructed Simona de la Vega to put soil from a cemetery under a pair of scissors placed in the form of a cross inside of a shoe under her husband's bed. This, she claimed, would keep him fast asleep while Simona could go out and have an affair. Simona Bonifacio told Fray Álvarez that Marfa had taught her how to make enchanted chocolate cooked in water that she had previously bathed in with a hint of lizard blood. Marfa also sold the women charms that she instructed them to bury at the spots where their husbands usually urinated.

Marfa wasn't the only witch; there were many more, such as one alleged to have made love to a snake once.[59] Two sorceresses named "La Memela" (the Pancake) and "La Rana" (the Frog) occupied some of Alvarez's time. They manufactured sleeping powders to keep husbands at home. Another, Juana Apodaca Pactle, or La Lozana as she was called, had her own school. Though not on the level of the alleged "School of the Devil" said to exist in a cave in the mountains, a school for witches it was. There she boldly proclaimed that the priests knew nothing compared to what powers she possessed. For instance, an African drummer from the soldiers' barracks told Father Alvarez that La Lozana and her followers would sometimes follow the men, gathering up the dirt they had just traversed as a means to bewitch them. Oddly, La Lozana would sing praises as she practiced her herbal magic. Maria de la Encarnacion, or La Chispa, on the other hand, once said, "When I ask the Devil he gives what is necessary." (An unfaithful husband put her on the path to magic when her prayers failed to keep him out of the arms of other women.)

Essentially, an interesting milieu of Aztec, Indian, Spanish and African witchcraft had been brewing in New Mexico in the time since the Spanish arrived over 100 years ago. However, whenever the accused were questioned about the use of Black Magic, they almost always blamed the Indians. A mulatto by the name of Josepha de la Encarnacion told Alvarez of a witch called La Naranja. She was the wife of one Pascual Naranjo, who would use a strange herb to somehow help her husband win at the game of Los Patoles sometimes. Other times she taught her clients enchantments by way of the Rosary in addition to the usual love potions.

Fearful of another Pueblo Revolt, the Holy Office of the Inquisition decided to let most accusations slide for the most part and turned their eyes to the sins of bigamy and sexual immorality instead.

JUANA DE APODACA VS. FELIPA DE LA CRUZ

In many instances, the wicked will often accuse the innocent of perpetrating a horrible act that they themselves instigated. Such a case was that of a Spaniard, Juana de Apodaca, against Felipa de la Cruz, of Tesuque, in Santa Fe in 1704. Apodaca accused de la Cruz of bewitching her and also that de la Cruz had damaged her reputation as an upstanding citizen of Santa Fe. As such, she wanted de la Cruz to be punished and made an example of. Ironically, the investigation ended up proving that Apodaca was herself the witch. Apodaca had bewitched and made sick an unnamed witness who also revealed that de la Cruz was only involved because she was trying to cure her of Apodaca's bewitchment. Likewise, Apodaca began going after de la Cruz after it was learned she was trying to cure Apodaca's bewitched victim.

DOÑA LEONOR DOMÍNGUEZ GETS BEWITCHED

In Santa Fe in 1708, Doña Leonor Domínguez, wife of Miguel Martín, brought charges to the governor, claiming she had been bewitched by three San Juan women while in Santa Cruz. In a written statement to Governor José Chacón Medina Salazar y Villaseñor, Doña Leonor claimed:

76

Being extremely ill with various troubles and maladies which seemed to be caused by witchcraft, . . . and although I am a Catholic Christian by the goodness of God, I know that there have been many examples in this Province of persons of my sex who have been hexed by devilish art, including, as is well known, Augustina Romero, Ana Maria, wife of Luiz Lopez, and Maria Lujan, my sister-in-law. Therefore I beg that Your Excellency may be pleased to send one of your agents to my house to take my legal declaration and solemn oath of what passed between me and three Indian women of the Pueblo of San Juan whom I suspect as witches. And I promise to declare the reasons for my suspicion, and your agent may observe the condition in which I find myself, which is a matter of public knowledge and notoriety.

This declarant, being on Holy Thursday last in the church of the Town of Santa Cruz, praying, saw beside her an Indian woman of San Juan, called Catherina Lujan, and further off another, who is the wife of Zhiconqueto, the painter; that she heard this Catherina Lujan say to the wife of the said Indian: "Is this the wife of Miguel Martin?" and she answered: "Yes, it is"; and that at this time this declarant heard the wife of the said Indian painter, and one of her daughters, say to the said Catherina Lujan: "Now"; and that the latter said; "Not yet"; and that, then, full of terror, this declarant left that place where she was kneeling, and fell on her knees further off, and this time the wife of the said Indian said to the said Catherina: "It would be better now"; and, being on her knees behind this declarant, the said wife of the Indian came close to her and put her hand on her back beside her heart; and then, as she did so, her entire body began to itch, and this declarant ... has not lifted her head since then, except that every day she... suffers and this declarant never knew that the Indian women had done her harm, but thought that perhaps they wanted secretly to steal the buttons from the mantle which she was wearing, and that she went out afraid and she has a horror of that place to the present day...

The above account was given to a magistrate, Juan García de las Rivas, on May 13, 1708, when he was sent by the governor when he started a judicial inquiry into the matter. On that day, the magistrate found Doña Leonor bedridden and near death. In fact, the woman was so ill she could barely speak and did well to make the sign of the

77

cross before giving her testimony. After having taken Doña Leonor's statement, the magistrate traveled north the twelve leagues to San Juan, where he arrested the three accused witches: Catherina Lujan, Catherina Rosa, and Angelina Pumazho.

In a departure from the usual New Mexico witchcraft proceedings, the women were charged with a criminal complaint outside of the Church. Soon after the arrest, the *alcalde* (the Spanish equivalent of a mayor under the old rule), began to mull over the case in his head. Doña Leonor had oddly stated that the three Indian women spoke Spanish between themselves when ordinarily they would have been speaking in their own language in Tewa. This was Alcalde García de las Rivas' first clue that not all was as it seemed. Furthermore, one of the accused witches claimed that she only touched Doña Leonor after she fell down in an attempt to aid her and determine the cause of her illness. The Indian woman said that she didn't want to be accused of witchcraft and that, 'Spanish women say that witchcraft is the cause of whatever sickness they have.''

The church in Santa Cruz, as photographed by William Henry Jackson in 1881.

Furthermore, that same Holy Thursday, Doña Leonor was seen slapping her husband in an argument in the churchyard. It was now becoming clear to the magistrate that rather than black magic at work, which all three of the accused denied, jealousy might be to blame. To aid Alcalde García de las Rivas, Governor Chacón instructed Sergeant Major Juan de Ulibbarí to help with the case. As the investigation continued under Ulibbarí, it was learned that the daughter of one of the women had a previous relationship with Don Miguel, Doña Leonor's husband. To Doña Leonor's logic, her husband would only cheat on her if bewitched. As for her illness, which was real, that, too, must have been the result of bewitchment.

However, rather than Doña Leonor latching onto local superstition as a scapegoat, she may have had reason to believe such things. According to her, witches from San Juan had in the past bewitched her sister-in-law, María Luján, and another woman she knew named Agustina Romero. Both persons had been healed by a Tewa curandero known as Juanchillo and his wife, Chepa. Ulibbarí went to San Juan to question the couple, and Juanchillo readily admitted to curing the two women named by Leonor. He had not, however, heard anything specifically about any of the three accused women from San Juan bewitching anyone. As far as who had bewitched Leonor's sister-in-law and Romero, he said that had been done by a Spanish-speaking woman from San Juan, who he did not name.

As Ulibbarí began to question Leonor's testimony, he decided to free at least one of the accused, Catarina Rosa, as she had crippled legs and was greatly distressed by the shackles binding her. Rosa's two accused companions would soon follow. Ulibbarí forwarded his finding to Governor Chacón on May 27th and, greatly irritated at Leonor, dropped the charges against the accused, stating that the claims had been "false, futile, and despicable, by reason of which and of the good effects resulting from the said proceedings, I must declare, as I do, the three Indian women to be free as regards the matter produced in this case."

It was a rare instance of New Spain's government siding with the native peoples as opposed to the Spanish.

KING OF PICURÍS PUEBLO

San Lorenzo de Picurís (1899).

In 1713, a litany of accusations were leveled against Jerónimo Dirucaca, the governor of Picurís Pueblo, by Lorenzo Coimagea, principal elder of the pueblo. In short, Dirucaca had greatly abused his power as governor of the pueblo, comparing himself to the king

79

of Spain, while his unfortunate subjects stated that he acted as though he were God. Dirucaca ignored the teachings and rules of the Church, encouraging and endorsing idolatry, concubinage, and witchcraft. Dirucaca himself had several wives and was accused of assassinating several people via sorcery. He also used love magic to bend women to his will, and those who didn't succumb to his love potions were killed. That the pueblo people actually turned to the Spaniards for help speaks volumes as to just how badly they wanted to get rid of Dirucaca, the dictator, who had been ruling the pueblo for two decades by this point. Ultimately, about fourteen persons from the pueblo, including some of Dirucaca's concubines, testified against him. Some of the pueblo elders notably stated that they felt they were "unable to speak" while he was in power.[60]

Similar to the case of "the Turk" who knew the way to Quivera years ago, Dirucaca was never executed or permanently imprisoned for his acts of sorcery because, as it turned out, he knew the way to a wealthy silver mine.[61] In exchange for showing the Spanish authorities the location of the mine, the charges against Dirucaca were dropped and he was eventually released under the provision that he leave Picurís Pueblo and also that he pay the court cost of 21 pesos!

> Similar to the case of Dirucaca was that of Pedro Munpa, who bewitched the fiscal of the San Idelfonso mission in 1725 after the fiscal had whipped Munpa for practicing witchcraft. The helpless fiscal asked Munpa to cure him, to which Munpa replied that he must deny "the law of the Spanish" and acknowledge that "only he [Mun-pa] was God." Furthermore, he should confess that it was only through Munpa that "the creatures lived, the plants grew, and rain fell." Before it was all over, Munpa proudly boasted to Spanish authorities that he had bewitched and killed many others in his time.

BRUJA OR CURANDERA?

Quasi similar to the case of Doña Leonor was this case from 1715, also involving witchcraft accusations aimed at a native of San Juan pueblo. In either 1712 or 1715 in Santa Fe, Antonia Luján was entertaining the wife of her neighbor, Francisca Caza, who was an

Indian from San Juan.[62] Rather abruptly, Francisca asked Antonia if she desired to be a rich important person with rich important friends. If so, she only needed to drink a special concoction of herbs. To illustrate the method, the woman pulled out a large shell and scraped a powder from it. If Antonia drank the concoction in warm water and rubbed the remainder on her hands, she would become wealthy and inherit important friends. Either skeptical of the process or not wanting to engage in witchcraft, Antonia refused the woman's potion and she left without saying a word, clearly angry that her offer had been refused.

A few days later, sores began to appear on Antonia's torso and left leg. In addition to that, great pain coursed through her body. Knowing she had been bewitched, she attempted to pay Caza with a colored blanket and four deerskins. This, however, apparently was not enough to appease the offended woman, and no cure was ever given. As such, Antonia returned and took back the blanket, though she was unable to get her deerskins back. Antonia next sought a curandera who provided her with a special herb from Galisteo. But still she was afflicted. So, in early July, she sent for the alcalde, Juan Páez Hurtado, who would go on to become an important figure in New Mexico. Hurtado listened to Antonia's story and was struck by the fact that Antonia thought that the whole incident could be related to the fact that her husband was having an affair with the accused witch. Having perhaps heard similar stories, such as that of Doña Leonor, Hurtado's hackles were raised.

Hurtado went to see Caza, who had already been imprisoned, to get her version of the affair. While Lujan acted as though Caza's offer of wealth came from out of nowhere, Caza claimed Lujan breached the subject when she complained that she "was very poor" and that "she did not even have a shirt" to wear. It was only after this point that Caza propositioned a special concoction that would cause God to "give her clothes" and to help her to find deerskins which she could use to buy clothes. And, contrary to the picture painted of Caza as a poor Indian, she and her mother both claimed to be wealthy, and Caza reportedly told Lujan that if she took the drink, she would become "equal to her." And, whereas Lujan claimed in her testimony that she rebuked Caza's offer by stating, "Look, we Spaniards follow the law of God," Caza claimed that Lujan did not, in fact, rebuke her or her offer. That said, it was still implied that Lujan did not drink the special potion.

It's interesting to note that Lujan's professed rebuke may have saved her from the wrath of the Church, even if she did confess to returning to Caza for a cure to her illness. Basically, as a Spanish citizen, Lujan was treated differently than the San Juan native. As the investigation continued, it was implied that Lujan had been in contact with Caza for about three to four years and that Caza may have acted as a curandera to her during that time. Or, in other words, Lujan only decided to file a complaint when she suspected Caza of sleeping with her husband. Unfortunately, the historical record is incomplete where Caza is concerned, and it is unknown exactly what happened to her. Caza's mother, however, did die in prison after being arrested in connection to Lujan's accusation.

THE WITCHES OF ISLETA

Charles Lummis photograph c. 1890 of citizens of Isleta Pueblo.

Sometime in the year 1733, Bicente García and his wife found themselves the victims of witchcraft at the pueblo of Isleta. According to a witness, Joseph Reaño, he had watched as a man named Melchor Trujillo gave the couple something to drink. Afterward, García and his wife appeared to die and then miraculously resurrect. A complaint was also filed against Trujillo by Captain Agosto Rael, who, in his declaration, claimed that he had observed the Garcias under Trujillo's spell. In the couple's home, he watched in astonishment as Trujillo seemed to go back and forth between healing the couple and causing them sickness. In his opinion, Trujillo had cast the evil eye upon them and made them ill. The charges were brought forward to the local alcalde, Don Gonsáles Bas, who launched an investigation into the matter. As it turned out, the strange liquid administered to the Garcias was peyote. Furthermore, Trujillo wasn't out to bewitch the couple, but to cure them of bewitchment.

When the alcalde called forth the Chief of Isleta, El Casique, for more details, it was he who revealed that Trujillo was acting as a curandera to thwart his own efforts to bewitch the couple. In case that wasn't clear, El Casique blatantly admitted that he was the real brujo. And it wasn't just him; he had a whole coven of fellow witches out to get the Spaniards. They comprised of an Apache woman named Manuela, a Hopi Pueblo woman named Maria la Moquina, and Francisco "El Flaco," the Thin One, also confusingly known as "El Gordo," the Fat One. El Casique went on to admit how he and his followers had bewitched the local priest, Fray Antonio Miranda, by means of a magical stone. He also confessed to bewitching Diego Padilla, Antonio Lopez, and Antonio Apache. The alcalde was stunned at these admissions, which didn't seem to stem from any desire to repent or even to gloat. El Casique stated these things as simple matters of fact, perhaps unaware of the consequences that it might warrant.

The Moqui Pueblo, as photographed by Charles Lummis, where María la Moquina hailed from.

El Casique next explained how the bewitchment was carried out via cursed idols. When asked if he would cooperate in turning over the idols, he not only agreed but even stated that upon their being relinquished, the bewitchment would cease. Next, María la Moquina was questioned via an interpreter on February 17, 1733. She seemed a bit more fearful in her testimony, perhaps suspecting a fierce punishment might be doled out. She denied being a member of the coven, more or less, and stated, "I did not cause the evil spirit. It was El Casique…" María had only acted as a message bearer for the coven and claimed that Manuela could also practice magic like El Casique. Maria accused Manuela of bewitching Martín Hurtado and also the wife of a man by the last name of Fernandez.

She then went on to confess she was present the night that the spell was placed upon the Garcias. She described El Casique, wearing a special robe, and his second in command, El Flaco, in a bright cloak, rubbing an enchanted dust from a small, enchanted stone onto their bodies in an unholy anointment. She said Maria and Manuela left before the main bewitchment commenced in the Garcia home. As for Martín Hurtado, he, along with his daughter, had been bewitched when monos in their image were pierced by pins.

When Manuela was questioned, she, too, like Maria, threw El Casique under the bus, claiming that he and El Flaco cast most of the spells. However, Manuela did oddly admit to bewitching Juan de Dios Martinez, Martín Hurtado, and the wife of Juan Hernandez. An old woman was in possession of the cursed idols, she claimed. Manuela was then questioned about Melchor, who had been called a brujo by some and a benevolent curandero by others. Specifically, Manuela was asked if she thought Melchor placed a spell on the Garcias. She answered that he did not; it was El Casique via a strange rock powder. Furthermore, Maria la Moquina was a bruja who had helped cast the spell. As for Melchor, he had found Maria inside of a gourd floating down the road. (Don't forget, New Mexico witches occasionally flew in pumpkins and gourds.) To stop Maria, Melchor placed three fingers in her mouth. (No, I don't understand the significance of this act, either.)

By this time the alcalde was thoroughly confused. Was Melchor a brujo or a curandero? Which of the two women was telling the truth about the other being a bruja? And, finally, why did El Casique confess so easily? Since most of the inquest was conducted via translators from the languages of the pueblos into Spanish, it is thought that much was lost in translation.

In any case, under pressure from the alcalde, they turned over the dolls and other items used in their magic. El Flaco willingly gave up four dolls and a strange string with three beads which he concluded were "not harmful in creating witchcraft or any harm." The women were also cooperative, and of the old woman Maria, she turned over "three other small dolls (*muñequillas*) and a medium size rock, and it was kind of round and bluish in color."

Next he went to El Casique's home, wherein he was told he would find nine dolls. The alcalde noted that "El Casique turned over to me a small oblong rock, pink in color and very smooth in texture. Then he turned over a buckskin bag containing a white rock wrapped in a small cloth, and then he turned over some of the idols as he had promised in his declaration. Then I threatened to whip him with whiplashes if he did not do as promised."

When El Casique refused to give up the whereabouts of the remaining cursed dolls, he was strung up by a rope tied to his hands and given ten lashes. According to one story, El Casique broke under the torture, claiming that he wanted to confess but that the Devil was holding him in bondage, and he could not do so. Other accounts simply acted as though El Casique was too proud and stubborn to turn over the idols. In either case, El Casique was given his ten lashes even as his coven cried out for him to simply hand over the idols.

The alcalde noted that "Realizing the obstacles I was facing, I called upon the Father Minister so that he might get him to confess, and again this was of no avail, but instead El Casique, playing a small deception on me, gave me a bag with a white rock and said this was an idol, and so he took up my time the whole day."

The perplexed alcalde gave up his search for the dolls and decided El Casique had received his penance upon the ten painful lashes.

SUCCUBUS OF SANTA FE

Accounts of sleep demons are common the world over. The two most common comprise of the incubus and the succubus. The former is male, and the latter is female. While typically a succubus only visited men and an incubus only women, the succubus of Santa Fe, if it should be called that, attacked and molested another woman.

On the night of April 17, 1734, around 8 PM, Maria Manuela de Armijo was attacked by a strange witch in Santa Fe. She said she was enjoying the day's end and all was quiet in her bedroom. Her

1889 sculpture "The Succubus" by Auguste Rodin displayed in Museo Soumaya, Ciudad de México.

85

husband, Cayetano Moya, and children were all asleep. Just as she began to fall asleep, she watched in horror as a bruja entered her home. She recognized her as Nicolasa Romero, a coyote (or person of Spanish, Indian, and African heritage). Romero was making noises like an animal, bellowing like a bull one minute and barking like a dog the next. She assaulted Armijo verbally at first, calling her the Spanish word for whore multiple times. When Armijo went to cry out, like many victims of a succubus, she suffered a form of paralysis as the witch began to fondle her body in a sexual manner— all the while, her husband was unaware of the supernatural activity going on next to him. Finally, Armijo managed to croak out, "Praised be the Blessed Sacrament!" followed by, "Glory be to Saint Anthony!" At that, the witch disappeared, and the story ended.

A Little Case of Love Magic

One day in the year 1751, a woman named Gertrudes Sanchez came before the Church to accuse a widow living in Sandia of witchcraft. Barbara Garcia was her name, and she had allegedly used a lock of hair to control her lover, a married man whom she was having an affair with. Garcia was instructed in this love magic by her friend, Katarina Guitierez, who told her to bind the hair in either her sash or her belt. The result of the matter was resolved swiftly. Barbara burned the enchanted lock of hair, ended the affair, and renounced love magic to return to the Church.

Plague of the Witches

My house has four corners
Four angels adore it
Luke, Mark, John and Matthew
Neither witches or sorcerers
Nor evil-doing man
In the name of the Father, the Son, and the Holy
Spirit. Amen.
—traditional prayer at Abiquiú

The prayer above was recounted by New Mexico state historian Robert Martinez during a presentation on the history of witchcraft in the state. And of all of New Mexico's witchcraft cases, the witch trials of Abiquiú, a small pueblo of Genízaros[63] in Northwest New

86

Mexico, is the most elaborate. And yet, for many years, the history of these fantastic events remained forgotten.

One of the first to mention Abiquiú was New Mexico historian F. Stanley, who wrote, "Abiquiú is to New Mexico what Salem is to Massachusetts."[64] Later, Mark Simmons only gave it a paragraph or so in his seminal *Witchcraft in the Southwest* due to a lack of information. In the late 1990s, Malcolm Ebright and Rick Hendricks began a thorough investigation into the full story, which resulted in a landmark tome entitled *The Witches of Abiquiú*. Thanks to them, the fascinating and somewhat unbelievable tale of Abiquiú resurfaced.

Fray Juan José Toledo, a Franciscan priest from Mexico City, was the main character in the drama. The primary villain, according to Toledo at least, was a devil-worshipping sorcerer by the name of Miguel Ontiveras, better known as *El Cojo*, the cripple. However, as Toledo would eventually learn, El Cojo was only one of many sorcerers, and it was debatable if he was truly the ring-leader of the bunch. Fray Toledo took charge of the mission in Abiquiú in 1756 but didn't report on the paranormal activities there until 1760. For a period of five years between 1760 and 1765, Toledo wrote to the governor to inform him of numerous "damages and deaths" that had occurred due to El Cojo's "explicit Pact with the Devil."[65]

Before Toledo became the main priest at the pueblo, his predecessor, Fray Félix Ordoñez, had been killed by methods of witchcraft. Also during Ordoñez's tenure at Abiquiú, Fray Toledo came to visit with another priest, Father Manuel Sopeña. There the elderly Sopeña was boldly confronted by a genízario sorcerer who rebuked him and told him that he should leave at once.[66] Sopeña was so taken aback that he was unable to speak[67] and dropped dead not long after—perhaps he had been stricken with the Evil Eye?

As such, Fray Toledo must have had some idea of what he was getting into when he took over Abiquiú from the late Fray Ordoñez in 1756. Soon after his arrival, a mysterious illness—or perhaps plague would be a better word—began to spread across the pueblo. The horrid sickness began with sharp pains in the stomach and led to dehydration, insomnia, and the drying of the bones. In the final stages, the victim's teeth would turn black, and blood would excrete from the mouth and nose. In the most extreme cases, the victim's stomach would swell until it burst. Allegedly, insects like spiders and worms would be found in the stomach according to locals.

Toledo himself had been afflicted by this illness twice and miraculously survived, though many others were not so fortunate. Toledo's sickness came about on July 30, 1757, at one in the afternoon. It had begun with coughing and choking that developed into an immense pain in his intestines, which he called a "ball in his stomach."[68] Basically, he was suffering from what they used to call "dropsy," which meant that there was an extreme buildup of fluids in his intestines. For three years he suffered this affliction. Medicine was no help and in some cases only increased his pain. Finally, on December 31, 1760, just when he thought he was going to die, a mysterious woman "dressed as a Spaniard"[69] appeared at his bedside. She was not an angel but a local curandera who began massaging him until he miraculously disgorged the ball in his stomach made of coagulated phlegm. Toledo wasn't out of the woods yet. Soon after, another ball began to form, and he again had to seek the aid of a curandera. The process repeated, and he was healed again. After this, his ailments were minor in comparison, limited to continued coughing, choking, and a heaviness in his legs.[70]

Franciscan Missionaries journeying across California.

Among those who succumbed was a woman named Dionista, who claimed to have become afflicted after eating a small piece of curd cheese from El Cojo. Her sickness was more agonizing than Toledo's, as the pain in her stomach was so extreme she could not even find solace in sleep. In addition to that was a feeling of internal burning and unquenchable thirst. No matter how much she drank, it would not cease. As with other victims, her teeth mysteriously began to darken, and blood secreted from her nose and mouth. All the while, her stomach swelled, and when she mercifully died, it was recorded that her abdomen had become "so massive, that the body could not be held to be buried."[71]

With the late Dionista having named El Cojo as the source of her illness, Toledo followed this somewhat tenuous lead and began to build a case against the sorcerer. Among those willing to come forward to accuse El Cojo was a genízario man who confessed to hiring El Cojo to kill his wife via sorcery. (This he did so that he could be free to cavort with his mistress.) The man had a change of heart, though, and came to Toledo to repent before it was too late for his ill wife, who ended up surviving.

To counter El Cojo, Toledo relented to recruit the help of a Ute curandera. (Oddly enough, the use of an opposing sorcerer was deemed acceptable if it was believed that it was the only way to counter another sorcerer's magic.) The curandera told Toledo that for the past two years she had observed El Cojo's magic killing off various peoples in the area. She then boldly offered to face off with him in front of the entire pueblo. What resulted could be considered similar to the classic stand-off made popular in the Western, only with magic. In front of the Abiquiú genízarios, El Cojo and the Ute curandera stared each other down. By use of the Evil Eye, El Cojo emerged the victor. Toledo noted that "El Cojo looked at the Ute with very angry eyes [causing her to] return to her nearby home deathly ill, bleeding from her mouth and nose. Then she dropped dead."[72]

This is interesting for a number of reasons. Firstly, it would appear as though El Cojo struck the woman with the same illness or some variation of it used to kill Dionista (as evidenced by the bleeding from her facial cavities). That El Cojo could inflict this via the Evil Eye as opposed to herbal magic is eyebrow-raising (if this he did indeed do, that is). Though, of course, some may argue that the plague was unrelated to witchcraft to begin with, and perhaps the Ute curandera was already suffering from it during the face-off. Toledo's attitude towards the woman's death is also disappointing on his part, as rather than being grateful for her effort, he denounced her by stating that El Cojo's devil had been more powerful than her own, and she had died in sin.

Before this, Toledo had also sought the aid of a renowned Apache medicine man called Son of El Canoso (El Canoso meaning 'the Gray-Headed One'). Son of el Canoso was called for during Toledo's first year at the pueblo in 1756. Upon investigating the strange illness, Son of el Canoso somehow identified that the cause of the plague was a magical poisonous snake in El Cojo's care. Under Son

89

of el Canoso's advisement, Toledo recorded that "A magic poisonous snake that El Cojo had, alive and concealed, was partially responsible." That this was deducted by an Apache medicine man is intriguing, as the Apache loathed snakes compared to other native peoples of New Mexico. In *Indeh*, Eve Ball noted that the Apache revealed little about their religion, but it was apparent to her that they were "very superstitious about snakes" and would not "use anything made of snakeskin."[73] Perhaps, for this reason, Son of el Canoso left soon after.

Depiction of Moses and the Bronze Serpent.

Snake worship among the Pueblos was not uncommon, the most famous of which being the giant snake of Pecos Pueblo that is quasi-related to Montezuma. On that note, one of the accused Abiquiú sorcerers was said to be a "follower of Montezuma" himself. Furthermore, was it possible that El Cojo was milking the snake's venom and placing it into food in some instances?[74] However, New Mexico didn't harbor any snakes with what is called boomslang venom, which causes bleeding from various orifices (snakes of that variety are only found in Africa). In any case, unfortunately no description was given of the so-called magical snake. While the magical snake may sound like pure hokum, the reptile was actually found and killed.

Though Toledo's train of thought was less pragmatic—he didn't seem to consider that perhaps the snake's venom was being used to cause the sickness—he decided the snake needed to be destroyed since it was being used as an object of worship. Somehow, he and other members of the pueblo found the snake and the genízaros beat it with sticks. The immobilized snake was then strung up on a

90

post, where it was noted that it took an unusually long time to die. Perhaps this was meant to mimic the story from Numbers, where the Israelites were plagued by venomous serpents:

"Then the Lord said to Moses, 'Make a snake image and mount it on a pole. When anyone who is bitten looks at it, he will recover.' So Moses made a bronze snake and mounted it on a pole. Whenever someone was bitten, and he looked at the bronze snake, he recovered.'" -Numbers 21:8-9

However, even with the snake dead, the sickness continued...

THE SCHOOL OF THE DEVIL

"I am at a loss how to begin my own declaration, for it is a contest with the Devil, from which, as a minister of God, I cannot excuse myself. It is within my jurisdiction and at my doorstep."—Father Toledo, January 1764

At the same time as the plague came news of the perennial "School of the Devil" common to witchcraft tales in New Mexico. Only in this case the school turned out to be real. It was first spoken of by an eight-year-old boy who worked as the doorkeeper at the Abiquiú mission. One day, as the boy took a nap, he was overheard talking in his sleep about this School of the Devil overseen by El Cojo.

The boy was brought before Toledo and eventually confessed to having attended the School of the Devil, which was located in a cave outside the pueblo. In the cave he saw drawings of individuals targeted for bewitchment, some of whom had already died. As this confession came about in private, Toledo brought the boy in front of officers of the pueblo. Only now, perhaps out of fear, the boy denied any claims of the School of the Devil. Toledo became angry, insisting that the boy show them the cave, and when he refused, Toledo whipped him. However, soon other attendees of the school came forward and confessed to Toledo, wanting to be forgiven before it was too late. El Cojo was placed in stocks due to these accusations, and though he promised to turn over the cursed items used in his ceremonies, upon release he would relent. Though he would not turn over the items or reveal the school's location, El Cojo did confess to killing Dionista and proclaimed, perhaps out of pride, that he was the head sorcerer in the area. El Cojo then proceeded to name some of the other witches, notably an Indian named Vicente Trujillo and his wife María, who had killed Toledo's predecessor at the pueblo, Félix Ordoñez.[75] Vicente had also bewitched a former

91

alcalde, Antonio Ulibarrí, who was struck ill along with his wife by the spurned sorcerer.

At a later date, during a trial in Santa Fe, more details emerged that pointed back to the old School of the Devil thought to be run by El Cojo. In fact, it was Agustín Tagle, known as *El Viejo*, who ran it and was the most powerful wizard.[76] El Viejo, it was said, "never went to confession or communion" and "followed the laws of Montezuma."[77] This would seem to be the case, as when the cave was later found, certain drawings on the cave wall were of Mesoamerican origin. Specifically, there was a reproduction of a circle divided into four parts. This symbol was used in the Aztec city of Teotihuacán to represent the underworld of Tlalocan. However, to Alcalde Fernández, this four part circle represented the four parts of the world and the four winds under the sway of the Devil.

Other accounts of the cave were given by the foster daughter of Vicente and María Trujillo, a genízario known only as Paula, whose parents died when she was fifteen. With her foster father now in jail, Paula apparently felt comfortable enough to inform on him. The story she told was remarkably similar to tales of the witches' sabbats related elsewhere in this book, only a bit less fantastic. So, either Paula actually witnessed a real version of the witches' sabbat, or she made up her own variation of it for reasons unknown. In any case, her account was as follows.

At some point in the past, Vicente and María took Paula to a cave outside of the village, presumably Toledo's long sought School of the Devil. Before entering, she was instructed to remove the cross hung about her neck, which was common to many tales of the witches sabbat. At the mouth of the cave, she was greeted by various animals, notably toads[78] and snakes, which she was instructed to kiss.[79] (Remember, the kissing of the snake was important in the witches' sabbat and also tied into the sacred serpent of Montezuma.) Upon entering the cave, somehow she was given the ability to turn into an animal herself, though she doesn't explain how. Nor did she mention being given peyote, though it would seem likely that she was, for soon she described transforming into a woodpecker. In her bird form, she tried three times to fly to Cerro del Pedernal a narrow mesa south of Abiquiú Lake. Despite her best efforts, her arms were too tired to make the flight and it caused her great pain. In the cave, she watched as some of the animals transformed into several Indian men and one Spaniard. She was then instructed to again kiss the toads and snakes, but this time she became fearful. She began to praise the Holy Sacrament. Unlike more fantastical tales where the person at the witches' sabbat found themselves magically transported away from it, in Paula's case, her foster parents were struck with great pain at hearing the holy words. As they howled in agony, they begged her to cease her mentions of God and the Virgin, but she refused. She was thrown out of the cave and the next day was also asked to leave their home.

THE DEVIL'S OWN:
ALLIES, ENEMIES, AND SHAPESHIFTERS

In his booklet on Abiquiú, historian F. Stanley falsely identified Father Toledo's greatest nemesis as a man called "Juachinillo" who "delved into the occult and master-minded the sorcery prevalent in the area."[80] Stanley was, in fact, confusing Toledo's greatest rival for his greatest helper. You see, in his battle against the Devil, Toledo recruited one of what he felt was one of the Devil's own, another sorcerer named Joaquinillo, codenamed *El Descubridor* (the Discoverer, or Finder).

As it stands, it's unclear if Joaquinillo was truly a devilish sorcerer or just a curandero, as those were synonymous for Spaniards at the time. Whether one or the other, he essentially became a spy or informer who supplied Toledo with much needed inside information.

Joaquinillo was discovered in April of 1763 when a genízaro woman claimed a sorcerer named Joaquinillo had bewitched her. Joaquinillo, in turn, told the local alcalde that it was not he who bewitched her, but a Sandia sorcerer named Antonio Menchero. Joaquinillo requested that his brother and fellow Medicine Man, Juan Largo, be allowed to help him prove that Menchero was a sorcerer, and this was allowed. However, the case against Menchero didn't appear to be pursued and somehow Joaquinillo became chief informant at Abiquiú.

One of the first sorcerers that Joaquinillo turned up was Agustín Tagle, El Viejo, who was said to be even more powerful than El Cojo. When Tagle was questioned in front of authorities, he denied claims of witchcraft. Juan Largo, Joaquinillo's brother, swiftly used his abilities as a medicine man to suck a foreign object from Tagle. Though this surely sounds strange, this practice was common among Apache medicine men to cure victims of shooting sorcery (see the following section on Apache and Navajo witchcraft). To do so, the medicine men had the ability to literally suck the object from the other person's body. In this case, Juan Largo grabbed Tagle's hand

93

and sucked from it a small piece of iron wrapped in buckskin. This piece of iron may have represented Tagle's heart as Juan Largo stated that Tagle's heart was just as hard as the piece of iron removed from his body. Around the same time, Joaquinillo sucked a heart-shaped flint from the back of El Cojo as proof of his witchcraft when El Cojo tried to deny ever bewitching anyone.

JOAQUINILLO'S HISTORY

Joaquinillo was not of mixed blood, but a Kiowa who had been captured by the Comanches at a young age and was later sold to the Spanish, which was how he eventually ended up at Abiquiú. In an interview with the governor in February of 1764, Joaquinillo explained that he had first learned the art of sorcery from his father as a boy but soon forgot it. To protect himself from the witches crippling and killing people in Abiquiú, he asked his brother, Juan Largo, to teach him again. Though Joaquinillo learned the art of sorcery in an effort to protect himself, some of his rituals were quasi-similar to those performed by María de Zamora back in 1605. If you'll remember, she used peyote in conjunction with a bowl of water from which a devilish creature would emerge. Joaquinillo explained to the governor how he would smear his body with certain herbs and spittle, and also chewed a special herb which was possibly peyote. He did so in front of a bowl of water in which was placed a white stone[81] with a small effigy representing an unknown deity. This ritual gave Joaquinillo foresight in that he could see reflected in the waters other sorcerers nearby.

It was at this point that El Cojo accused a man named Pedro Trujillo of witchcraft. Specifically, he accused him of bewitching people while he was in the form of a cat. Joaquinillo backed up this claim by stating he knew of others bewitched by Trujillo.[82] After this, Alcalde Carlos Fernández had El Cojo, Augustin Tagle, and Vicente Trujillo arrested and taken away to Santa Fe to be imprisoned.[83] With three of the head witches now gone, more Abiquiú residents were less fearful of pointing the finger at other suspected witches.

Shooting Sorcery at Abiquiú

Though shooting sorcery was more common to the Navajo and Apache, it was also semi-prevalent at Abiquiú. Through the sucking cure of medicine men, out of victims' bodies were removed anything from strands of hair to arrowheads, beads, pebbles, and pieces of wood. These objects could literally be shot into the victim's body through a tube. Some were also shot via means of magical incantations after they had been placed upon a cloth or piece of buckskin. The objects traveled so quickly that they were said to be invisible to the naked eye. The most notable example of shooting sorcery at Abiquiú came from Vicente Trujillo. One of his victims, Prudencia Trujillo, was cured of an illness when Juan Largo sucked from her body several small shells and strands of hair. Juan Largo told her to take these items and place them on Vicente's doorstep. If he became ill, he was indeed the sorcerer who had fired them. Prudencia did as told, and Vicente soon became ill.

However, Toledo still had it out for El Cojo, who Joaquinillo promised that he would capture, whether it be in his regular human form or in his animal form as a black cat. Yes, like other New Mexico and Mesoamerican sorcerers, El Cojo could take the form of animals.[84] Though Joaquinillo only mentioned a cat, other Abiquiú residents claimed to have seen El Cojo in the form of a dog. They knew it was no ordinary dog when they shot at it with arrows but were unable to hit it.

Another of Vicente's disgruntled students, Isabela "La Pastora," became an informant and revealed more shapeshifter tales.[85] She claimed that she had seen Vicente take the form of an owl. Juan Largo gave a report on Vicente that was more liken to a skinwalker, as he claimed to see Vicente transformed into some kind of animal— he couldn't tell what kind—only from the waist up. Other Abiquiú residents claimed that they had seen Vicente as a dog.

While Toledo certainly believed that the Devil gave supernatural aid to the sorcerers, he was not so sure that they had the ability to actually shapeshift. In a letter to the governor, he wrote that the sorcerers managed this change via their "artifices" through which they "appear as domestic animals, most of the time cats."[86] From this statement it's a bit unclear just what Toledo was trying to say. In the same letter he gave an account of Joaquín Mestas, who killed an attacking animal that had invaded his home. Mestas subsequently burned the animal's body, and the next day, in San Juan Bosque, found a "certain Indian dead and singed."[87]

A Priest Encountering a Werewolf from the Irish Legend of the Werewolves of Ossory from Topographia Hibernica by Gerald of Wales, c. 1200.

At a later date, Toledo encountered Vicente Trujillo in the form of a wolf. What had happened was that Toledo had convinced two bewitched women to confess in front of the whole pueblo that Trujillo was the cause of their sickness. Never before had Trujillo been outed like this publicly, and he sought vengeance against Toledo as described in a May 15, 1763, letter. Toledo claims that while riding on horseback, he saw a small whirlwind approaching him, out of which emerged a wolf that he somehow knew to be Trujillo. In his letter, Trujillo wrote that

He arrived in a small swirling of dust (and apparently turned into a wolf). He attacked me and I stopped him many times with my hands. He fought with great force, punches, and bites

96

although I kept him down [and] remained firmer in the saddle, holding onto the mane between both ears.[88]

In the ensuing fight, Toledo hit his head against a branch and his horse fell to the ground with the priest, his foot caught in the stirrups. Toledo lost consciousness and the wolf was gone when he woke up. This is as odd as anything, as surely the wolf would have gone for the kill with the priest on the ground and unconscious.[89]

The mini-whirlwind that Trujillo arrived in was notable as well, since there were claims that Popé traveled by whirlwind while planning the Pueblo Revolt. The fact that Toledo described the wolf as punching him is also interesting. Was this something akin to an anthropomorphized wolf-man later made popular in movies? Looking into the lore of Old Mexico, there were tales of a Devil Dog called the Cadejo that was known for punching its victims with its snout rather than biting them. Perhaps this also fits into the story in some way. Or am I giving this report too much credence, as Toledo may have simply been telling a tall tale? This, of course, we can never know for certain. What the governor thought of this account we can only imagine. The only evidence we have as to his reaction is the fact that the governor didn't seem to react at all. He never bothered to address the outlandish claim, which greatly damaged Toledo's credibility.

EXORCISM AT OJO CALIENTE

In Toledo's arsenal against the Devil he had a book that taught him what to look for regarding witchcraft. For instance, the rope used in a hanging execution could be worked to perform magic. Even teeth and bones of the dead, plus hair, fingers, and toes, figurines made to represent the targeted victim, bird feathers, and certain plants could be used to work magic. The guidebook was called the *Itinerario* and was written especially for priests when dealing with bewitchment. It listed four primary methods with which to deal with curses and other supernatural maladies. First, the sacraments of confession, the Eucharist, the Mass, plus prayer and fasting were recommended. If not those, then the power of the cross or certain saints were to be used. If these methods failed, exorcism should be attempted. The use of herbal medicine was not looked down upon as being some type of magic; it was simply believed that herbs could not prevail against black magic and the Devil.

In addition to the *Itinerario,* Toledo also turned to his Bible. After a long study, Toledo pointed specifically to Asmodeus as the chief devil in this case as opposed to Lucifer. In Toledo's words, Asmodeus, mentioned only once in the Bible, was "the prince of injustice" and "the third from Lucifer down."[90] Why exactly he chose this devil above all the others is unknown, but surely he had his reasons. Whereas before Toledo was only countering examples of herbal magic and witchcraft, he would soon go toe to toe with devils and demons in the form of possession.

Stone Ruins photographed at Ojo Caliente c.1891.

In May of 1763, Father Toledo performed an exorcism at Ojo Caliente. If these possessions came about solely from the Devil, then he could exorcise them. However, if these were afflictions from witchcraft, Joaquinillo would be needed as a medicine man to cure the ailments of the afflicted. Indeed, the first case of possession turned out to be sickness caused by bewitchment, and Toledo allowed Joaquinillo to treat him on the condition that he did not perform the strange sucking magic that removed foreign objects from the body. The treatment was successful, and the next case the duo worked did indeed turn out to be a case of possession that sounded as though it could have influenced *The Exorcist* (1973).

The possessed person's name was Mauricio, a genízaro from the area. When Toledo placed his hands on Mauricio's head and began to read scripture from the Gospel of John, the priest began to shake uncontrollably. When Toledo launched into an exorcism, Mauricio began to taunt the priest, unveiling an obsidian-edged wooden club. He then sat naked in a heap of burning coals, the flames arising on

98

either side of him doing him no discernable harm. According to Toledo, "Then he took some coals and put them in his mouth and began to expel sparks and flames from his mouth and eyes."[91]

Later that night, a remorseful Mauricio approached Toledo and begged him to let Joaquinillo remove a bewitched item from his body. Seeing as his exorcism didn't work, Toledo relented, and Joaquinillo sucked a stone from Mauricio's body. Toledo saved the stone and sent it to Alcalde Fernandez with the instructions that it be forwarded to the governor as proof of the strange happenings. If there was anything notable about the stone itself other than the fact that it had been sucked from Mauricio's body is unknown.

Toledo's next exorcism, that of a man caused to hate his wife, was more successful. The man's wife had come to Toledo with the claim that her husband beat her anytime she tried to go to church. When Toledo confronted the husband about this, he claimed that a powerful sorcerer called Cascabel[92] had made advances on his wife, which she rebuked, and so Cascabel had bewitched him with "a devil so that he would hate his wife..."[93]

Toledo made the husband drink from the waters of San Ignacio and then successfully exorcised him. With that, Toledo and Joaquinillo returned home. As it turned out, this was only a prelude of far more terrifying things to come at Abiquiú.

THE POSSESSIONS AT ABIQUIÚ

"In the year 1764 some women possessed by the devil broke loose in this kingdom." –Fray Francisco Atanasio Dominguez, 1777.

Not long after Father Toledo returned to Abiquiú from Ojo Caliente, an Abiquiú woman fainted in the middle of an exorcism prayer at church in June. The woman's name was María Trujillo, though she was not the same María Trujillo accused of witchcraft and married to Vicente.[94] In her sickness, María became covered in purple spots on the palm of her hand, on her knee, and on her right shoulder and elbow. When Father Toledo exorcised her, these strange maladies vanished. However, new ailments took their place soon after in the form of depression, headaches, and indigestion.

That summer also marked the three year anniversary since Toledo had first petitioned the governor about the plague of witchcraft affecting the pueblo. Perhaps not knowing what else they could do, Fray Toledo, Alcalde Fernández, and several others went to a mysterious site about two thousand varas from Abiquiú called *El León Fuerte* (the strong lion), where Toledo performed an exorcism.

Their mission was to destroy and annihilate as many of the heathen temples as they could. Some devilish petroglyphs were eradicated at the spot and a cross was erected in their place. There was also a second site where El Viejo, Augustín Tagle, took his followers to perform strange rites of some kind. The petroglyphs there were also erased, and crosses were apparently drawn in the vicinity to replace them. Feeling that they had at least accomplished something, they trudged back to Abiquiú, where the real mayhem was only beginning.

Spanish Priests Destroying Aztec Idols During the Conquest.

In December, María Trujillo's symptoms became unmanageable and she kicked off a plague of possessions in Abiquiú. That month she fainted in church and began to writhe, "tearing at herself" as though possessed of "unnatural forces."[95] On December 17th, she came to Toledo begging for deliverance and he performed another exorcism successfully. However, the demon spirits would return yet again before it was all over.

The next to be possessed was eighteen-year-old Francisca Varela the following day on December 18th. She had walked from her house to a nearby spring to draw water when all of a sudden, her body began to quiver in fear of some unseen force. Then, in the distance, she heard a strange squealing akin to a pig. Quickly she hurried home where she fainted. Upon coming to, she was no longer herself, making strange animal-like noises. Swiftly she was rushed to see Toledo. The priest was informed of the girl's strange ailments, such as a sensation of ants crawling inside of her body. Father Toledo alleviated this particular ailment, though he noted that the girl continued to make "unbelievable screams" that sounded like "pigs, cows, burros, owls and other animals"[96] in addition to writhing about and flailing her arms. It was only with great difficulty that parishioners held her down as she bit and clawed at them while Toledo performed the exorcism. As Toledo did so, Varela cursed him, calling him an "insolent, kid goat, Mulatto."[97] Again, it was not unlike a scene from *The Exorcist*. As the all-night exorcism proceeded, Varela contorted and twisted her body in strange ways as she attempted to escape the grasp of those holding her down while also emitting loud howls. Only upon the rising of the sun did she finally relax.

There would be no rest for poor Father Toledo. That very morning, yet another possessed girl, twelve-year-old María Chávez, emerged. Perhaps due to exhaustion, Toledo called for Joaquinillo to help. It was his opinion that the girl was a victim of herbal magic and that she had eaten a small bun containing "an evil spirit" that had made her ill. As it was, the girl was experiencing extreme pain on the right side of her body in addition to convulsions. Joaquinillo felt that the culprits were Jacinta, a pueblo baker, and her mother, known as Atole Caliente.

The next time Toledo tried to perform Mass, the possessed girls, including the alleged witches, all began to convulse and fall to the floor, making great noise as they did so. Toledo and his choir continued the service, but the noise made by the possessed women was so great that neither he nor the choir could be heard. Still, things got stranger. When the group of possessed women marched to church, a group of crows seemed to follow their every move in what Toledo called a "Satanic procession." As Toledo described it, he saw "crows flying around their heads and escorting them in front and behind their bodies every time they go out."[98] On December 21st the afflicted women were particularly bad, and a new girl in the group demonstrated such possessed strength so as to overpower four to six men. The next day things escalated when Toledo witnessed Atole Caliente assaulting two of the afflicted girls on December 22nd. And so, Toledo began to whip Atole.

As the month winded down towards the New Year, the possessions increased to the point that Toledo would sometimes try to exorcise as many as five women at once. As things continued to escalate, the demons possessing the women began to converse with Toledo in Latin. The genízaros did not speak Latin, so either one of two possibilities existed: Toledo was making things up, or the girls were actually possessed. And, as it would turn out, Toledo would not be the only one to hear the women speak in Latin, so the latter seems to be the more likely explanation. One of these devils also told Toledo in 28 days that all the demons would depart from Abiquiú. Toledo took this statement as deception and as an effort to get him to cease his exorcism ceremonies, which he would not do.

In one of his conversations, Toledo even learned the name of one of the demons, which was given as Diablo Cojuelo, which told him that he had possessed María Agueda in Chimayo in order to abuse her and end her community. Though Toledo drove Diablo Cojuelo from María's body, the demon next entered several other women.

In one case, María Trujillo, the first possessed girl, invited the Devil into her. María was having an argument with her husband and invited the Devil to intervene. When the Devil did so, the house began to tremble. Toledo was called to exorcise María and was greatly incensed that she had invited the demon into her life again. When exorcising her, this time, María choked out of her throat a horse's tooth! In yet another instance, María became possessed again in a field near her home where she said there were legions of demons.

The litany of exorcisms at Abiquiú were finally enough to make the governor get serious about an investigation into the manner. Joaquinillo was called before the governor to make a testimony and a list of alleged witches not just in Abiquiú, but in northern New Mexico in general. For instance, he identified 24 witches at Taos alone though seven of them lacked names and only descriptions were given.

A new governor had taken over at Abiquiú by the name of García Perejas, who was bound and determined to put an end to this "Empire of the Devil." One of his first acts of business was to destroy idols worshiped in secret by the genízarios. As had been done years earlier with the previous governor, Toledo and Joaquinillo and a few others traveled to a hidden site with Perejas. Toledo soon found a stone on which was inscribed what he considered to be a contract with the Devil. Toledo smashed the stone and broke it into several pieces, then exorcised the remaining sections afterward in a rebuke of the Devil. In the spot where the stone had been found, he erected a six-foot cross.

After this excursion, things began to intensify yet again. Toledo and Perejas encountered another demon-possessed woman of particular note. Unnamed, the woman slapped Toledo in the middle of his exorcism because the demon possessing her had things it wished to say before departing. In particular, it wished to prove to Perejas that it was a real spirit with knowledge unknown to normal human beings. The demon went on to divulge private moments from Perejas's life that only he knew to his astonishment. The demon told him that his rosary kept his home safe from the evil spirits swarming about the edges of his property line. It was at this point that the lines of good and evil began to blur, the motive unknown. The demon began to give Pereja personal advice as to private home matters involving his wife and daughters in addition to divulging the locations of more pagan idols in need of destruction not revealed by Joaquinillo. The purpose of these seemingly benevolent revelations puzzled both men for some time. In fact, Toledo began to believe the demons, advertently or not, were helping guide the genízaros towards true salvation by giving them a taste of Hell.

Pictographs within Bandelier National Monument.

Specifically, the demon mentioned a site thought to be in current day Bandelier National Monument south of Abiquiú containing an effigy of stone lions. Though there do today still reside two stone lions in the area, it would seem the demon was referring to two other stone lions previously destroyed by Toledo, as the demon stated that Toledo's destruction of the idols had taken away the power from that particular site. The other two idols listed included a stone serpent hidden away at Ojo Caliente by the San Juan Indians. The other was a "powerful stone located in an ancient ruin of an Indian pueblo near the ranch that belonged to [Juan José] Lobato."[99]

Mystery of the Stone Lions

The Stone Lions Shrine of Bandelier National Monument, seen above, is of special note. The lions are carved into the tops of two side by side boulders near Yapashe, an ancient pueblo. However, there is another shrine sporting a singular stone lion as well. Jack Kutz wrote of what appeared to be paranormal activity associated with that statue in his book *Mysteries & Miracles of New Mexico*. Kutz related how a team of anthropologists from the University of New Mexico worked tirelessly to transport the stone lion away to save it from vandals on March 7, 1970. However, the operation was plagued with a string of bad luck eerily preceded by an eclipse of the sun that day. In addition to an injury that ensued from a falling boulder when moving the statue, a helicopter used to transport the stone lion also experienced difficulties from harsh winds, and the stone lion nearly crushed one of the anthropologists as it was being lowered onto a truck bed below. The stone lion was taken to the Maxwell Museum, but eventually the lion was returned due to protests by the people of San Felipe Pueblo in 1981.

Eventually, the woman, still possessed some time later, led the men to another site sacred to the Indians described as a huge tower almost forty feet high. It was constructed of mud and stone and appeared "miraculous" to Alcalde Perejas. On the stones nearby along with the ones used to build the tower could be found numerous petroglyphs and pictographs. A pyramid-shaped rock depicted the Devil in the shape of a two-headed snake according to Perejas's interpretation, while another featured a horned serpent likely representing the snake deity Awanyu. As much of the site as possible was destroyed and Toledo performed an exorcism.

THE INQUISITION OF ABIQUIÚ

After the exorcisms performed at the pagan sites, the possessions still continued at Abiquiú. Finally, Governor Vélez Cachupín took action in a written statement on January 31, 1764, vowing to take responsibility for the outbreak of witches. That same day he also appointed a commission of the top ecclesiastics of New Mexico to thoroughly discuss the matter. For two days, they debated whether or not evil spirits truly possessed the women. Their verdict was that they were indeed real evil spirits, but also that perhaps their purpose was to help convert the genízaros. Furthermore, it was decided that Fray Toledo was partially to blame for not better mastering the language of the genízaros and knowing more about their customs. To some degree, it would seem the commission was more interested in placing the blame than fixing the problem. The only real solution they came up with, which did not come to pass, was to build a second pueblo for the genízaros at Abiquiú.

Other recommendations included that the governor interview Joaquinillo in person and that the list of witches from Joaquinillo and Toledo be forwarded to the offices of the Inquisition in Mexico City. Spaniards on the list should be dealt with, but Indians were a bit out of their jurisdiction. For some reason, it was noted that the witches of Chimayo should be treated with caution.[100] As for any remaining pagan idols, they should be destroyed. Lastly, the governor put an end, for the time being at least, to the ceremonial Turtle Dance conducted at some pueblos, as it was associated both with Poheyemo and the Pueblo Revolt. Actually, it was Joaquinillo who had informed the governor that during the ceremony, the Devil—possibly meaning Poheyemo in this instance—appeared before the participants to give them both instructions and predictions as to the coming year.

MENCHERO

Along with El Cojo, another sorcerer of note that several witnesses seemed to have heated feelings about was Antonio Menchero. A Spaniard by the name of Salvador Garcia claimed that Menchero had bewitched and killed his wife. Initially, Garcia reluctantly approached Menchero and paid him to come cure his wife, somewhat similar to a ransom or extortion case. Menchero tried various methods to heal the woman, the most macabre of which saw him place flaming coals in his mouth and blow smoke on her. (This was similar to the feat accomplished by Mauricio in Ojo Caliente.) Though Menchero sucked various stones from the woman's body, she never recovered and soon died. Likewise, Joaquinillo accused Menchero of killing a woman, María de la Luz, he made advances upon with a bewitched bone. Joaquinillo also claimed that Menchero had tried to kill the priest at Sandia. Menchero naturally denied these allegations. All that Menchero admitted to that was some time ago a sorcerer from San Felipe pueblo had tried to teach him the dark arts. Specifically, he gave Menchero some powders to ingest, after which he was to swallow an arrow. Menchero claimed the act of swallowing the arrow was too much for him and he renounced witchcraft then and there.

Around this same time, María Trujillo made a second attempt on Fray Toledo's life when he came to visit Miguel Tenorio and Corporal José Maldanado, in whose home she was being sequestered. While there, Toledo foolishly ate some of the food she prepared (perhaps he thought she was on her best behavior under the watchful eyes of Tenorio and Maldanado). Toledo became ill just as he had back in 1756 with the same ball in his stomach. Knowing María to be the cause, she was tied to the wheel of a gun carriage with her hands bound behind her back. After eight hours of the very uncomfortable ordeal, she finally confessed to poisoning Toledo.

106

It is unclear if María's confession was referring to events in the recent months or years ago, before she was a witch. In any case, she claimed to be out in the wild hunting for parsley and wondering if she might meet someone who could teach her the art of witchcraft and work herbal magic. The Devil then appeared to her in the form of a dark-skinned man.[101] The Devil instructed her to pick a wild herb called Dragon's Blood, dry it, and then grind it into powder which she could sprinkle into the food or drink of who she wished to bewitch. This she did for certain when Toledo came to visit, but again, it's unclear if she used a different herb or method to poison Toledo back in 1756. While she was confessing, María also added that she was unsure of whether or not her husband was a sorcerer, but he was known to be away from home in the middle of the night. She also claimed to once overhear her husband tell Juan Mascarenas of Chimayo that he had the ability to devour priests! (If he meant figuratively in some spiritual sense or in a literal physical sense is unknown.)

The Governor saw to it that María administered a cure to Toledo, which she did by way of the very same herb that had poisoned him somehow. The governor made sure that María's cure was purely herbal with no magical incantations to go along with it. Toledo revived and María went back to acting as a servant and no more people were bewitched by her thereafter. Furthermore, her confession inspired the other imprisoned genízario sorcerers and brujas to do the same, perhaps taking note that María was not put to death for poisoning the priest. In fact, it took only one day for the prisoners to begin confessing after they heard about the incident between María and Toledo.

The first was María's husband, Vicente, who said he never practiced sorcery or made pacts with the Devil. He also denied his wife's allegation that he claimed to know how to "devour priests". Next up on the round of confessions was Pedro Trujillo, who El Cojo once accused of transforming into a cat. Pedro didn't really confess anything of himself, and instead, his confession was that El Cojo was the main sorcerer of Abiquiú. Other imprisoned witches followed suit and began to point the finger at El Cojo. In essence, things were coming full circle, considering El Cojo was always Fray Toledo's main culprit.

Diego Tagle gave the most interesting testimony of all regarding El Cojo, who, it should be remembered, was also imprisoned at this time. Tagle claimed that one day in their cell, he began singing a strange song that summoned a Swallow that appeared in their skylight. The bird then began to speak to El Cojo, though Tagle didn't reveal what their conversation entailed. He only noted that if El Cojo could conjure such things while in jail, who knew what terrible things he could conjure as a free man?

Abiquiú many years later, c.1920s.

In the end, there were no executions for witchcraft at Abiquiú. Even though men like Vicente Trujillo were accused of killing as many as 22 people, he and other sorcerers were allowed to go free under certain conditions. Only Joaquinillo and Juan Largo, despite being sorcerers, were allowed to go free without any consequences, with the governor noting that despite the fact that they confessed to practicing magic, neither had ever used it in an attempt to harm anyone that he knew of.

In all, four accused sorcerers died while imprisoned including Augustín and Diego Tagle, Antonio Ulibarrí, and another called Antonio, El Chimayo. The rest of the prisoners caught a lucky break upon the marriage of Spain's Prince of Asturias in September 1766, as it was customary for the Spanish Kingdom to grant pardons to celebrate important marriages. The prisoners knew this and petitioned the prince for just that and the governor honored it. Though not all of the accused were allowed to go completely free, some were at least let out of jail with no extreme conditions. Suspected sorcerers accused of malicious acts were sentenced to serve Spanish masters for an undetermined—or perhaps we should say unrecorded—amount of time. The sorcerers were also banned from Abiquiú[102] and forbidden to practice anything resembling witchcraft, including curanderism.

108

It was actually the women who received the most extreme sentences. María Trujillo was told if she tried to escape her masters, she would be given fifty lashes and four years imprisonment in Encinillas, while practicing witchcraft again would put her in prison for life in addition to two hundred lashes. A suspected witch named La Come Gallinas, meanwhile, was given the Spanish equivalent of being tarred and feathered. (She was covered in honey and feathers while naked from the waist up. She was put on display that way for several hours in Santa Fe Plaza.) As for her crime, she had been accused of poisoning several Spaniards with poison derived from dead toads.

Ultimately, the Inquisition in Mexico City was at a loss for what to make of the Abiquiú witch trial. Their main point of contention was the possessed woman who became an ally to Toledo and Perejas. As they saw it, no demon would ever aid the Church. The Inquisition was also snakebit, so to speak, from the fiasco that was the Querétaro Witch Trials of a few years before in Mexico. On March 5, 1765, almost ten years since the ordeal had started, the Inquisition closed the book on the Abiquiú case. Fortunately, the devils had by this time departed.

Today many see the acts of the possessed genízaros as a rebellion against the Catholic Church solely on the part of the Indians without any demonic influence. But, if this were so, how did some of the genízaros develop the ability to speak Latin in addition to the gift of premonition? While Father Toledo's initial reports, such as accounts of shapeshifters, were regarded as far-fetched, García Perejas corroborated everything that happened with Toledo after he arrived in Abiquiú, which included the possessed woman with psychic abilities. Either Toledo and Perejas were both exaggerating to the point of outright lies, or Abiquiú really did endure an outbreak of witchcraft and possession.

THE EXECUTION OF CRISTÓBAL

After the strange events of Abiquiú, our next known witchcraft case occurred in 1796 in the vicinity of Sandia. There, a suspected brujo called Cristóbal was accused of somehow using witchcraft to aid an Apache raiding party in running off some of the village's livestock. Supposedly, Cristóbal had done so as an act of vengeance, though it wasn't stated why. As such, Juan Domingo, the village governor, and Diego Antonio, the war chief, called for the villagers to assemble in a ceremonial kiva at the pueblo. There they decided that Cristóbal should be tortured until he confessed.

Cristóbal's feet were placed in stocks, while his hands were bound with a rope from a horse halter. Next, his arms were raised up and suspended from the roof beam of the kiva, and he received about twenty lashes. Cristóbal confessed to being a witch and he was further beaten. Later he died from his injuries. The death was brought before Governor Fernando de Chacón in Santa Fe, who chose not to pursue an investigation seeing as evidence was thin and witchcraft tended to be a powder keg issue in the pueblos.

Though the image above is said to represent a Zuni witch execution it seems to fit this story.

THE POISONED PRIEST

An incident at San Ildefonso in 1799 proved to be rather interesting in that all parties involved did wrong in some way or another and all were punished for it. It all began when Fray Antonio Barreras was bewitched and fell ill. Barreras traced the spell that made him sick back to three of the Pueblo Indians, those being herbal specialist María Varguer Lucero, plus Juan Domingo Caracho and Joseph Antonio Paez. When Barreras brought his claims before Alcalde Don Manuel García de la Mora, he only halfway fulfilled his duties. Rather than arresting all the accused and placing them under trial, he only arrested the two men, but not Maria. He then handed the two men off to the priest himself, which was not the proper channel. Barreras then proceeded to torture the two men until one of them, Caracho, died. When the governor learned all the details of the incident, he punished Barreras by permanently exiling him from New Mexico. But he also punished Alcalde Garcia de la Mora by removing him from office and he was not allowed to hold another office for eight years. Lastly, since all evidence seemed to indicate that the accused enchanters had indeed poisoned or bewitched

110

Barreras in some way, Paez was sentenced to four years in a Chihuahua, Mexico, sweatshop in ankle chains. María, like María Trujillo years before in Abiquiu, was sentenced to servitude with a Christian family for four years.

NAMBÉ'S FIRST RECORDED ACCOUNT OF WITCHCRAFT

The pueblo of Nambé was mentioned earlier in this tome in relation to the accused witch Juana Chavez, an account which was undated and possibly nothing but folklore. And, though Táhwi the Nambé medicine man, was accused of witchcraft for stealing holy water, really it was just a case of curiosity. As such, this 1822 story could be considered the first true witchcraft account from Nambé. When his nephew Santiago was struck ill, Spaniard Gaspar Ortiz made a formal claim before authorities that the young man had been bewitched by a Nambé Indian named Juan Inocencio. The accused witch denied nothing, and even told how he had bewitched the boy. According to him, he had gotten a cluster of his hair, then intertwined it with feathers and cotton. This somehow worked Inocencio's magic and the boy began to go crazy. However, Inocencio also stated that he could administer a cure that would work within five days time. What happened to either the bewitched young man or Inocencio went unrecorded, but it marks a somewhat inauspicious start to much wilder witch tales from Nambé to come.

PECOS PUEBLO AND THE GREAT SERPENT

"A long time ago, say the mountaineers, there used to be serpientes, or serpents, in New Mexico that were large enough to swallow a man."—Wesley Hurt Jr., "Spanish American Superstitions" El Palacio.[103]

Perhaps it's appropriate that since we started this section on the myth and magic of Pecos Pueblo that we shall also end this section with the desertion of the pueblo. As recorded earlier, it was whispered that within a hidden kiva or cave was kept Montezuma's sacred flame and along with it, a rattlesnake so large that it could swallow a human being whole. Allegedly, the tribe's elderly were fed to the monster, as were infants at certain times as ritual sacrifice. Other accounts claim that the giant snake was fed fresh game from hunters rather than human beings, while others point out that there has never existed a rattlesnake large enough to devour a baby, much less a full-grown adult. However, this was no ordinary snake; it was magical. And so the legend goes, when the mystical serpent either

111

left or died, so did Pecos Pueblo. That, they say, is the real reason that in 1838 the last of the pueblo's dwindling population left for Jemez Pueblo.[104]

Old Mission Church and Ruins, Pecos, 1846.

It was in the aftermath of this abandonment that secondhand stories of the sacred serpent began to surface. Tales of the eternal flame and the giant snake were even said to reach the ears of Albert Pike. Its most noted mention came about when Willa Cather utilized the legend in her novel *Death Comes for the Archbishop*, which featured a scene where a priest stayed the night in the sacred cave. This was where most people were introduced to the tale of the giant snake. Perhaps due to Pecos Pueblo's relationship to the Aztec ruler Montezuma, it didn't take long for the giant snake to be conflated with Quetzalcoatl.

The Santa Fe New Mexican covered the giant serpent on November 27, 1966, mentioning it in relation to a folk pageant of sorts being performed entitled "The Plumed Serpent." The article was one of the first sources to describe the giant snake as an "enormous, fantastically plumed serpent which was housed in one of the kivas." It also noted that the play "involves the incident of [infant] sacrifice which turned the benevolent yet powerful serpent into the destructive force that drove the Indians from their homes and left Pecos in the state of ruin in which it is seen today."

New Mexico historian Alice Bullock compared it to Quetzalcoatl as well, writing in *Living Legends of the Santa Fe Country* that

112

... there are those who say the holy serpent still sleeps today in a hidden cave somewhere close to the old ruin, awaiting the return of his worshippers. There are even stories that say the feathered serpent is lethargic because it has been so long since he has been fed a pueblo virgin...[105]

Pecos Pueblo church by Heinrich Balduin Möllhausen (1858). Note the rather ominous flock of birds hovering over it.

Of course, Bullock was far removed from the heyday of Pecos Pueblo when she wrote of it. To go back to sources closer to the period, folklorist Aurelio Espinosa commented on the "Monster Viper" in his piece on New Mexico folklore in 1910, relating:

The belief is that the Pueblo Indians of New Mexico have in each pueblo a monster viper (*el viborón*) in a large subterranean cave, which is nourished with seven living children every year. I know absolutely nothing about the origin of this myth, and have had no time to study it; but I am inclined to believe that this is a pure Indian myth, probably of Aztec origin. The interesting thing about it is, that the Indians themselves have very vague ideas concerning it, some even denying it. The belief among the New Mexicans of this Indian myth is widespread, and the gradual disappearance of the New Mexico Pueblo Indians is explained by the myth in question. In the pueblo of Taos it is said that an Indian woman, when her turn came to deliver her child to the monster viper, fled to her Mexican neighbors, and thus saved her child.[106]

LEGENDS OF PECOS CHURCH

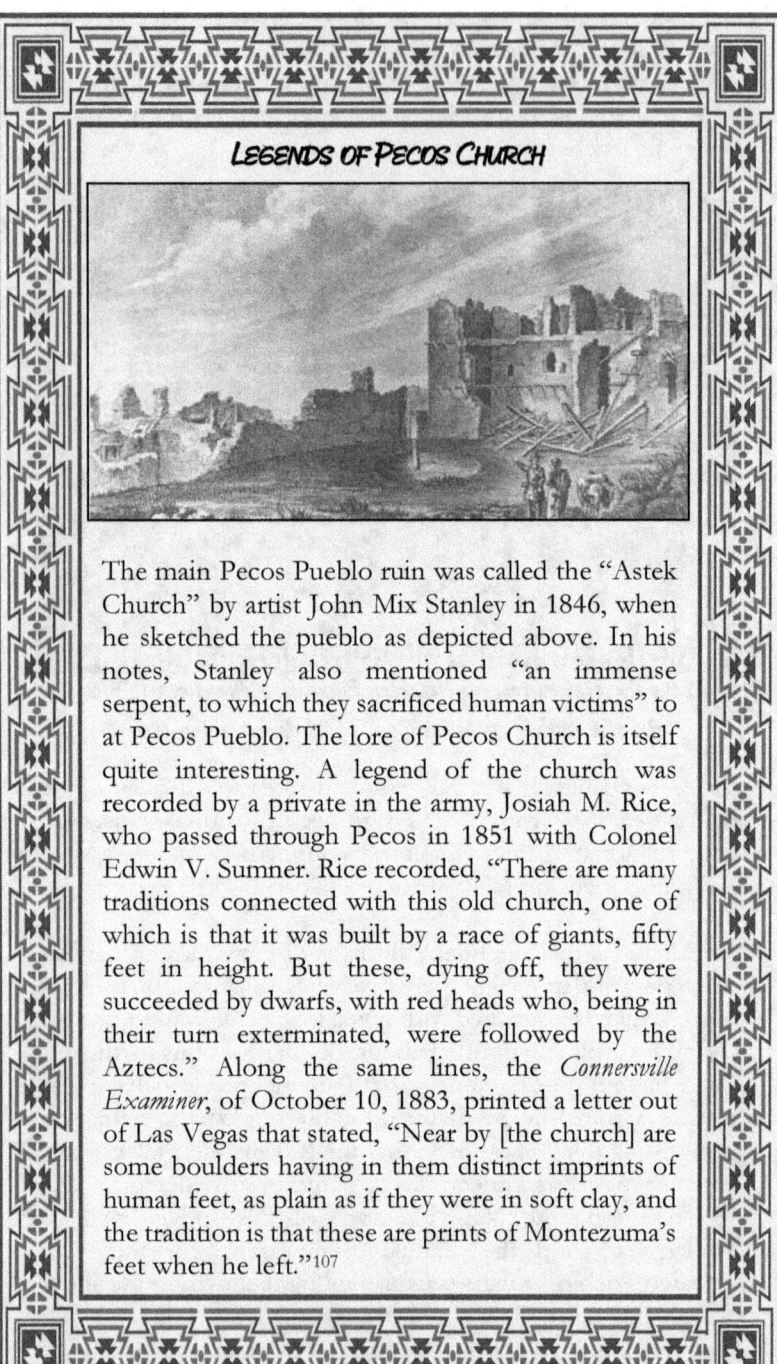

The main Pecos Pueblo ruin was called the "Astek Church" by artist John Mix Stanley in 1846, when he sketched the pueblo as depicted above. In his notes, Stanley also mentioned "an immense serpent, to which they sacrificed human victims" to at Pecos Pueblo. The lore of Pecos Church is itself quite interesting. A legend of the church was recorded by a private in the army, Josiah M. Rice, who passed through Pecos in 1851 with Colonel Edwin V. Sumner. Rice recorded, "There are many traditions connected with this old church, one of which is that it was built by a race of giants, fifty feet in height. But these, dying off, they were succeeded by dwarfs, with red heads who, being in their turn exterminated, were followed by the Aztecs." Along the same lines, the *Connersville Examiner*, of October 10, 1883, printed a letter out of Las Vegas that stated, "Near by [the church] are some boulders having in them distinct imprints of human feet, as plain as if they were in soft clay, and the tradition is that these are prints of Montezuma's feet when he left."[107]

Oddly, Espinosa said nothing of Pecos, which was the origin of the myth. Instead, he seemed to confuse it with Taos Pueblo. But, as you'll soon see, nearly everyone had a different iteration of the snake story. One of the most quoted sources for the giant snake was Josiah Gregg, a pioneer merchant and explorer who wrote of Pecos Pueblo in his book *Commerce of the Prairies*:

> The task of tending the sacred fire was, it is said, allotted to the warriors. It is further related, that they took the watch by turns for two successive days and nights, without partaking of either food, water, or sleep; while some assert, that instead of being restricted to two days, each guard continued with the same unbending severity of purpose until exhaustion, and very frequently death, left their places to be filled by others. A large portion of those who came out alive were generally so completely prostrated by the want of repose and the inhalation of carbonic gas that they very soon died; when, as the vulgar story asseverates, their remains were carried to the den of a monstrous serpent, which kept itself in excellent condition by feeding upon these delicacies. This huge snake (invented no doubt by the lovers of the marvellous to account for the constant disappearance of the Indians) was represented as the idol which they worshipped, and as subsisting entirely upon the flesh of his devotees: live infants, however, seemed to suit his palate best. The story of this wonderful serpent was so firmly believed in by many ignorant people, that on one occasion I heard an honest ranchero assert, that upon entering the village very early on a winter's morning, he saw the huge trail of the reptile in the snow, as large as that of a dragging ox.[108]

Around the same time as Gregg's recollections came another first-hand account published not long after Pecos Pueblo was abandoned. It was published in various newspapers and the author was identified only as E.T.F., said by the paper to be a "son of one of our citizens now on a trading expedition to Zacatecas." His letter was dated and addressed as "Pecos, New Mexico, Oct. 14, 1846." It, too, offered another variation on area legend, likely due to mistranslations and details that became jumbled in translation. For instance, the author noted how the "temple," or Pecos Church, contained "The bones of the descendants of Montezuma." Basically, the way he understood the legend was the opposite of the usual telling. Instead of

Montezuma originating at Pecos, it was Montezuma's royal family who came and built Pecos Pueblo after his death during the conquest of Mexico. The author also gave his rendition of the giant serpent, the eternal flame, and, most noteworthy of all, the current status of the flame:

In the grand plaza they dug three deep cisterns; these all communicated with each other by an underground passage. In these cisterns they kindled fires which never went out for more than 300 years, indulging the vain superstition that Montezuma would again visit them before the flame expired. (It was only 10 years ago that governor Armijo put a stop to their devotions, and caused the flame to be extinguished.) Only a peculiar kind of person was permitted to feed this fire, for they supposed if any one of the "Profanum valgus" descended into the cistern, he would be immediately swallowed by an immense serpent. One year's labor over the fire, generally proved fatal yet as fast as one devotee passed away, there were found many willing and anxious to fill his place. But disease and the wild mountain tribe of the [sic] Apachas have lopped off all their royal scions, save two, and these have gone far beyond the Rio del Norte, rekindled again the flame, over which will expire in a few short years, the last of the Montezumas.

E.T.F.'s account was one of the only ones I've ever seen that claimed the sacred fire was rekindled elsewhere, or that Governor Armijo had something to do with the pueblo being abandoned. A later letter, dated October 4, 1883, out of Las Vegas, NM, also recorded a variation of the desertion of Pecos Pueblo and presented yet another fate for the eternal flame:

In 1837 the tribe was reduced to 15 persons, of whom but seven were warriors. All this time they had kept the sacred fire burning, but they could do it no longer, as they were too few, and tradition says that three warriors went into the woods with the fire and that Montezuma himself appeared and relieved them of it. Then they packed their goods and went to join their brothers at the Jemez Pueblo, west of the Rio Grande. [109]

Later, it also blamed the great serpent for the abandonment:

116

The town was abandoned, some say, [sic] Commanches attacked it and so reduced it that it could no longer continue, but another tradition has it that a sacred serpent was kept in the council house where the fire was burning; and that it was fed every day a child, and that reduced the Pueblo finally to a point where the few remaining could not hold out alone.[110]

Alternatively, Adolph Bandelier heard the sacred snake had been taken by the last surviving Pecos residents to Jemez Pueblo. Bandelier's source for the tale was a man named Mariano Ruíz in 1880. Ruíz had been among those to leave in the 1838 exodus. According to him, once a year the Pecos people really did elect one member of the tribe to tend to the sacred fire and the giant serpent that it kept at bay.[111] Ruíz said he was relieved that he was never chosen for the deed, as he heard that anyone who left the tribe after attending the fire would die. (Ruíz was not a native of the pueblo and had been adopted.) Years later, Ruíz's grandson also mentioned the serpent to the famous photographer Edward S. Curtis in 1924. In Curtis's *The North American Indians* (Volume 17) he recorded from Ruiz's grandson the tale of the giant snake. Actually, it also recorded the death of the snake:

The snake, he said, was kept in an underground room in the village, and at stated intervals a newborn infant was fed to it. The elder Ruiz was asked to assume the duty of custodian of the sacred fire, an annual office, which he declined because he had observed that the fire-keeper always died soon after being released from confinement in the subterranean chamber where the fire burned. (Whether the fire and the serpent were housed in the same cell the grandson did not know, but possibly such was the case and the refusal of Ruiz to accept the proffered position was really due to his horror at the idea of spending a year in proximity to the reptile. But there appears to be no good reason why he should not have imparted this information to Bandelier, if such was the case.) Strolling about the environs of the village, Ruiz one day came upon his most intimate friend bowed in grief. To the Mexican's inquiry the Indian responded that his newborn child had been condemned to be fed to the snake, that already he had been forced to yield several children to the sacrifice, and had vainly hoped that this one would be spared. This was the first time Ruiz had heard that children were fed to the snake. He proposed that they hoodwink the priests, and acting on his advice the Indian poisoned a newborn kid [baby goat] with certain herbs, wrapped it up as if it were a baby, and threw it to the reptile. That night terrifying sounds issued from the den as the great snake writhed in its death agony, and in the morning it lay with the white of its belly exposed. The populace was utterly downcast, for this presaged the extinction of the tribe.

ANOTHER FATE FOR THE SACRED FLAME

Yet one more account of the Sacred Flame's ultimate fate came from roving journalist Matthew C. Field. In 1839, Field spent the night in the old Pecos Church and wrote an article on the legend of the pueblo. According to him, in its last days, the peoples of Pecos had chopped down so many trees to keep the sacred fire burning that the land was becoming barren. He claimed that eventually only the chief, his daughter, and her betrothed remained. The old man died, and so the daughter and her mate went to the hidden cave and retrieved the sacred fire via a brand they carried with them into the wilderness. The night sky then lit up with a red glow and "the lovers lay in each other's arms, kissing death from each other's lips, and smiling to see the fire of Montezuma mounting up to heaven." Considering that Field was also an actor with a flare for the dramatic, it's likely he simply made this version of the legend up.

Yet another variation of the end of the snake was unearthed by Helen H. Roberts in her article "The Reason for the Departure of the Pecos Indians for Jemez Pueblo" appearing in issue #34 of *American Anthropologist* in 1932. Roberts had gathered the account during the summers of 1929 and 1930 as she collected songs in the Rio Grande pueblos. At San Ildefonso she met 70-year-old Ignacio Aguilar, who told her the "real reason" that Pecos Pueblo had been abandoned. The story came from Ignacio's grandfather, who knew of the "snake god" the Pecos people kept concealed in a kiva. According to him, the snake god gave all that they asked so long as the hunters supplied fresh meat to it. (Notably, no mention was made of human sacrifice in this instance.) "The snake was very

118

hungry and required much meat. It was just after a war, and the kiva men were very busy, or perhaps for some other reason they did not feed the snake god," Ignacio told Roberts. He continued that the snake spoke to the men, asking for food, and when his pleas were ignored, he told the men, "Since you will give me no food, I cannot stay and help the people any longer. I must go away from here."

And so, the snake god slithered out of the kiva and left a "track like a small arroyo" in his wake. Ignacio's grandfather and a party of San Ildefonso Indians happened to be out hunting near Galisteo when they saw two Pecos Indians coming from the river. The two hunters asked Ignacio's grandfather and his companions if they had seen the giant snake on its way to the river. When they replied that they had not, the Pecos men replied, "It is well that you did not, for he might have bitten you. We have tracked him this far, but we cannot find him."

The two Pecos hunters traveled down the valley, tracking the snake's path down to Domingo, where they lost it. The trail led into the river and the snake was never seen again. After that, Ignacio's grandfather claimed, the magic left Pecos Pueblo, and so did its residents.

However, we will give the final word to our friend Charles Lummis, who had something to say not just about the giant snake but snake worship in general, his view of it being a bit more skeptical. In his book *Mesa, Cañon and Pueblo*, he explained:

But while all snakes are to be treated well, the Pueblo holds the rattlesnake actually sacred. It is, except the rare Pichucuate (a real asp), the only venomous reptile in the Southwest, and is the only snake dignified by a place among "The Trues." Ch'a-ra-ra-de is not really worshiped by the Pueblos; but they hold it one of the sacred animals which are useful to "The Trues," and credited with wonderful powers. Up to a generation ago it played in the marvelously complicated civilization of these people a much more important part than it does to-day. In days of old, every Pueblo town maintained a huge rattlesnake, which was kept in its own sacred room and fed with great solemnity once a year. My own pueblo of Isleta used to support a sacred rattler in a volcanic cave of the Cerro del Aire; and there was great consternation when it escaped. Old men have told me that it was nearly as large around as my body, which may be discounted. But I myself saw a sacred snake that escaped from Acoma and was killed by an

American teamster; and it was as large as the thickest part of my thigh.[112]

Lummis also spoke to the stories of Pecos Pueblo, which he did not believe:

There used to be gruesome stories of human sacrifices to these sacred rattlers—even that a baby was chosen by lot from the pueblo once a year to be fed to the snake. That of course was a foolish fable. The Pueblos never practised human sacrifice in any form, even in prehistoric times; and the very grandfather of all the rattlesnakes could no more swallow the smallest baby than he could fly.[113]

Whether Pecos Pueblo ever sheltered a giant snake or not, its desertion foreshadowed a greater shift to come in New Mexico. Soon the land would no longer be under Mexican Rule and would become a territory of the United States of America. And then would begin a new era of witchcraft and confusion in the Land of Enchantment...

Chad Arment compiled a collection of giant snake articles from newspapers entitled *Boss Snakes: Stories and Sightings of Giant Snakes in North America.* He managed to dig up an account of alleged snake worship and sacrifice still going on in 1905. And though the paper lists a "Zae" Pueblo, presumably they meant Zia Pueblo, which was near Albuquerque, where the grand jury was mentioned. The *Daily Press* out of Middleton, New York, on December 21, 1905, reported:

The United States grand jury at Albuquerque, N.M., is investigating reports that the Indians of the Zae, the most isolated of the Pueblo tribes of New Mexico, feed a certain number of newborn babies each year to a mammoth snake which is worshiped by the tribe. The interior department will probably be asked to interfere.

120

THE ENCHANTED TREE OF PECOS

Though Pecos Pueblo had been deserted before the outbreak of the Mexican-American War that resulted in New Mexico becoming a territory of the United States, there exists a curious legend tied in with the Pecos Pueblo, the scared flame, and a new addition in the form of a magic tree of sorts. From the *El Paso Daily Herald* of November 12, 1900, on page two:

A PRETTY LEGEND.
It Is Told of the Ruined Indian Pueblo of Pecos.

Marion Hill, in Frank Leslie's Popular Magazine tells the following romantic legend about the ruined pueblo of Pecos, around which so much romance has been woven:

"Through all the grotesque darkness of Pueblo superstition runs a bright thread of poetic legend: and one legend is woven around the ruined estufa in the ruined pueblo of Pecos. Pecos was founded by the man god, the great Montezuma himself, and he therefore probably felt a protective interest in it; at any rate, when the usurping Spaniards lay upon the conquered Pueblos the cursed rule of restraint and wrong. Montezuma invoked against them the aid of his brother gods in heaven. These told him to plant a tree upside down beside the chief estufa of Pecos, and to light a holy fire upon the altar, and if the fire kept burning until the tree fell, then would there come to the rescue of the oppressed a great pale face nation and deliver them from the Spanish thrall.

So the fire was lit and a sentinel was posted to guard its sacred flame; and the tree was planted—under the circumstances the planter would be excusable in planting the tree as insecurely as possible. But year after year passed, and the tree remained standing. Sentinel succeeded sentinel and the flame lived on. Generations withered away, yet deliverance seemed no nearer. One day there came a rumor from old Santa Fe that the city had surrendered to a white-faced people. Was this the band of deliverers? That day at noon the sacred tree toppled and fell. Spanish rule was no more. The prophecy had been fulfilled.

"If there be an unbeliever of this legend, let him go to the ruins of Pecos and see for himself that whereas the city was built upon a mesa so barren that no trees are there nor ever have been there, yet across the crumbling estufa lies the fallen body of a pine of mighty growth. The like of it is not for many miles around. "Whence then, did it come?"

Section Notes

[1] Dobie, *Coronado's Children*, p.204.

[2] At Pojoaque, the cacique, Juan Felipe was listed as the son of Poseyemu.

[3] Bandelier, "'Montezuma' of the Pueblo Indians," *American Anthropologist* (Vol.5. October 1892).

[4] Mason, "The Papago Migration Legend," *Journal of American Folklore* (Vol. 34, No. 133, Jul. - Sep., 1921), p.259.

[5] According to *Indian Stories from the Pueblos*, Poheyemo took on the name of Montezuma after achieving priesthood, meaning they were one and the same in some stories.

[6] This is not meant to be the same Malinche that served as the interpreter and mistress for Hernán Cortes. However, during the looming Mexican American War of 1846-48, the Tewa Indians' reverence of Montezuma was used against them. Mexico circulated a document claiming that Malinche was the daughter of Montezuma given in marriage to Cortes. This was a vain effort by the Spaniards to try and make the Tewa Indians feel a kinship with them against the American invaders.

[7] Another variation says that rather by eagle, Montezuma traveled to Mexico via a pair of golden shoes. These special golden shoes were taken by the Spanish, and as such, Montezuma could not escape back to New Mexico during the conquest.

[8] According to the article "La Sierra Glorietta" published on page eight of the *Terre Haut Saturday Evening Mail* of June 21, 1884, the route was as follows, though where they got this information is unknown: "The first place the Eagle alighted, the city of Santa Fe was founded; the second was where the city of [sic] Albuquerque now is, then came Socorro, then El Paso and after a great flight the Eagle at sunrise rested on a Cactus bush and caught a snake. There was founded the city of Mexico and named in honor of Mexitt, the Aztec God of war."

[9] Bandelier, *A Visit to the Aboriginal Ruins in the Valley of the Rio Pecos*, p.112.

[10] Gregg, *Commerce of the Prairies*, p.59.

[11] Ibid, p.57-58.

[12] In the Guadalupe Mountains there is a similar tale of a giant rattlesnake in a cave kept by a dark tribe of witches called the Snake People who also fed babies to the snake.

[13] Hammond & Rey, *Benavides' Revised Memorial of 1634*, pp. 40-41.

[14] Milich, *Relaciones*, p. 91.

[15] Horgan, *Conquistadors in North American History*, pp.144-145.

[16] His brother, Pedro, participated in such skirmishes as the battle of Acoma Pueblo. His acts there were romanticized by the writer Gaspar

Pérez de Villagrá in his epic poem "Historia de la Nueva México" in 1610.

[17] *Witchcraft in San Gabriel: Accusations of Sorcery against María de Zamora San Gabriel, New Mexico*, 1607.

[18] María was from Barrio de San Sebastián in Mexico City.

[19] *Witchcraft in San Gabriel: Accusations of Sorcery against María de Zamora San Gabriel, New Mexico, 1607.*

[20] Ibid.

[21] Martinez, "Brujeria: A History of Witchcraft in New Mexico."

[22] *Witchcraft in San Gabriel: Accusations of Sorcery against María de Zamora San Gabriel, New Mexico, 1607.*

[23] An alternative to this tale, and concerning old stories likes these there are always variations, stated that Beatriz wasn't actually attempting to kill Bellido. Instead, she was feeding Bellido a concoction of worms harvested from dung called *gusanos ciegos*. This concoction was meant to lure back wayward husbands from adulteresses. Bellido became violently ill when he drank a bowl of milk containing the worms. Beatriz did her best to neutralize the concoction by giving him another composed of an unknown oil. But instead, he died and the incident drew the attention of a local commissary, Estevan de Perea. Yet another variation was printed in *Medicine Women, Curanderas, and Women Doctors*. In that version, Beatriz was said to bury a clay idol of Bellido under her hearth, and she also hung a clay effigy of him from a tree. In that case, Governor Osorio ordered her to heal Bellido, but she was unable to reverse the spell in time.

[24] Or, if not her husband, accounts went that she poisoned the man she was having an affair with, Hernando Marquez Sambrano.

[25] This tale taken from *Ghosts-Murder-Mayhem: A Chronicle of Santa Fe* by Allan Pacheco.

[26] Perea had experience with the Inquisition in Mexico City during the trial of Governor Juan de Eulate from 1618-1625.

[27] In the version recounted in *The Witches of Abiquiú*, instead of Gruber and two friends, it was simply Gruber and a friend named Juan Martín Serrano who climbed up into the loft.

[28] Horgan, *Great River*, p.267.

[29] Stanley, *Abo Story*, p.14.

[30] Also responsible were the two priests in charge of the investigation, Fray Juan de Paz, and Father Juan Bernal. After Gruber's long imprisonment and escape, the duo were highly criticized and it reflected poorly on the Inquisition.

[31] Applegate, *Indian Stories from the Pueblos*, p.66.

[32] Ibid.

[33] According to F. Stanley in *The Nambe (New Mexico) Story*, an Indian was lynched in Nambe a few days before the Pueblo Revolt in August of 1680.

[34] Simmons, *Witchcraft in the Southwest*, Kindle Edition.

[35] Horgan, *Great River*, p.271.

[36] Applegate, *Indian Stories from the Pueblos*, p.68.

[37] Those with an interest in numerology and the repeating of certain numbers may find it interesting that later, during the revolt itself, exactly 47 Indian prisoners were taken by Spanish forces during a battle on August 20, 1680.

[38] That four died was an interesting coincidence, or perhaps it was deliberate. The number four is significant if not sacred for many Native American tribes. Furthermore, of the three that were hanged, each was meant to represent a certain pueblo. Of the three pueblos to have a man hanged were Nambe, Jemez, and San Felipe.

[39] Furthermore, so devoted to the rebellion was Popé that he killed his own son-in-law, the Spanish-placed governor of San Juan Pueblo.

[40] Espinoza, *The Pueblo Indian Revolt of 1696*, p.33.

[41] Ibid.

[42] Ibid.

[43] Applegate, *Indian Stories from the Pueblos*, p.71.

[44] Ibid, p.70.

[45] Ibid, p.72.

[46] Ibid.

[47] Ibid.

[48] Ibid.

[49] Aragón, *New Mexico Native American Lore*, p.64.

[50] Horgan, *Conquistadors in North American History*, p.215.

[51] Hackett and Shelby, *Revolt of the Pueblo Indians of New Mexico*, p.5.

[52] Ibid, pp.15-16.

[53] Chavez, "Pohé-yemo's Representative and the Pueblo Revolt," *New Mexico Historical Review* (Vol. 42, #2), p.99.

[54] Ibid, p.115.

[55] Ibid, pp.95-96.

[56] Ibid, p.89.

[57] Bullock, *Living Legends of Santa Fe*, p.98.

[58] Turzillo, "The witches of Santa Fe," Dark Hearted Women (October 17, 2018) https://darkheartedwomen.wordpress.com/2018/10/17/the-witches-of-santa-fe/

[59] Though probably not related, in parts of New Mexico there were whispers of a diabolical tribe called the Snake People who were said to have been interbred with rattlesnakes.

[60] Presumably they meant this figuratively, though it's possible they were implying he had bewitched them into silence, perhaps? Similarly, at Abiquiú a few years later, it was said that a priest was "unable to speak" in the presence of a sorcerer.

[61] Remember, the Turk was only executed after Quivira turned out to be a bust.

[62] It is unclear if the complaint was only brought forth in 1715 or if the incident occurred in 1715.

[63] The genízaros were a mix of different native peoples including the Hopi, Pawnees, Pueblo, Kiowas, Comanches and Plains Indians.

[64] Stanley, *The Abiquiú (New Mexico) Story*, p.1.

[65] Ebright & Hendricks, *Witches of Abiquiú*, p.121.

[66] This sorcerer was later revealed as Vicente Trujillo.

[67] Was this similar to the case of Picurís Pueblo where the elders claimed they could not speak? Or, was this just a figure of speech?

[68] Toledo would not report this until a full six years later in 1763.

[69] Ebright & Hendricks, *Witches of Abiquiú*, p.154.

[70] It's unclear if this occurred before or after the main illness struck him, but Toledo specifically claimed that when he walked to someone's home to take confession, his feet would suffer terrible pains that he blamed on evil, interfering spirits.

[71] Ebright & Hendricks, *Witches of Abiquiú*, p.123.

[72] Ibid, pp.126-127.

[73] Ball, *Indeh*, p.170.

[74] However, that would still not explain El Cojo afflicting the Ute curandera with this illness via the Evil Eye. Nor did killing the snake end the plague sweeping the pueblo.

[75] He became ill at Abiquiú and died soon after at Laguna Pueblo.

[76] Juan Tagle, a son of the Agustin Tagle, was said to possess an owl's claw that he used for macabre purposes, such as killing the wife of Felipe Roybal. (If Tagle simple held onto these claws, or if his hands supernaturally morphed into these claws isn't clear.) Yet another Tagle brother, Diego, also used an owl's claws, but in his case it was for love magic to make women fall in love with him.

[77] Ebright & Hendricks, *Witches of Abiquiú*, pp.136-137.

[78] Ointment made from toads gave some witches the ability of flight according to trial testimonies from the Spanish Inquisition.

[79] In one of his many letters to Governor Marín del Valle, Toledo noted the use of snakes and toads in ceremonies, and seemed to imply the creatures could become possessed to carry out the devil's deeds as he wrote that "these animals respond to what is asked of the Devil."

[80] Stanley, *The Abiquiú (New Mexico) Story*, p.6.

[81] Joaquinillo and his brother both held white stones in significance, as Juan Largo told the governor of a sacred white stone at the foot of Sandia Mountain kept by the cacique of San Felipe. The cacique sold portions of the stone, so perhaps Joaquinillo's white stone came from it?

[82] It's a bit confusing, but among the others inflicted were Joaquinillo's other brother named Vicente and his wife María—possibly the same couple that were unknowingly the cause of Toledo's illness—it's a bit hard to sort out.

[83] It's unknown if the following incident occurred during this trip, or a subsequent one. But the man tasked with taking the witches to Santa Fe was Gregorio Trujillo. On a trip wherein he escorted Juana Pacheco and María Trujillo, wife of Vicente, Gregorio was poisoned by the women. They did so by hiding a pebble from an ant hill in a meat-stuffed tortilla consumed by their escort. (See the next section for an explanation as to how ant hills tie into witchcraft.) Gregorio became ill and began vomiting profusely upon his return to Abiquiú.

[84] Though no events ever occurred again at Abiquiu to rival the witch craze there of the 17th century, the old village still had its witches even into the 20th century. Paul Garcia told one such tale in *Adobe Angels* of a shapeshifting witch living in the village who used to prowl about as an animal at night gathering information. One night, as a large black owl circled the village, a hunter etched a cross into a bullet and shot it. The bullet hit its mark, and an explosion of black feathers fell to earth as the owl winged off to the mountains. The next day, the suspected witch was seen with a bloodied bandaged shoulder.

[85] As for La Pastora herself, it was said that she once cured an ill woman by placing a toad on the nude woman's body and dancing around her.

[86] Ebright & Hendricks, *The Witches of Abiquiú*, pp.147-148.

[87] Ibid, p.148.

[88] Ibid, p.156.

[89] Another story also circulated about Father Toledo being assaulted in his sleep by a half-man half-beast creature. I found no mention of this in *The Witches of Abiquiú*, and surely a fantastic story such as that would have been included. Was this a conglomeration of Toledo's battle with the wolf and Juan Largo's report of a half-man half-animal, perhaps?

[90] Ebright & Hendricks, *The Witches of Abiquiú*, p.155.

[91] Ibid, p.180.

[92] Cascabel was eventually among those arrested for witchcraft. It was said that he carried a very powerful small black stone that he used in his magic.

[93] Ebright & Hendricks, *The Witches of Abiquiú*, p.181.

[94] If you'll recall in another footnote, Joaquinillo had a sister-in-law by that name, perhaps this was her?
[95] Ebright and Hendricks, *The Witches of Abiquiú*, p.181.
[96] Ibid, p.182.
[97] Ibid.
[98] Ibid, p.184.
[99] Ibid, p.192.
[100] It was never adequately explained what made the witches of Chimayo special, but there were said to be about 55 in total: 35 Spaniards and 20 genízaros. Only the brujo Cascabel was charged in the Abiquiú witch trials, the others were never bothered it seems.
[101] Curiously, this harkens back to reports of the Pueblo Revolt and siege of Santa Fe nearly one hundred years ago.
[102] María and Vicente Trujillo were supposed to be banned from Abiquiú for life, but returned about 20 years later. Neither committed acts of witchcraft, though Vicente did steal a golden cross and rosary from the church once.
[103] Hurt, "Spanish American Superstitions," p.194.
[104] They migrated there because they spoke the same language.
[105] Bullock, *Living Legends of Santa Fe*, p.52.
[106] Espinosa, "New-Mexican Spanish Folk-Lore," p.403.
[107] Mexico has similar legends at spots where Quetzalcoatl left his footprints, and so on.
[108] Gregg, *Commerce of the Prairies*, p.58.
[109] "FROM NEW MEXICO," The Clermont Sun (October 9, 1883), p.4.
[110] Ibid.
[111] According to Bandelier's recounting of Ruiz's story, the sacred flame was kept in "a sort of closed oven" and was not actually "permitted to flame".
[112] Lummis, *Mesa, Cañon and Pueblo*, pp.147-148.
[113] Ibid, p.148.

Special Section
APACHE & NAVAJO
WITCHCRAFT

Amongst New Mexico's tribes, the Apache and the Navajo were unique from the peoples of the pueblos, and less was recorded about them in the early days as opposed to the Tewa Indians. This is probably because whereas the pueblo peoples stayed in one place, the Navajo and the Apache roamed freely. This is also why in the mid-1800s, the Apache and the Navajo were singled out by the U.S. government and forced onto the Bosque Redondo Reservation at Fort Sumner. This government experiment proved to be a disaster, not just because the land itself was unsuitable, but because the Navajo and the Apache were adversaries.[1]

Though enemies, both had similar concepts of witchcraft and superstition, which were notably different from the Tewa Indians—in my opinion, at least. In his masterwork *Navaho Witchcraft*, Clyde Kluckhohn touched on the similarities between the Apache and the Navajo as well, but in his view, some of the commonalities stemmed from Tewa beliefs.[2] For the most part, the Navajo and the Apache agree that witchcraft stems from hatred, greed, and jealousy. Witches possess power in the same way as their medicine men, only used for evil rather than good. The difference between the two is basically day and night. What medicine men do in public to heal; the witches work in the dark to do harm. Ghosts are abhorred by both, but more so by the Navajo, and in the two tribes there is such as thing as "ghost sickness." Incest is associated with witchcraft by both as well, and to gain the dark power of a witch, Apache and Navajo sorcerers are said to kill a close relative, usually a sibling, something not as prevalent in Pueblo witchcraft, in my opinion.

A typical Navajo or Apache witch encounter would usually have the victim poisoned during the night in their hogan. The next morning tracks would lead away from the dwelling to the abode of the suspected witch, who would either be executed or banished from the tribe.

Famous picture of Geronimo, far right, with some of his men in 1886.

"Power" was one of the more distinct similarities that I picked up on between the Navajo and the Apache. The "Power" was predominantly believed in and quantified more so by the Apache, though the Navajo certainly had their own version of it. In pop culture, one might compare the "Power" to the Force in Star Wars or the presence and intuition of the Holy Spirit in Christianity in the real world. All people, animals, objects, and other forms of life might possess a certain amount of power, be it good or bad. Different Apache chiefs and medicine men possessed different power. Chief Nana was said to have power over rattlesnakes and was adept at procuring ammunition when needed, while Geronimo had a vast array of "power" abilities. Though less apparent in the Navajo realm, they, too, had a belief in power among certain healers and witches in regards to specific animals and elements, like snakes and lightning.

As stated before, both tribes have a particular abhorrence for ghosts, which the Navajo call *chindi*. A chindi could easily bring about more death or sickness and an unnamed Apache informant once told anthropologist Morris E. Opler that "A witch can send a ghost to bother a person.[3] This is one way of witching."[4] Both tribes called the condition "ghost sickness," and it was even believed that some witches continued their magic as ghosts. (Though typical ghosts were not considered witches themselves despite some confusion on the matter on the part of outsiders.)[5] As with the Navajo, it was impolite to utter the name of the dead after they had passed among

130

the Apache. The deceased's belongings were either destroyed or buried with them. Sometimes the burial site of a Mescalero Apache would not even be disclosed for fear of the ghost being disturbed or a witch going to rob the grave.

Three Navajo performers dressed as Tó Neinilii, Tobadzischini, Nayenezgani in 1904 as photographed by Edward S. Curtis. Ironically, many captions incorrectly label these men as skinwalkers as opposed to ceremonial dancers representing the Hero Twins or Twin War Gods that often killed witches.

As it was among most first nations peoples, the number four was revered among the two tribes. For many tribes, the number four is sacred in a similar way that the number seven is God's holy number in Christianity and Judaism. For instance, Geronimo was the fourth male child born to his family, and for that reason may have had unique powers. There were also strange superstitions attributed to the first four hunting excursions of a young Apache brave, while a taboo associated with the number four for the Navajo was refusing a request four times in a row. If I had to guess, I would say the significance of the number comes down to the four corners of the winds and the four directions north, south, east, and west.[6]

HOPI SNAKE DANCE, ARIZONA.

The Apache and Navajo greatly feared snakes compared to other tribes, like the Hopi, who performed the Snake Dance (pictured above), or Pecos Pueblo, which allegedly worshipped a giant snake. John G. Bourke wrote of the Apache superstition of snakes, which other historians, like Eve Ball, had trouble getting them to speak of. In *Indeh*, Ball mentioned that the Apache were "very superstitious about snakes" and would not "use anything made of snakeskin."[7] According to Bourke, "The Apache will not let snakes be killed within limits of the camp by one of their own people, but they will not only allow a stranger to kill them, but will request him to do so. They made this request of me on three occasions."[8]

The other big similarity I picked up on between the two was a particular reverence for bears, snakes, and lightning. For instance, the Apache fear snakes greatly and try to keep away from bears as they think those might be the dead reincarnated,[9] while lightning is vastly powerful to them. Examples of these taboos included stepping on a rattlesnake skin, which could cause sickness, or eating beef from a cow that was struck by lightning. Drinking from a water source that a bear had trudged through was also not a good idea amongst the Apache. While the Navajo are less specific in regard to their reverence of snakes, bears, and lightning, one of Kluckhohn's unnamed subjects notably said that Navajo witches weren't afraid of snakes, bears, or lightning.

The power of the name is another interesting concept the world over. Exorcisms are conducted in the name and authority of Jesus Christ, for instance, while in Judaic folklore, the demon woman Lillith took flight by uttering the ineffable name of God. Particularly in Navajo and Apache beliefs, the name is a very powerful thing. Uttering a skinwalker's true name could render its witchcraft powerless, just as a witch or sorcerer used the victim's name to inflict sickness. "The name of an American Indian is a sacred thing, not to be divulged by the owner himself without due consideration," Bourke wrote in *Apache Medicine Men*, because, when a person knew your name, they could then properly bewitch you if they so desired. Likewise, Kluckhohn noted that "...the use of the personal name enters in all four techniques [of witchcraft]," and also that "They used to say you can't witch a person until you know his name."[10]

With those similarities in mind, we'll now take a closer look at the different varieties of Navajo and Apache witchcraft individually.

NAVAJO WITCHCRAFT

"Witches are just like ghosts. They like to eat dead people."-unnamed informant in Navaho Witchcraft[11]

In the Navajo creation myth, First Man and First Woman, more or less the Navajo Adam and Eve, were the first to bring witchcraft to the world along with the trickster god Coyote. Witchcraft has been a plague to the Navajo ever since. Witchcraft has never been accepted by the Navajo, and there are no ambiguous loopholes wherein its usage might be accepted. For them it is a simple case of good and evil. In fact, to this very day, Navajo are reluctant to discuss witches. Nor do they go out alone at night, for that is when witches are about, especially when the wind blows.

Whereas in Spanish culture, more women than men were often witches, among the Navajo, the opposite is true; more men are witches than women. (That said, there are a few female witches—typically older or childless women that were whispered to be practicing the dark arts.) When found, witches were often beaten to death with clubs or axes. There was also a belief that if a witch escaped detection by other members of the tribe, they might be dealt with by good supernatural forces, which would see to it that the

133

witch was struck by lightning (another belief shared with the Apache).

As stated before, despite often being labeled as a Skinwalker, this is a Navajo man portraying Nayenezgani, aka Monster Slayer.

THE HERO TWINS

The concept of two heroic twins or siblings that come along to slay primeval monsters is an important aspect of both Mesoamerican and Native American creation stories. Though they mostly fought giants and monsters, occasionally the hero twins tussled with witches. As such, twins occasionally factor in Native American superstition and witchcraft in interesting ways. Though the Hero Twins were benevolent heroes, twins born within tribes were sometimes feared to grow up and become witches unless protective measures were taken at once, more so among the pueblo peoples as opposed to the Navajo and the Apache. To ward off the possibility of twins growing up to be witches, the mother would urinate on them at birth.

The flesh of children was said to be the most appealing to witches for consumption, especially that of twins. "One man says twins is the best medicine they have. Use that bone in the back of the head. Cut it in circle shape. After they cut that bone out, then they shaped it very round with a rock," said an informant in *Navaho Witchcraft* on page 134. And again, on page 136, twins were brought up: "People say their best medicine is made from twins—either part of the back of their heads or skin whirls. Twins are especially supernatural."[12]

According to the Navajo, there were four types of witchcraft that could be perpetrated, identified as Witchery, Sorcery, Wizardry, and Frenzy Witchcraft.[13] (Frenzy witchcraft, lumped in with love magic and the pursuit of wealth through good luck in gambling, is mostly similar to the love magic of the Spanish and Pueblo witches, so it will not be discussed in depth.) The four categories begin with the worst of the bunch, that being Witchery Way which includes the dreaded skinwalkers.

Skinwalkers began drifting into the public eye in the 1980s when beloved New Mexico novelist Tony Hillerman began including them in his murder mysteries starring Joe Leaphorn and Jim Chee. Utah's Skinwalker Ranch further propelled that name into the forefront when strange things began happening there in the 1990s. Now one will see skinwalkers in just about any movie or TV series with a werewolf theme. However, almost all Navajo wish the secret of the skinwalker would have stayed hidden. If one reads the works of Hillerman, one will notice that the Navajo characters are loath to even say the word skinwalker, lest they attract the attention of the witch. This wasn't an exaggeration for the sake of the books. To this day, many Navajo will not say the word skinwalker. I have even heard of non-Navajo Spanish residents of northern New Mexico today that will not utter the word.

In recent years, the Navajo Skinwalker has come to be thought of as the Native American equivalent of a werewolf. As already stated, skinwalkers are really just witches, as were many of the so-called werewolves of medieval Europe. If one reads up on European werewolf folklore, one will learn that most werewolves were simply practitioners of black magic. None had been bitten by a wolf and turned into one. Almost always they had made a pact with the Devil, and to induce their transformations, they would typically rub their body with a magical salve. As they did, they might recite some type of incantation whilst wearing the pelt of the animal they desired to transform into, usually a wolf. Overall, the traditional European werewolf has more in common with the Navajo skinwalker than it does the Hollywood version of a "Wolf-Man."

That said, Kluckhohn's *Navaho Witchcraft* actually refers to skinwalkers as werewolves in the text. (However, I think this may have just been Kluckhohn's way of making the text understandable to readers of the time as it was published in the mid-1940s.) I'm also not so sure when the term "skinwalker" came to be widely used, but for certain, the Navajo themselves called shapeshifting witches *yee naaldlooshii*, which translates to "with it, he goes on all fours." (*It*, in this case, meant to indicate power, witchcraft, or perhaps even the animal pelt itself.)

To induce the transformation from man to beast, the skinwalker must wear the pelt of the animal they wish to transform into. Sometimes they might also wear the skull of the animal atop their heads, as it was thought this increased their power.[14] They pick their animal based upon the task at hand. If they want speed, they might choose a fleet four-footed animal like a wolf, or even a mountain lion of some sort. If they want brute strength, they might choose a bear, for instance. For this reason, one won't see a regular Navajo wearing the pelt of a predatory animal, as the skinwalkers made it taboo.[15] The skinwalker's powers don't stop at shapeshifting, either; they are also able to possess people in a manner of speaking. Or, that is to say, though it isn't implied that their spirit enters their victim's body, it is thought that they can gain control over a person after locking eyes with them.

As to how one achieved these powers, the finer points are still shrouded in mystery, but the final phase of the initiation occurred after one had killed either a sibling or a close relative. One informant in *Navaho Witchcraft* told how his father pressured his mother to learn witchcraft, telling her that "she must allow her favorite brother or sister to be given to the were-wolf people so that they could kill him or her."[16]

"It has to be a *full* brother or sister that you kill," another informant said in the same book. "That's why people get stuck and don't learn all of it. If you do kill your brother or your sister, they put it right into this medicine."[17] (Putting it into the medicine would seem to imply that perhaps the murderer ingested part of their sibling in an act of cannibalism.[18])

The were-witches of Acoma, apart from jumping through a magical hoop to induce their transformation, seem to have a similar initiation ritual to the skinwalker. These men were from what the Acomans called the "Witch Society," which congregated in a cave on the north side of Enchanted Mesa, the original home of the Acoma people. In the tale of the hero Arrow Youth, who is kidnapped and taken to the cave of the witches on Enchanted Mesa, he is given a bowl of food to eat as part of his forced initiation. (Since they all eat of the bowl's unspecified contents, perhaps it was corpse meat?) The Witch Chief then tells Arrow Youth of the next step: "Tonight you shall bring me the heart of the brother you like best. I will change you into whatever animal you wish to be." However, Arrow Youth cannot bring himself to kill either of his two beloved brothers and instead kills a goat and takes its heart to the Witch Chief.

And how might one spot a skinwalker? In human form, they are said to have animal-like eyes, while in animal form, their eyes appear more human-like and will also glow red when a bright light is shown upon them. This attribute comes from modern sources, though. In the days of Kluckhohn, none of his informants mentioned this trait. One of his informants said, "Witches wear masks—that's how they talk. The masks are made of unwounded buckskin."[19] Another said that witches painted their faces and bodies with the same white clay used in chants. The more descriptive witnesses said that skinwalkers painted their foreheads white, their noses black, their mouths blue, and their chins yellow. (Presumably this had something to do with the fact that in the Navajo creation myth, the four clouds containing the elements of the First World were colored black, white, blue, and yellow in that order.)

"Medicine Man, Performing His Mysteries over a Dying Man" by George Catlin from a ceremony he saw performed at Fort Union of the Upper Missouri River in 1832.

Apart from the animal hides, which were said to drape down to the wrists, most thought the witches went about naked, though some wondered if perhaps they wore g-strings and they just couldn't see them since no one could ever catch a witch, to begin with. Some thought the witches merely ran about on all fours in the animal skins as opposed to actually being an animal. Along that train of thought, one informant gave the following statement:

Those were-animals take the whole hide off a bear or mountain lion or they take any kind of hide. They take the bones out and leave the claws. They put sticks in the legs to move the skin. With strings they move the ears of the hide up and down. If you shoot at the head of one of these were-animals, the shot will just go through the hide. Shoot at the animal's neck and then the shot will go right through the real head of the witch.[20]

TRACK OF THE SKINWALKER

In the Navajo nation, there are many stories of large wolf tracks found heading away from disturbed graves and burials. Europe has some interesting folklore regarding the footprints of wolves relating to werewolves. Supposedly, if one were to drink rain from the footprint of a large wolf, they would turn into a werewolf. The Navajo are superstitious when it comes to the tracks of either a wolf or a perceived skinwalker. An informant told Kluckhohn, "If you see the tracks of a were-animal, you must be sure to step across them. Never go in front of them."[21] Another informant reiterated this, stating, "If you ever see the tracks of were-animals be sure to step across them, don't go in front of them."[22] What would happen if you didn't? The informant didn't say.[23]

In talking about how fast and fleetfooted the skinwalkers were, one informant said that not even a horse could catch them. The lone hope was for the skinwalker to trip on a prairie dog or gopher hole. (While this may not seem important on the surface, gopher often used his burrowing ability to aid the witch-slaying Hero Twins. So, perhaps that was the real reason they got tripped up?) A few witnesses have also claimed that they've seen a skinwalker transform into a ball of light, as in the sightings of the Spanish and Pueblo witches.

Typical skinwalker accounts of the old days had the witch climb atop the hogan of their intended victim at night. They would peer down at them through the smoke hole and then sprinkle a deadly potion made of corpse powder onto them. Sometimes they would also use pencil-thin sharpened sticks to break the victim's skin.

Having heard strange noises the night before, the victim or a member of their family would walk out of their hogan to see dirty tracks leading to the top of the smoke hole. They would then find larger than normal animal tracks of some kind, usually those of a wolf, and follow them back to the witch's abode, which could be another hogan or sometimes a cave dwelling.

If caught along the trail or in the act of witching itself, the witch might offer a bribe in the form of valuable beads. A cautious and proper Navajo would reject these beads, usually out of fear that they were stolen from a grave and belonged to the dead. If one accepted the beads as an act of sorcery was in progress, they would likely become sick. If they rejected the beads, the witch would come down with the very sickness they were attempting to inflict.

And, as with many common Spanish accounts, an animal thought to be a witch would be shot, and later a Navajo would turn up dead or with a wound in the same spot the animal was shot. There were also many variations of a tale where a Navajo is going to shoot some animal—anything from a coyote to a horse—only to have the animal speak, saying, "Don't shoot, brother, it is your sister."

But why did the witches commit their heinous acts? Navajos believe that greed often leads to witchcraft. Thus, a victim might be murdered by a witch and their possessions stolen when buried with them. Basically, the witch would murder someone knowing that their valuables would be buried with them and then go and dig them up after burial. (Ironically, the Navajo and other tribes buried their dead with their valuables because they felt this would protect the elderly from greedy young relatives who wished to inherit said valuables.) There was also a method of scamming wherein a witch might team with a healer. The witch would cause the sickness, the healer would treat it, and then the duo would split the healer's fee. Or, sometimes, the witch and the healer were just one and the same.

Skinwalkers and workers of Witchery Way were thought to have a wealthy leader. They would all meet within a hidden cave, nude aside from masks, jewelry, and beads, plus body paint in certain areas as described earlier. The cave would be adorned with the heads of victims, plus baskets or piles of corpse flesh. Sometimes the witches would eat the flesh. Other times, they would make corpse powder out of it. Vile acts of necrophilia would be committed against the bodies of dead women.

Whereas werewolves were defeated by silver bullets, in the movies at least, skinwalkers had a few unique weaknesses as well. The best way to render a skinwalker powerless was to learn its true name and utter it. (Remember the earlier section where we discussed the power of the name.) This is also perhaps not coincidentally similar to a little-known method to defeat the European werewolf, being that one could negate the creature's supernatural power by uttering its Christian name three times.

Just as werewolves abhorred silver, skinwalkers were said to abhor white ash. This could be because in curing ceremonies some medicine men anointed their bodies with ashes and another secret substance to help them locate foreign objects in a person's body. White ashes might also represent the residue from a purification ceremony. However, I saw no mention of white ash in Kluckhohn's book, so I'm not sure when this information was divulged or how accurate it is. Some have also argued that perhaps white ash refers in some way to bark from the White Ash tree, but whitened ashes from a purifying ceremony seem more likely.[24]

The popular website Legends of America specifically says, "Another alternative is to shoot the creature with bullets dipped into white ash. However, this shot must hit the witch in the neck or the head."[25] Also, according to Legends of America, "These witches live on the unexpired lives of their victims, and they must continually kill or perish themselves."[26] If not killed, it is thought that a skinwalker can live far beyond a normal human being's lifespan according to today's version of the mythology.

Down the hierarchy from skinwalkers/witchery way next comes sorcerers, who may participate in witches' sabbats even though they don't transform into animals. Sorcery in the Navajo context referred to the burial of property of victims or pieces of the victims themselves. Essentially, a sorcerer tended to work long-distance magic against their victim. To do this, they collected anything containing their target's DNA. The obvious options included hair and nail clippings, but dirt recently urinated upon could also work.[27] After obtaining the needed DNA, a ritual would commence where the object or objects were buried in a grave. Specifically, the item might be stuffed in the mouth of a corpse, or sometimes the opened stomach of a corpse (see an entry on the Navajo Witch Purge of 1878 for a notable instance of that). A chant would then be offered which included how many days the victim had left to live. If not placed in a grave, the item might be sat or buried under a tree struck by lightning.

Just as an Apache witch might recite the victim's name four times, or walk around their abode four times, a Navajo sorcerer will also sometimes circle a victim's hogan an unspecified number of times while chanting. After this is done, the victim is said to expire four days later. However, if a witch is caught and confesses to their dastardly act, they will themselves expire within a year from the same affliction.

The most dreaded method of sorcery was shooting sorcery, in which people were hit or injected with foreign projectiles.[28] Though anything could be injected into the body, the bone dart was and still is the most dreaded weapon of many Native American cultures. In addition to bone darts, stones, quills, charcoal, and ashes could be fired into a victim. To be even more specific, chips of bone and teeth from the dead were thought to be ideal, along with ashes from a ghost hogan (or a hogan where someone had recently died and it had been burnt down). Grains of sand from a red ant hill were another favorite, along with pieces of yucca and sometimes the whiskers of a wild cat.

> The grains of sand from the red anthill wasn't random, as ants often dug up fossils and other remnants of dead things. As it stands, ants coexisted with the dinosaurs, a fact that most Native Americans remarkably knew before naturalists ever did. In her masterful work *Fossil Legends of the First Americans*, author Adrienne Mayor wrote of the connection between ants, Native Americans, and Navajo witchcraft:
>
> Ants, unchanged since that era [the days of the dinosaurs], still live in our world and travel between layers of Earth and time/space. Like the monsters, ants are unfeasible entities, and in my reading of Gladys Reichard, I had learned that Navajo witches used the tiny smooth pebbles that ants carry up to the surface for evil spells (notably, ants also bring up minute fossils of extinct creatures from past worlds).[29]

In literal instances, projectiles would be fired into the body in a manner likened to a blow-dart. However, rather than literal shooting sorcery, the witch would fire a symbolic arrow from an imaginary, spiritual bow in many other instances. As they imagine the arrow entering the image of the victim, they then believe that the spell can manifest.

In the old days, before photographs, Navajo witches would draw a representation of their intended victim via sand paintings, some say out of colored ash. As witches plotted harm for the victim, they may have also engaged in necrophilia and cannibalism in their evil cave. Then a form of long-distance, voodoo-like shooting sorcery commenced. By use of a ritual bow (smaller than normal and allegedly made of a human shin bone), the witch would fire a turquoise bead arrow at the sand painting of their victim. Where it struck, an injury would occur. In addition to this, sometimes the witches would curse, urinate, and spit upon the sand painting.

Kluckhohn had good reason to believe that shooting sorcery came about after the Navajo internment at Fort Sumner. This theory was evident in the fact that Navajo medicine men and healers seemed unable to cure cases of shooting sorcery via the sucking way ceremony. As it is, if stricken with a bewitched projectile, the Navajo typically seek healers from other tribes, such as the Hopi, the Ute, and the Apache. And, whereas it appeared that medicine men magically sucked out the foreign objects at Abiquiú, in cases involving the Navajo and Apache, it is clearer that medicine men rubbed the patient's body with a special salve to locate the foreign object. After that, they would take out a special knife, make an incision, and then suck the cursed object out after the incision was made. In at least one instance, it was reported that the foreign object moved within the body as if trying to avoid the sucking way cure, but eventually, the medicine man was able to trap it and use an Olivella shell to somehow pull it out.

If one considered typical close-range shooting sorcery as being not dissimilar to an assassin carrying out their hit with a sniper rifle, then one could consider the next method to be the equivalent of a heat-seeking missile. This ritual is purely magical and less physical than the usual method. For the long-range method of shooting sorcery, the wizard rubs their body in ashes to prepare for the ritual. The object they intended to shoot would be placed in a special basket or on a buckskin. Upon a special chant or incantation, the deadly projectile would rise into the air and then fly to its intended victim.

Sorcerers also utilized voodoo dolls, though Kluckhohn wondered if Navajo witches learned this trick from the Spanish settlers. Whatever the case, the effigies were often made of clay or carved of wood and then stuck with cactus needles or other sharp objects. One of Kluckhohn's informants, Richard Van Valkenburgh, claimed that he saw such an effigy carved out of a pine tree struck by lightning, and in its center, representing the heart, was a piece of turquoise.

While we're on the subject, it was said that a doll made of wet earth, urinated upon by the intended victim, was the most effective. Throwing in hair or nail clippings from the target also made it more effective. Essentially, anything that might have their DNA made it more powerful. Along these same lines, sorcerers also had a macabre method of targeting pregnant women and their unborn children by killing a horned toad and stuffing its stomach cavity with a unique item of some kind.[30] There were also stories of live snakes being sent out to strike certain victims as well. Or, a witch might kill a snake and point it in the direction of the targeted victim.

Another method of instilling sickness was to go to a ghost hogan, where someone had recently died. There the witch would draw the victim's face on a stone and leave it facedown in the hogan whilst also saying their real name. A sorcerer might also target one's livestock or crops. In the case of the latter, they might send locusts or grasshoppers. To ruin a corn crop, the witch could also place a cornstalk over a cliff, and when the wind blew it over backward, the targeted victim's corn crop would die. In the case of livestock, they simply caused sickness to fall upon them as they did people.

Typical Navajo hogan.

Another very significant aspect of both witchery way and sorcery is that of corpse powder. As the name suggests, corpse powder was made from dried flesh and sometimes bone. When dried out and ground to dust, corpse powder was said to resemble pollen. "They take and dry all this meat and when it is real dry, they grind it. Grind it like baking powder, make it soft," said one of Kluckhohn's informants.[31] It would then be administered to the victim in the old days by the skinwalker crawling to the top of the victim's hogan. The witch would then let the pollen-like substance drift down until it filled the sleeping victim's mouth and nostrils. Other methods included infusing a cigarette with corpse powder. Or, if in a large crowd or gathering, a witch might approach their victim with a furrowed stick, or perhaps a straw, and blow the powder in their face before disappearing into the mass of people. Typically, after inhalation, the tongue would become black and swollen, fainting might occur right away, and sometimes lockjaw (to inhibit the consumption of a cure from a medicine man) would befall the victim. If not treated, the victim would wither and die.

Of course, the Navajo had plenty of methods to counteract sorcery. Similar to the Apache and Spanish methods of turning witchcraft back onto the perpetrator, the Navajo have the Shield Prayer, the Bringing Up Prayer, and the Bringing Out Prayer. Gall medicine made from an eagle, bear, mountain lion, or even a skunk among other animals, may be useful against corpse poison. Or, if a witch threatened to strike someone with lightning, that person needed to find a tree struck by lightning and place a turquoise offering there.

APACHE WITCHCRAFT

As stated before, Apache witches aren't terribly different from Navajo witches apart from not transforming into animals. Other minor differences included the fact that rather than greed, the Apache singled out the cause of all witchcraft as hatred, certainly tangential to jealousy, though. Essentially, if hatred were to disappear, so would the witches. Another difference between the two schools of witchcraft is that if an Apache wants to become a witch, they can pay a witch to learn.

Like the Navajo, the Apache are reluctant to so much as discuss witchcraft. Even the great writer and friend of the Apache, Eve Ball, rarely got them to discuss it. When she did, the results were always fascinating and provided a rare peek into the world of the supernatural as the Apache understood it. For instance, she once interviewed the grandson of Cochise, Christian Naiche, who told her he and many other Apache believed the great chief didn't die of cancer as was said. Instead, Cochise died from bewitchment.

"To the Apaches witchcraft is real and to be feared," Ball wrote in one of her masterworks, *Indeh*.[32] Another of her informants, Eugene Chihuahua, told Ball the account of a man who had a mysterious gathering of butterflies fluttering about him. This, he said, was a sign that his first wife was bewitching him and trying to get him to come back to her. Chihuahua further claimed that when a man was bewitched, he could be made to do anything, even murder. He would not be held entirely accountable for his actions as would someone who was conscious of it. Instead, upon death, he would have to come back for a time as a bear before going on to the "Happy Place," the Apache equivalent of Heaven.[33]

The Apache structure their universe into three broad categories basically revolving around living and non-living things, and to a degree, animate vs. inanimate objects. For instance, *hinda* refers to things capable of moving under their own power. Obviously, this includes all life-forms, but also certain machines like automobiles. The second class describes objects incapable of moving under their own power. The third class, *Godiyo'*, refers to holy objects like turquoise and elements like rain and thunder. The power belongs to this class. As Keith Basso put it in *Apache Witchcraft*, "The Apache are very specific about which things possess power and which do not, but they are quite unable to explain just what power is. Moreover, they are certain that any attempt to do so is doomed to failure."[34]

Power was a very important aspect of Apache witchcraft, more so than it was for the Navajo since Apache witches were essentially the

146

evil equivalents of medicine men. As it stands, certain medicine men have certain power.[35] A man who could converse with bears, which Apache sometimes believed to be reincarnated humans, had "bear power" while a man bitten by a rattlesnake who lived without treatment would be considered to have the "snake power." A witch, in reverse, might have the power to send a snake to do harm. Simply put, some have power and some don't, and to be either a witch or a medicine man, one had to have power.

Apache Medicine Man identified as "Loco".

The good power could be obtained through prayer and presumably time with Ussen, the one god of the Apache. As for bad power, an individual could attain it through a person inviting evil powers or spirits to enter them. In both cases, lightning was the most revered form of power, hence why tree bark struck by lightning was used in certain forms of Apache magic. If an Apache claimed to have power over lightning, they would be greatly feared.

The difference between medicine men and witches is fairly simple for Apache. Basically, everything the medicine man does in public to heal, the witch will do in secret, unseen in some dark cave to do harm.[36] For instance, whereas medicine men make sand paintings, Apache witches do not make sand paintings at all, it is claimed. Unlike other tribes, the Apache consider it impossible to be both a witch and a medicine man at the same time. But a medicine man can become tainted and angry and become a witch if he chooses.

Actually, the Apache could be weary of the powers of medicine men as well. In *Apache Odyssey*, Morris E. Opler recorded, "It was believed by a number of Apache tribes that when his time comes to die, a shaman with evil inclinations might prolong his own life by allowing or encouraging supernatural power to substitute another person instead."[37]

The idea of taking the life of a loved one to gain magical powers, similar to the skinwalker, was also present in at least one Mescalero Apache account from *Apache Odyssey*. The medicine man was known

147

as Old Elk, and had harnessed something called "buzzard power" from a buzzard spirit. The spirit animal informed Old Elk that if he wished to keep using his power, he would have to offer up the life of one of his children or another close relative.

While we're on the subject of the skinwalker, there were a few accounts of Apache medicine men and witches alike taking the forms of animals.[38] A notable instance of shapeshifting was discussed in *Apache Odyssey*. The narrator, Chris, told Opler that "In the old days those who knew Bear used to go around in the form of a bear. But since the white man has come they don't do it, for fear of the gun."[39] In a footnote conjoined to this statement, Opler elaborated that some but not all Mescalero believed that a shaman could assume the form of the animal that he derived his power from. In this instance, the skin of the animal might not be necessary to induce the transformation, as opposed to the skinwalker. In any case, Chris went on to describe a shapeshifting shaman that could assume the forms of bears, wolves, mountain lions, and horses. Even Chris's father implied to his son that he could become a bear if he desired. Chris also spoke of a witch that had grasshopper power that could turn herself into an insect. But, as stated before, shapeshifting is something of an outlier in Apache witchcraft compared to the Navajo variety.[40]

There are three main types of sorcery for Apache: poison sorcery, spell sorcery, and shooting sorcery.[41] Like the Navajo, the Apache considers a witch and a sorcerer to be two different things. Similar to the Navajo, sorcerers are greatly feared because they are more dangerous than, say, a witch practicing love magic.[42] Also like the Navajo, sorcerers are more often men than women because, according to the Apache, men experience the emotion of hatred more intensely.[43] A sorcerer is quite similar to a Navajo skinwalker apart from the were-animal aspect. A sorcerer is said to be active at night, they might attack a person during a large gathering so as to go undetected, and sorcerer's footprints are often found leading away from graves but are hard to identify. Lastly, a sorcerer caught in the act might try to buy their freedom with goods—if they don't threaten whoever caught them with sudden death, that is.

The witches' sabbat of an Apache witch is vaguely similar to the Navajo equivalent. In the Apache case, the witches dance naked around a fire holding the remains of corpses over their heads that they recently obtained from a grave. Unlike the Navajo witches, there is no necrophilia. Instead, intercourse occurs with a close clanswoman who is menstruating as a form of incest. Basso noted

148

that "Although these witch dances bear a striking resemblance to the Navajo 'witches' sabbath' described by Kluckhohn (1944), I found no evidence that the Apache conceive of them as part of an initiation procedure through which all neophyte witches are required to pass."[44]

Apache sorcerers had their own version of corpse powder as well. Naturally, dried-up ground human flesh was the main ingredient, but it also included bear feces, rattlesnake skin, wood from a tree struck by lightning, bear urine, and menstrual fluid (hence the act previously mentioned at the witch's dance). The sorcerer carried this deadly powder at all times and was often administered through food or through the top of a hogan skinwalker-style.

Next up is spell sorcery, which is less herbal and more magical. It is pretty similar to the Navajo equivalent. The victim's real Apache name must be used and is usually chanted four times since that number holds special significance for the Apache. A line from a ceremonial chant uttered backwards might also play into the spell as in the Navajo version. Keith Basso clarified that to make a spell more effective, one of the following four methods could be implemented:

1. By walking around the intended victim four times. (This method is said to be most frequently employed at ceremonials.)

2. By circling the victim's dwelling four times.

3. By placing four pieces of wood, one at each of the cardinal points, around the victim's wickiup or shack.

4. By burying some object (usually a piece of wood or a small stone) in the ground near the victim's dwelling or at some spot where he habitually goes to drink or relax. Although spells are directed.[45]

In addition to humans, livestock could also suffer a sorcerer's spell, and even an inanimate object like a saddle could be cursed for a specific purpose. While poison sorcery comes from ingesting bad food, and shooting sorcery is self-explanatory, for spell sorcery, the bad power enters through the victim's ears; hence it having to be spoken. Spell sorcery was reportedly the most commonly used method of witchcraft to cause harm. Like those stricken from sickness by corpse powder in the Navajo realm, an Apache might suffer a swollen tongue before expiring. According to lore, the body of a person killed by witchcraft would decompose at an "unusually rapid rate."[46]

Lastly, there is shooting sorcery, which is basically the same as the Navajo equivalent. The objects shot were mostly similar to the Navajo version, with a few exceptions. In Apache shooting sorcery, the more magical long-distance method seemed to be the one utilized. Informants described projectiles that "travel[ed] unerringly over great distances" and were "propelled at such high speeds" that they became "invisible in the air."[47]

An epidemic of Apache shooting sorcery occurred as late as the 1920s. Between 1920 to 1925 within Fort Apache and the San Carlos Reservations, many victims fell prey to shooting sorcery until it was quashed by a medicine man named Silas John. According to the Apache, that was the last big hurrah for shooting sorcery and the method has nearly died out—at least according to the subjects interviewed by Basso.

Just as the Spanish had unique charms and objects to ward off witchcraft, the Apache believed eagle feathers, cattail pollen, and turquoise beads were a form of protection. Also similar to the Spanish custom of a witch's power coming back against the witch, Apache healers often tried to turn a witch's power against them via either a lightning, bear, or snake ceremony. If successful, the bewitchment would come upon the witch who sent it and the witch would die.

Frederick Schwatka observed in the 1880s that the accusation of witchcraft was a fairly carefully done procedure with the highest ranking chief of the area being called in to investigate the matter. The entire tribe would take part in the proceedings, which would usually end in an execution wherein the accused was stripped naked and hung by their thumbs. They would then be beaten by mesquite bushes until one of two outcomes occurred: the accused confessed to being a witch and was swiftly beaten to death; or, assuming the accused never confessed, they would be beaten until the tribe tired of doing so. The individual would then be left to die an even slower death from neglect and sustained injuries. Other methods sometimes included hanging an individual upside down over a fire. Occasionally, an accused witch might just be banished from the tribe in addition to being banned from joining any other tribe, in essence making them a nomad for life. After a witch's execution, the family of the accused would be allowed to bury the dead, minus the usual mourning rituals. Also, said witch's home and belongings would all be burned.

Conclusion

In conclusion, though enemies, the Apache and the Navajo share a great many of the same beliefs when it comes to the realm of witchcraft and superstition. Beyond that, both have a shared trauma in the form of their internment at Bosque Redondo, which is referenced in the passage to follow, and which seems to provide a fitting conclusion to this section. An informant identified as Mr. Left-Handed from Crownpoint, New Mexico, concluded Kluckhohn's appendices in *Navaho Witchcraft* with the following prophecy:

I heard that all the Navaho that had died at Fort Sumner and all those who had been killed by enemies were coming back to life. The Navaho were all to go back to where they had been living before and all the whites would have to go back to their own country. This came from a round Tohatchi. There was no dance connected to the coming of the ghosts. As a rule it was not believed by the majority. Most of the people thought that this [rumor] was started by the witches."[48]

Section Notes

[1] The word Apache translates to enemy, which the Apache adopted proudly.

[2] Kluckhohn said, "Association with incest, trial and execution of witches and other traits are also found among the western Apache. Incest connection, killing of witches, ambivalent attitude toward ceremonial practitioners, the sacrifice of a close relative and other parallels likewise turn up among the Chiricahua Apache. But it is very difficult to find any trait shared by the various Apache groups and the Navaho which both of these do not also share with Pueblo culture. Indeed, it is my impression that Navaho witchcraft as a whole has more in common with Pueblo witchcraft... than it does Apache witchcraft." (Kluckhohn, *Navaho Witchcraft*, pp.70-71.)

[3] Zuni witches also did this. To summon the ghost, they planted a prayer stick in the ground and called the ghost by name, then told it which person they wanted it to torment.

[4] Opler, *Apache Odyssey*, p.149.

[5] *In the Days of Victorio* tells a story of the Apache Chief Nana apprehending seven riders, six of which were professed witches and one of whom was a captive boy who Nana set free. The six witches threatened that if they were executed, they would return as ghosts to haunt them. Nana had the witches burned and wisps of smoke were seen from the canyon as Nana and his men rode away with the boy they had freed.

[6] For yet another example, there are four distinct types of Thunderbirds. The same is true for their counterparts, the Water Serpents.

[7] Ball, *Indeh*, p.170.

[8] Bourke, *Apache Medicine Men*, p.20.

[9] In some cases, the Apache believed that witches could come back as bears.

[10] Kluckhohn, *Navaho Witchcraft*, p.241.

[11] Ibid, p.137.

[12] As to why Navajo witches were particularly infatuated with the skin whorls of a victim, perhaps the spiral-like patterns on the fingertips reminded them of the spirals so often depicted in petroglyphs.

[13] Special plants are used, and frenzy witchcraft is not to be discussed around children "whose bones are not formed." (Kluckhohn, *Navaho Witchcraft*, p.37) It is one of the less deadly forms of witchcraft, and nor did someone who practiced it have to be part of a witch's coven performing their obscene rites in hidden caves. Nor were the dead involved.

[14] Along these same lines, some seem to think that antlers will give the skinwalker additional power.

[15] That said, some of Kluckhohn's informants said the hides of goats and horses might also be used.

[16] Kluckhohn, *Navaho Witchcraft*, p.138.

[17] Ibid, p.139.

[18] Some interesting rumors about Navajo witchcraft went that witches had to rip the hearts out of their siblings during the killing ritual, though Kluckhohn said his informants told him that was false, as was the idea that twin colts were killed at once because witches liked to ride upon them.

[19] Kluckhohn, *Navaho Witchcraft*, p.137.

[20] Ibid, p.140.

[21] Ibid, p.136.

[22] Ibid, p.137.

[23] Another superstition would seem to have to do with a normal coyote, and not a skinwalker in coyote form. It was believed that if a Navajo glimpsed a coyote, that meant that their brother or sister was about to die. To undo impending death, the witness needed to place turquoise in the coyote tracks.

[24] I used the White Ash tree version in my novel, *Once Upon a Time in Fort Sumner*, since it was more conducive to the story.

[25] Recently, on Peter Santenello's YouTube channel, a Navajo man explained that the white ash lacing the bullets penetrates the spirit of the skinwalker and therefore reinforces the fact that it is white ash from a purifying ceremony.

[26] https://www.legendsofamerica.com/navajo-skinwalkers/

[27] This is why some people in the Southwest pick up their hair clippings after a haircut, for fear that a witch might procure them.

[28] Kluckhohn actually attributes shooting sorcery to wizardry, the third category of Navajo witchcraft. However, all three of the first varieties of witchcraft seem to utilize this method.

[29] Mayor, *Fossil Legends of the First Americans*, p.132.

[30] It was said that rather than making pouches out of typical, furry mammal hides, witches preferred horned toads and other things that crawled on their bellies.

[31] Kluckhohn, *Navaho Witchcraft*, p.135

[32] Ball, *Indeh*, p.230.

[33] Apache healers go to the Happy Place, the Apache version of Heaven, while witches will go to a place where there is little light, or air for that matter.

[34] Basso, *Western Apache Witchcraft*, p. 30.

[35] John G. Bourke (1846-1896) wrote of supernatural abilities had by medicine men in his book *Apache Medicine Men*, stating that he had heard of one who could light his pipe by simply holding it up to the sun. Another could fire a gun without touching it, or so he had heard. Bourke also wrote of one medicine man, Nakay-do-klunni, operating at Camp Apache in 1881 who claimed he had the power to raise the dead, and that also he would drive away the whites from the land. However, he died later that year in August in a confrontation at Cibicu Canyon.

[36] Geronimo, though not necessarily thought of as a medicine man in the public realm, had power and displayed it in public. Therefore he would be considered a medicine man among the Apache rather than a witch, though there were some who certainly called Geronimo a witch.

[37] Opler, *Apache Odyssey*, p.135.

[38] John G. Bourke also conflated Apache medicine men with skinwalkers. Or, that is to say he claimed that Apache medicine men were reputed to be able to turn into coyotes or other animals, though that doesn't mean that they utilized the skinwalker method of doing so. Afterall, traditions of were-animals are worldwide. The medicine men of Honduras, for instance, are also said to be able to turn into lions and tigers and so on.

[39] Opler, *Apache Odyssey*, p.185.

[40] In a footnote relating to page 34 in *Western Apache Witchcraft*, Keith Basso wrote, "My informants repeatedly denied that witches became were-animals. In this respect, Western Apache witchcraft beliefs contrast sharply with those of the Navajo."

[41] Considering the Apache significance of the number four, it seems rather strange that it's one category short of four types of witchcraft.

[42] The Apache love witch uses love magic called *godistso*. It is not terribly dissimilar to the many instances of love magic used amongst the Spanish and Pueblo peoples and so doesn't warrant much discussion here.

[43] Conversely, according to an investigation by Frederick Schwatka in the 1880s, from what he could ascertain, more women than men were accused of witchcraft among the Apache. (Of course, that's just one researcher's perspective.)

[44] Basso, *Western Apache Witchcraft*, p.34.

[45] Ibid, p.35.

[46] Ibid, p.38.

[47] Ibid, p.36.

[48] Kluckhohn, *Navaho Witchcraft*, p.218.

Part II
THE TERRITORIAL PERIOD

Similar to the culture shock that occurred when the Spanish conquered Mexico and the southwest portions of North America was the aftermath of the Mexican-American War fought from 1846 to 1848. When the dust settled, the United States acquired control over Texas and what would later become the states of California, Nevada, and Utah, and most of New Mexico, Arizona, and Colorado, plus parts of Oklahoma, Kansas, and Wyoming via the Treaty of Guadalupe Hidalgo, signed on February 2, 1848. In addition to the land, the U.S. government also inherited the superstitions of the Southwest. Whereas in the old days, witchcraft-related conflicts had sprung from the Spanish coming into conflict with the religious practices of the indigenous peoples, now it was the U.S. government that was puzzling over the practices of the Spanish and the Indians alike. In the past several hundred years of Spanish occupation, Old World witchcraft from Europe had slowly blended itself with the Native American supernaturalism of the New World.

Long before U.S. newspapers marveled over superstitious New Englanders conducting strange rituals to ward off vampirism in Rhode Island in the early 1890s, they were scratching their heads at the practices of the residents of the newly acquired territories. New Mexico, in particular, had many cases of witchcraft wherein the alleged witches were executed as in the days of Salem. For just one example: "Witches and wizards merited tribal punishment which was death. Two witches were clubbed to death in 1880," F. Stanley wrote in regards to Zia Pueblo.[1]

Likewise, the Spanish and Native American peoples were equally appalled that their new Anglo-American rulers thought of the dangers of witchcraft as the stuff of fairytales and ignorant peons. Oftentimes, accusations of witchcraft were brushed off by the U.S. courts, leaving the old residents of what used to be New Spain to take matters into their own hands, and the results were never pretty.

"Conquest of New Mexico" engraving of General Kearney proclaiming New Mexico part of the United States, Plaza, Las Vegas, New Mexico, 15 August 1846.

CANNIBAL WITCHES OF NAMBÉ

Nambé Pueblo 1880 as photographed by John K. Hillers.

Popularized in films such as *Hocus Pocus*, and also based upon the real practices of witches, is the idea of witches going after children to eat them or drain their youth in some way. One of the few documented instances of alleged child abduction at the hands of witches in New Mexico occurred in 1854 at Nambé, north of Santa Fe. Two Indian men identified in newspapers as Luis Romero and Antonio Tafolla were accused of child abduction and eating of the children in a despicable ritual of some sort. Actually, so far as can be pieced together, the two men were never seen eating the children, but witnesses claimed that they did see the accused witches pull the bones of their victims from their mouths and noses. As witches, the two men were marched outside of town to be executed by firing squad. At dusk, a four-man execution squad did just that, forcing the accused to kneel side by side, and then felled them both with a single shotgun blast to the head.

The order came from the governor of Nambé, Juan Ignacio Tapolla, and was an instance of the alcalde, or old Spanish rule, being at odds with the recent American rule of New Mexico Territory. As such, it caused a great stir in the newspapers, which will be quoted from, specifically the *New York Herald* of June 5, 1854. The trial, held not for the witches but for the men who executed them, occurred in March of 1854. The paper said that the trial could be considered "new and strange" to United States readers of the time and, "Who would have imagined that the scenes of the early days of

Salem would be reenacted in the middle of the nineteenth century..."
The paper explained that the defendants had shot the two witches
"a short distance beyond the borders of the Pueblo."

The first witness called to the stand was Juan Ygnacio Tafolla, who
gave the following statement:

> I live in Nambé; I know Luis Romero; he lived in Nambé; I
> also knew Antonio Tafolla; he lived in Nambé; they are now
> both dead; I know Juan Diego Tafolla, Juan Jose Trujillo, Juan
> Jesus Tafolla, and Juan de los Reyes Mirahal; these four men
> came and reported to me they had killed Luis Romero and
> Antonio Tafolla, in accordance with the order of the Pueblo.
> It was done in the beginning of this month; they only said
> they had killed them; did not see them after they were killed;
> they were killed not quite a league from the Pueblo in a north
> direction; they killed them at twilight; I saw them going out
> with the deceased; they had a shot gun; Juan Diego carried
> the gun; I saw them when they came back to report to me...

Thus ends the particulars of his testimony, which was one of the
more detailed accounts. Next up was the Nambé governor, who
stated that he sentenced Romero and Tafolla to death because they
had "done great wrongs to the Pueblo." He explained that the two
men confessed that they had committed witchcraft and sorcery and
had "eaten up the little children of the Pueblo." The governor
continued that it had "always been our custom to put a stop to and
check bad acts." He further explained the times and new governing
system in an interesting way: "We have not exercised this custom of
killing witches since the Americans came here, because there had not
been much bad doings before; we have always governed ourselves
as an independent community; and Governor Calhoon said, as we
were poor and ignorant, and could not serve as jurors, we might
govern ourselves."

The next witness offered a few new insights into the alleged
witches, clarifying that both were young men. Romero was basically
a vagabond living on his own with no property, while Tafolla had a
home and a wife. A slew of other witnesses then testified how they
didn't know where the men were killed and simply had not seen
them for a few days. As for the governor's remark that he had told
the Nambé peoples they could govern themselves, Governor
Calhoon claimed that he didn't remember if he ever said such a
thing—not exactly an outright denial.

The papers concluded that "Although the act of the killing was sufficiently proved to the jury, there was no evidence it was done in the county of Santa Fe, without which they could not find them guilty. The trial was conducted in three languages—English, Spanish, and the dialect of Nambé; and during its continuance a deep interest was manifested." In other words, the executioners of the alleged witches couldn't be charged over confusion as to where the Santa Fe County line was.

A year later, another execution was carried out at Nambé of three men and one woman accused of witchcraft. According to papers they were "butchered in a most horrible manner." Again the executioners were taken to court, and again they escaped punishment, though this time, they did have to pay $400 in court costs.

BRUJOS OF TRUCHAS

"Owls are not only hated as chicken-killers but as bearers of ill-fortune and witchcraft. The old people say that the owl is a bruja, or witch, that can only be killed with a bullet that has a cross incised upon its point. Others say that it necessitates a silver bullet." –Wesley R. Hurt, "Spanish-American Superstitions," El Palacio.

Folktales of hunters shooting and wounding an animal in the night only to meet a human with a similar injury in the morning are common across the Southwest. After a certain point, one has to wonder if there is indeed some truth to them or if the same tale was simply repurposed over and over again using different people, locations, and animals.

This variation of the tale took place in Truchas, a small settlement located halfway between Taos and Santa Fe. Even today, Truchas remains remote, as a paved road was not created for the community until the early 1970s. Furthermore, the old Spanish Land Grant laws still stand; cars must share the road with cattle, and so on. Though still a very remote community, for many, it is best known as the primary filming locale for *The Milagro Beanfield War* (1988).

Our story centers on an unnamed trader who frequently traveled between Santa Fe and Taos in the old days. He often stopped along the way in Truchas, where, after peddling his goods from his covered wagon, he would spend the night at the home of his friend, Don Melitón Vigil. One such night, after a nice long chat in front of the fireplace with his elderly friend, the trader went to retire for the night. After grabbing his bedroll from his covered wagon, he laid down to rest in the front room of his friend's home.

After sleeping a short while, his rest was interrupted by an unnerving noise he had grown to know well over the past few weeks. Lately, a pair of owls had been following him from village to village. This was a bad omen, as owls were solitary creatures, and to see two together was unusual. Stranger yet, the trader had recently had some trouble with two Tesuque Pueblo men over a horse trade gone bad. The two men, whispered to be brujos, had vowed to get even with him. There were always two owls following him; could it be the brujos in animal form? Nervously, he opened the front door to look outside. There on the cross-pole of his host's front gate were perched the two unusually large owls. Perhaps his tired eyes were playing tricks on him in the bright moonlight? The trader crossed himself and shut the door. He marched into his friend's bedroom to find him up rolling a cornhusk cigarette. The owls had disturbed his sleep as well. The trader asked the old man if he might have his gun to shoot the tiresome creatures. Vigil obliged but warned him, "If you think that those two owls are sorcerers out to do you harm, you had better carve a cross into the bullets. Otherwise, the bullets will be useless."

The trader remembered the two men said to be witches and didn't argue with his friend. As instructed, he took out his pocketknife and carved a cross into two of the bullets. He loaded his friend's rifle and collected his nerves. If these were witches, he would need to act fast. In his mind's eye he remembered the exact spot the owls perched upon the gate, swung the front door open, and fired two shots in quick order. One owl fell dead onto the patio, while the other flew into the night with one leg hanging down. It had been hit, but the wound would not be fatal. The trader marched across the moonlit patio and picked up the dead owl, then threw it across the road and down the hillside.

On his trip home, the trader received news that one of the two Tesuque men had died recently. The man and his companion, suffering a broken leg, had gone on an unfortunate hunting trip. One

160

of the men had accidentally shot himself and died. His companion slung him across the back of his horse and rode back to the pueblo. On the way there, his horse tripped and fell on him, breaking his leg. Or that was the story told, at least. But the trader knew that he, along with his old friend Vigil, knew the real truth of the matter. The men were witches. The trader was never bothered by the surviving witch again and presumed he either gave up his quest for vengeance or quit practicing witchcraft altogether.

SKINWALKERS ON THE LONG WALK

"Fort Sumner was a major trauma, the full calamity of which it is difficult to convey to white readers."—Clyde Kluckhohn, Navaho Witchcraft.[2]

Between August of 1864 to the end of 1866 occurred the tragic "Long Walk" of the Navajo, who made the arduous trek from Arizona and Western New Mexico to the Bosque Redondo Indian Reservation in Fort Sumner, New Mexico. During the course of those two years, thousands of Navajos in over fifty separate groups were forced to make the traumatic journey across the desert to Bosque Redondo. To make matters worse, they would have to share the Bosque with their enemies, the Mescalero Apache. While there, the Navajo also picked up a few tricks from the Apache.

According to more than a few sources, it was at the Bosque that Navajo medicine men learned both the "shooting way" and the "sucking way" to cure it from the Apache. Backing this theory up, in *Navaho Witchcraft*, Clyde Kluckhohn stated that shooting sorcery had, according to certain informants, been "known only since Fort Sumner."[3]

161

The Navajo also picked up another Apache cure called the "wind way," which was to treat sickness brought about by the wind in some way or another, which was different from witchcraft. In any case, there was much sickness at the Bosque, and a decent amount of it was attributed to witchcraft.

In addition to witches, the Navajo also had to watch out for ghosts, especially the ghosts of aliens—aliens, in this case, meaning non-Navajos. Navajos were at risk of alien ghosts killed in battle by other Navajos, and sometimes the departed spirit of a non-Navajo with whom sexual relations were had. Actually, something as simple as accidentally touching a corpse or stepping on its grave could induce ghost sickness. Being around so many whites and Apache, there were many "alien ghosts" to contend with at the Bosque. To counter these sicknesses, they performed the Squaw Dance semi-often it was said. Occasionally the Navajo left the Bosque to enact vengeance on other tribes that had attacked them. Out to get some Comanche one night, a coyote appeared in the warrior's camp. This was why four Navajo died in the assault, it was said. Though in that case, the coyote had been an omen as was typical, later, the Navajo performed the Coyote Way Ritual, an act that they believe led to their freedom. The *New Mexico Historical Review* explained:

According to Navajo oral tradition, it was not pleading alone that secured the Navajo's release, but also the performance of the Coyote Way ritual. Although some informants claimed that the ritual was divinatory, indicating that the government was now ready to free the Navajo, other Navajo attributed their freedom to this ceremony. The years of pleading had been unsuccessful, they claimed, until the performance of the Coyote ritual, "during which our leader was blessed with Coyote power." Because of this ceremony, the next request to leave was approved.[4]

By 1868, the experiment at Bosque Redondo was officially acknowledged as a failure, and all the Navajo were allowed to return home to the place they called Dinehtah, or Navajoland. But the horrors and ramifications of the Long Walk weren't over yet. It was said that many individuals tainted by hate and anger took to the skinwalker way at Bosque Redondo to get by. This epidemic of skinwalkers and witchery way would follow the Navajo back home and eventually result in the Navajo Witch Purge of 1878, to be covered later.

162

WITCHCRAFT MISTRIAL AT SOCORRO

The Albuquerque Morning Journal ran a small item by H.R. Whiting, a former court clerk in Socorro County in the 1860s, on witchcraft on August 11, 1915. He told of a pitiable trial held in La Joya where a husband and wife were falsely convicted of witchcraft, in his opinion. Whiting recollected,

> In the middle of the 60s of the last century there was a trial in Socorro before the justice of peace at La Joya of two poor ignorant persons, natives of New Mexico, husband and wife, and advanced in years, on an accusation for witchcraft. I do not give the names of any of these parties, as all are now dead and it might bring discredit on their families, if they have left any. The justice was a man of no education, not being able to even read or write. The prosecutor was a member of the bar of the district court of the second judicial district of New Mexico in Albuquerque. He brought the accusation against the two old people, who had nobody to defend them, and pretended at the trial to read from the compiled laws of New Mexico of 1865, a section defining witchcraft and the penalty for its violation. The justice heard the evidence, and, deceived by the attorney, found the defendants guilty and sentenced the man to twenty-five lashes on the back and ordered all of their effects consisting principally of bedding and two or three burros to be taken for the costs. The sentence was carried into effect.

LA RUBIA, WITCH OF FORT UNION CAVE

Our next story takes place either before, during, or after the Civil War in the vicinity of Fort Union. Stationed there were three good friends who had grown up together in Taos by the names of Pablito Martinez, Manuel Esquibel, and Miguel Archuleta, the teller of the tale. During their time at the fort, they heard tales of a nearby enchanted cave harboring a woman known as La Rubia. She was very beautiful, with flowing red hair. She would be seen at the mouth of the cave during the early morning and the evening. She appeared to men passing by the cave and would beg them to disenchant her and set her free, though she never revealed how or why she was bound to the cave.

163

"Three men ventured into the cave at different times," Don Miguel, told FWP writer Lorin W. Brown when he was around 96 years old. "Of these, only one had stayed in overnight, and not only overnight, but forever as he never came out again."[5] As such, people began to surmise that La Rubia was more witch than enchanted maiden that enticed men to their deaths.

Don Miguel told of how one night, Pablito returned to their barracks in a state of great excitement. He was struck with love at first sight, for he had seen La Rubia and intended to go back to the cave at once, even if it meant deserting his post. His two friends convinced him to wait until they could accompany him during their next scheduled leave, and he reluctantly agreed. However, even in his sleep that night, he tossed and turned, muttering about La Rubia.

As planned, the three friends set out together on their next leave. With them they took guns and provisions and even made sure to make one last confession to the priest before leaving lest anything happen to them on the way. Pablito wondered if the beautiful woman might be a princess from Spain, and if he wed her, he might inherit her riches.

"*Pobre* Pablito, he was dreaming we knew. What could be found in a hole in the ground in these sun-baked hills except that maybe it was the home of some *bruja* who took the form of the *Rubia* to lure men into the caves for her own wicked ends?" Don Miguel mused.[6] Eventually, they made their way to the cave, the entrance of which was obscured by brush and a large overhang. They made camp and ate one last meal before entering, their pistols ready to shoot down any brujas they encountered. At first, the cave was troublesome and narrow, but eventually it opened up into a large room. The men inspected the cavern for footprints, and Pablito excitedly exclaimed that he had found one. It must belong to La Rubia, he thought. Pablito dashed down a new corridor, following the footprints and shouting all the while that he would fight every devil in the place to free La Rubia. His two companions followed, though they noted they saw no footprints other than Pablito's. Pablito, in his frenzy, ran so far ahead of his friends that they lost sight of his torch when he turned a corner.

Upset with their friend, Miguel and Manuel stood at the spot where they lost Pablito, which branched off in three different directions. Miguel decided he would explore one of the branches while Manuel stood and waited for Pablito in case he came back. During his exploration through the labyrinthian cavern, he came across two skeletons, which he guessed to be Indians due to some pottery shards found nearby. Eventually he gave up his search and returned to Manuel, still alone, standing sentry for Pablito. After some time, their friend finally returned to them, greatly disenchanted with the enchanted cave. As they passed a large drop in the cave floor on their way out, Pablito shouted, "Rubia, if you are down there, you can stay there!"

The men had a good laugh at their adventure, which had been for naught, and walked back to Fort Union on foot as their horses had deserted them long ago. To their shock, they had spent three days and two nights in the enchanted cave. At least La Rubia didn't make them permanent residents...

THE NAVAJO WITCH PURGE

Ordinarily, this witchcraft account wouldn't belong in this book, as it predominantly occurred in Arizona. However, the incident has deep ties to events in New Mexico via the tragic Long Walk of the Navajo. When the Navajo returned to their homeland from Fort Sumner's Bosque Redondo in 1868, they did so without adequate provisions for the journey. As such, when they settled back to what they thought would be their old lives in Dinehtah, they fell upon hard times. There was great sickness among the people and their livestock alike. Arousing suspicions was the fact that some families prospered with their livestock and farms while others suffered badly. Some blamed this sickness, along with other hardships, on witchcraft. Over the next decade, the whispers of witchcraft would grow more prominent until they finally reached a fever pitch in the summer of 1878.

Though witchcraft had always been a despised but acknowledged part of Navajo existence, what kicked off what would later be known as the Navajo Witch Purge was the chilling discovery of a "cursed item" in the first half of 1878. Apparently, a Navajo had found the "cursed item" buried in the Arizona desert near Ganado Lake; only being a Navajo, this person couldn't touch the cursed item. As such, a trusted trader named Charles Hubbell was recruited to do so. Charles was the less well-known brother of Juan "Don" Lorenzo Hubble, who, along with his brother, was born in San Miguel County, New Mexico. Together the two established a franchise of trading posts across the Southwest.

Eventually, the brothers developed quite a rapport with the Navajo and began trading with them. One of the ways in which the Hubbells benefited the Navajo (and themselves) was by helping them to determine which patterns on their blankets were the most popular among consumers so that they would know what to produce more of.

Of Hubbell, it was said that "Sentiment about him varied. Euro-Americans viewed him as the dean of Indian traders in the Southwest. Some Navajo customers said it was good to have trader Hubbell as a friend, while others said Navajos did everything around his trading ranch for low wages."[7]

Hubbel's Trading Post.

As stated before, the Navajos requested that Charles Hubbell go and remove the cursed item found near Ganado Lake. Hubbell agreed and made a chilling discovery. Though accounts differ on what he found, the most interesting alleges that within a shallow grave, Hubbell found a dead body with the stomach split open. Within the stomach, he found either a curse scrawled across a random piece of paper or the actual 1868 treaty between the Navajo and the U.S. government that had released them from Bosque Grande—accounts differ.

Juan Lorenzo Hubbel.

A grandson of a tribal member named Hash keh yilnaya years later recollected to researcher Martha Blue that "the collection that these witches gathered was found wrapped in paper and this paper was I think the Treaty of 1868. . .buried in the belly of a dead person in a grave. . . ."[8]

Whatever it was, the unearthing of this cursed item set about a series of events comparable to the Salem Witch Trials of the late 1600s, only much less publicized. The Navajo Witch Purge, as it would later be known, resulted in an estimated 40 people being executed as skinwalkers or witches. While some of the dead may well have been actual skinwalkers, it is believed that plenty of others were just the victims of malicious false allegations motivated by jealousy and petty feuds.

The first witch to die was killed right in front of Hubbell's Trading Post, possibly in the doorway itself. Years later, an elderly tribesman named Yazzie T'iis Yazh related the following to researcher Martha Blue:

Hastiin Jieh Kaal/Digoli was first killed in the doorway of Hubbell's first trading post near the lake after he told about his companion killing young people. After that the trading post was relocated to the present site because Navajos were afraid of the trading post where Hastiin Jieh Kaal/Digoli was slain and considered the building haunted.

Whoever killed the witch in front of Hubbell's lucrative trading post made a poor decision in location, as the Navajo belief system warns that the dead spirit of a violent killing will linger at the kill spot. As such, Hubbell moved his post to a location nearer Ganado Lake.[9] Yazh said,

> ….in the doorway there was blood all over, so the people living around there told [Hubbell] that he shouldn't live in a place where someone dies.[10]

Soon after, the Navajo went after Hastiin Jieh Kaal's companion whom he had accused of killing young people. Yazh related to Blue that,

> [H]is companion was Hastiin Biwosi and was in the vicinity performing a ceremony so some Navajos went there to kill Hastiin Biwosi.[11]

According to some accounts, as many as 50 people went out in search of Biwosi. A grandson of one of the posse, Hash keh yilnaya, said that "people gathered... from Ganado, and some from Greasewood, and others from Klagetoh... they prepared themselves... armed themselves with guns, arrows, clubs... there were many people riding horses... fifty... or hundred."[12]

Where exactly the posse found Biwosi has never been specified, but find him they did in some kind of residence. They stated their business to the inhabitants of the structure, all of whom left, and the party then dragged Biwosi outside. There, a respected leader of the tribe, Totsohnii Hastiin, officially pronounced Biwosi as a witch and all but one were set to kill him, that being Ganado Mucho, who cried, "[H]e's my relative... my older brother!"[13]

In some accounts, it was also stated that Mucho made the case that as dangerous as a skinwalker was in life, its ghost could be even more deadly. However, Hash keh yilnaya argued that Biwosi had "cut off [his] chance for a good life. . ."[14] Totsohnii Hastiin then gave the go-ahead to kill Biwosi, and the group shot him and then stoned him to death.[15]

Following Biwosi's death, tensions continued to escalate throughout Dinehtah. Charles Hubbell and his employees feared that since their post had been the site of the first killing that they may be implicated in it somehow. By late spring, Hubbell was concerned enough with the "Witch Purge" to write a letter to "W.B. Leonard, Fort Defiance, Arizona Territory, Yavapai County" on May 31, 1878. In the letter, he requested that he be sent rifles and ammunition because he was expecting a "big row" among the Navajo. Specifically, he felt that a large band of them may arrive from Canyon de Chelly, Arizona, to attack most of the Anglo settlers, and in particular, he feared for his store being destroyed.

Fort Wingate, New Mexico.

In another letter written on the same day, Hubbell revealed he had received intel from an informant he identified only as Ganio, that certain Indians were arming themselves and had intent to harm him specifically. As such, he requested that soldiers from Fort Defiance come and protect him, his family, and their post.[16]

Sometime later, Manuelito—another Navajo tribal leader— arrived at Fort Wingate with a letter he had written to J. L. Hubbell— stating that "the Navajos had tied up six medicine men accused of

169

witchcraft" and that he was convinced many Navajos would start murdering each other without military intervention. As it was, Manuelito's own cousin had been executed earlier that summer.

Eventually, the military intervened as requested. Ten accused witches were then brought before a military council presided over by Lieutenant D. D. Mitchell. Instead of having them executed as the Navajo would have done, he let them go and gave a stern speech condemning the wanton killing of the alleged witches. After this, the killings lessened in number, though a few still occurred in isolated areas from time to time. But, for the most part, the Navajo Witch Purge of 1878 was over.

Of course, today we brush off the 1878 witchcraft claims as pure unfounded superstition. And while most of them probably were false claims based upon petty feuds, how many more might have concerned true supernatural evil? After all, there are still many sightings of skinwalkers in Navajo country today...

THE WITCH OF LINCOLN COUNTY

View of Lincoln village in 1888.

Interestingly enough, a witch was said to be practicing in Billy the Kid country sometime in the 1880s. The sole source of this story is the late author Jack Kutz in his classic *Mysteries and Miracles of New Mexico*. In it, he tells of an informant named Maria Candelaria Trujillo y Rudolph, who lived in Lincoln County in the 1880s. This woman told of a witch that lived in Lincoln County around this time, and unfortunately the details as to exactly where in the county are limited. (Back in the 1880s, Lincoln County was huge and technically comprised most of southeastern New Mexico. But, since Kutz wrote the book in the 1980s, presumably he meant Lincoln County as it is considered today.)

The witch of Lincoln County was named Doña Peipeiuta and had a talent unique among New Mexico's witches. According to witnesses, she could take her own body apart limb by limb. Maria Candelaria's great-uncle was walking by Doña Peipeiuta's home one night when he witnessed the act himself. He claimed that he peeped into a window to see the witch sitting on a wooden bench over a steaming tub of hot water. He watched with grotesque fascination as she took off one of her legs and washed it in the water, which boiled any time she submerged a limb in it. The man watched her do her arms as well, and it all became too much for him when she detached her head and began to scrub it in the tub as well.

This is all purely folkloric of course, but one has to wonder what truth, if any, this tale is based on. And, though I said earlier the bit about being able to detach limbs was unique to New Mexico witches, it was not unique to the witches of Old Mexico. Up until the mid-1960s, the Tlaxcala region kept a strong belief in the Tlahuelpuchi, a shapeshifting, bloodsucking witch that fed upon infants. According to lore, the Tlahuelpuchi would detach its limbs to lessen its size and therefore turn into a bird of some kind so that it could fly out into the night to commit its heinous acts.

Every resident I asked within the village of Lincoln today had no recollections or knowledge of any witch. However, according to Kutz, she lived in Lincoln County in general, so perhaps she was holed up somewhere in the Hondo Valley?[17]

THE CRIPPLING OF JUAN REYES

Though the exact year of this short tale is unknown, the location was Santa Cruz, 30 miles north of Santa Fe. There lived Juan Reyes, who suffered a curse put upon him by his father. While his mother lay dying, in such a weakened state that she could not speak, Juan asked her about his inheritance. She pointed to Juan's father, who promptly denied that any inheritance awaited him. Sure that he was lying, Juan threatened his father with a dagger. Juan's father then put a curse on him, shouting, "May the Earth swallow you. Not money, but a deformed and twisted body shall be your inheritance."[18]

According to the legend, the ground opened up beneath his feet and swallowed Juan up to his waist. When Juan pulled himself out, his legs were now deformed and his right arm had become useless, thus rendering him a beggar for the rest of his life. A true story, or just a cautionary tale not to mouth off to one's parents?

MA'AM JONES AND THE MAGIC OF THE SPANISH

Seven Rivers Cemetery. (Southeastern New Mexico Historical Society/
Near Lovingsbend.org)

Immortalized in Eve Ball's now classic work, *Ma'am Jones of the Pecos*, the Heiskell and Barbara "Ma'am" Jones family eventually became legendary figures in southeastern New Mexico. Through this family, which would one day have ten children in all, one of the great frontier trading posts of New Mexico was born. It was located in the vicinity of Seven Rivers and was known from South Texas to Kansas. But, more than anything, it was known for Barbara "Ma'am" Jones's famous food and hospitality.

Barbara Jones was also considered something of an unofficial doctor and healer in the Seven Rivers region. Had she been of Hispanic heritage, she probably would have been called a curandera. (That said, Barbara was schooled in the art of Spanish herbs and local cures by her Hispanic neighbors.) Among her patients was a scrawny young man who would one day be known as the legendary outlaw Billy the Kid, who was counted as family among the Joneses.

Barbara herself witnessed an instance of what they would've termed "Indian Magic" in those days when she observed a Spanish woman divert a hail storm. Barbara had ridden to the abode of one of her neighbors with two of her children when copper-colored storm clouds descended on the range. Barbara wanted to ride away

172

and beat the storm back to her home, but her neighbor, Juanita, stopped her. She beseeched Barbara to stay there while she stopped the storm.

On page 33 of *Ma'am Jones of the Pecos*, Ball wrote:

> Juanita returned to the house, took a handful of salt from a pottery jar, and advanced into the path of the approaching hail as though repelling an enemy. From the hills came the terrific roar of crashing ice pellets as they struck trees and rocks. Juanita threw pinches of salt into the wind. She muttered strange words. Barbara overtook her and attempted to pull her toward the house. Juanita shook her head and jerked loose. 100 yards ahead the hail battered the earth.

To Barbara's shock, just as the storm was about to be upon them, it suddenly changed course and passed by the woman's home, heading towards the Ruidoso River, missing them by only a few yards.[19] As Barbara rode home safely, she pondered the strange phenomenon she had just witnessed. Ball filled in her wonderings thusly: "[Juanita's] mutterings had seemed more like those of sorcery than supplication [prayer]. There was something very queer about it, something she had better not mention to her husband or sons. And Juanita had cautioned her not to tell the *padre*."[20]

ZIA WITCH

"In the Pueblo world, a coyote can either be a witch or a witch's pet… or it may contain the spirit of a dead person. Sometimes, women unwittingly married were-coyotes and became witches themselves."-
Jack Kutz, Mysteries and Miracles of New Mexico.[21]

At Zia Pueblo in the early 1880s, a witch there was causing the deaths of numerous children. The Puebloans called a nearby priest to come help, but he refused to leave the neighboring village where he lived to come to their aid. In his absence, the villagers turned to the next best thing, the local sacristan. Charles Lummis related the scene in *A New Mexico David*:

> He marched at the head of the mob, carrying a jar of holy water, which he had taken from the church. As they came near, the poor old woman fled, with the mob in howling pursuit. Just as they were about to overtake her, she suddenly turned herself into a dog, and soon distanced them. They got

their horses and ran her down; but she changed again to a coyote and ran faster than ever."[22]

Zia Pueblo c. late 1880s as photographed by John K. Hillers.

After a full day of trailing the were-coyote, the pursuers cornered it near a tree. The coyote transformed into a cat and raced up the tree. The villagers shook it in a vain effort to make the were-witch fall to the ground. In the end, the sacristan had to toss his holy water into the tree. Hitting the cat, it transformed back into a human and tumbled to the ground. The villagers then proceeded to beat the old witch profusely, but still she would not die. "Untie the knot! Untie the knot!" the witch shouted until one of the men stooped down to examine her body and found the little knot of which she spoke. It was on a bloodstained blanket, which he untied, and her spirit fled from her dead body.

BEWITCHED TREASURE OF QUARAI RUINS

One night several boys were playing ball near the ruins of Quarai. Eventually, the ball rolled away, and as one of the twelve-year-old boys went to fetch it, he saw a tiny man, or *duende*. (In Spanish folklore, duendes were enchanted dwarfs which often caused mischief and were tangentially related to bewitchment.) This duende was around three feet tall and spoke to the boy in a language unknown to him. Frightened, he ran back to the house where they had been playing ball. The boy told a neighbor and a young man of his strange encounter, and so they ran outside themselves to look.

Quarai Ruins.

Instead of a dwarf, they saw a floating orb of light that was nearly blinding in its intensity. Thinking it to be a bruja, they followed it as it traveled towards a cattle tank west of the home. As was the common practice, they drew a circle in the earth, and as a witch ball was wont to do, it shot into the circle like a bolt of lightning and disappeared. Normally, a witch would be found in the circle after this. But, as no witch was found, the men wondered instead if the glowing orb was really a sign of buried treasure.

175

The men grabbed shovels and began to dig. Two feet down the ball of fire reappeared and leapt out of the ground. They paid it no mind as it bounced around in the air, deciding to dig deeper for the supposed treasure. At six feet down, they were shocked when a rooster's crow came from the hole. As they dug deeper into the ground, more strange noises emanated from the earth—this time, it was the sound of men riding fast horses. Frightened of the bewitched hole, they ceased their efforts and never dug into it again, letting the supposed treasure rest there lest it be cursed.

FOR WHOM THE BELL TOLLS

One of the greatest collectors of folktales in all of New Mexico was Lorin W. Brown. Like many other writers, he collected his stories during the 1930s as part of the Federal Writer's Project. He specialized in the area of Taos and Cordova. One day while in Cordova, he was making casual conversation with Manuel Trujillo, the best moccasin maker in the village, when suddenly the church bells began to toll. Due to the unexpected time of day at which they rang, that could mean only one thing: someone had died.

The bells were tolling for a woman with a saintly reputation by the name of Teodorita Garduño of Taos. She had earned her pious reputation for being the one to always ring the bell for the vesper services during the month of May in Cordova. It was an arduous task for the old woman as she had to climb a ladder to do so. As Brown complimented the deceased on her seemingly saintly behavior, Trujillo told him otherwise. According to him, Garduño had been proven to be a witch on multiple occasions and started her godly deeds to deflect unwanted accusations.

The first time Garduño was proven to be a witch was in the home of José de la Luz Chávez. However, Garduño wasn't invited to the home for a routine social call. Mrs. Chávez had reason to believe that Garduño was out to bewitch either her or her baby. As a test, she took two sewing needles and made a cross out of them and placed them above the doorframe after Garduño had entered the home. Several times, Garduño prepared to leave but found herself perplexed as to why she couldn't bear to cross through the doorway. Eventually, Mrs. Chávez removed the needles and showed them to Garduño, stating, "Now I know you are a witch, and I want you to promise never to harm me or my family!"

Garduño threatened the woman and her baby with unspeakable horrors before fleeing the house. This encounter was reported to the alcalde, who then threatened to whip Garduño if she did not renounce her threats upon the Chávez family. Aiding the alcalde was a man known as Salvador Martinez, who, according to Manuel Trujillo, had "helped kill that witch in Chimayo." According to Trujillo, Martinez had been harmed by witches in his youth and so took every opportunity that he could to kill or drive them away.

THE WITCH OF CHIMAYO

The witch that Salvador Martinez killed could have been this one, reported in the New Mexican Review of September 8, 1884. The "Death of a Witch" reported that:

Major T. D. Burns, merchant of Tierra Amarilla brings in word of a shocking outrage that occurred recently in Rio Arriba County. A Mexican woman, aged about 40 years, whom the natives of the small village known as Chimayo believed to be a witch in league with the Devil, was taken from her lonely adobe hut by three roughs on Thursday last and murdered. They stripped her of all her clothing and shot and stabbed her many times. It is said the perpetrators of the crime are known to the authorities, but are desperate characters and no attempt whatever has been made to arrest them.

Martinez, under the authority of the alcalde, went to Garduño's home along with several other men to confront her. In his hands he carried a lariat with which to tie her if need be. At first, Garduño denied the claims. But, when she saw Martinez with the rope, due to fear of his well-established reputation, she finally confessed to being a witch and swore not to harm the family she had threatened. On her knees, she begged for mercy. Rather than sentencing her to death, the alcalde decreed that Garduño pray the Rosary on her bare knees on coarse gravel taken from an ant den. Even after this, strange things happened around the home of Garduño.

Namely, balls of fire were seen floating near her abode. Sometimes they would fly down the hillside from the direction of Truchas to enter her chimney. Then there was the matter that owls seemed to congregate near her home. People stayed away from the place apart from gazing upon it in curiosity. If they saw her on the streets, they would cross themselves or might go the other way. As Trujillo put it, "She never had any visitors except those which came through the air."

El Santuario de Chimayo, 1918.

Trujillo reported his own supernatural encounter with Garduño one night as he and some friends were walking to the nearby village of Chimayo. As they sang happily on their walk, they suddenly noticed one of those peculiar fireballs following them from atop the ridge. As the ball of light floated towards them, a man in the party named Juan Mondragon stepped in front of it, made the sign of the cross, and then drew a circle in the air. This immobilized the ball and within it could be seen the eyes of Garduño glaring at them. The witch implored Juan to set her free. Instead, Juan made her transform back into a normal human and walk with them to Chimayo and back to Cordova barefoot. Once again, Garduño swore not to revert back to her witchy ways. Presumably, that's when she began ringing the church bell before she moved away to Taos with her granddaughter.

LOS VOLADEROS, VILLAGE OF THE WITCHES

In New Mexico folktales is occasionally mentioned a mystical spot known as Los Voladeros, a hidden village inhabited entirely by witches. Where it was allegedly located is hard to pinpoint, but the most prominent accounts point to it being somewhere in the vicinity of Truchas and Mora. According to Ray John de Aragón in his book *Enchanted Legends and Lore of New Mexico*, Los Voladeros was settled on the highest peak near Mora. Though not named, this is likely Truchas Peak, which has an elevation of just a little over 13,000 feet. In *Enchanted Legends and Lore of New Mexico*, Aragón explained that Los Voladeros, meaning "The Flyers," was "a hidden village... up in the clouds surrounded by mountains at the highest point near Mora."[23]

Truchas Peak among the Sangre De Cristo Mountains.

The star of the tale Aragón told was a man named Buenaventura Angel, who had a burning curiosity to visit the forbidden village his elders had warned him of. So, despite their warnings, one day Angel saddled up his horse and set off into the mountains to find the mysterious settlement. He arrived at the crest of the mountaintop at nightfall and could no longer see well. He thought back to what the elders had warned of. They said that if one approached the village at dark, one needed only to look for a narrow, moonlit path. Whatever happened, one was not to stray from the path, as that would mean death. Lastly, one would know they were nearing the village upon hearing the hooting of many owls.

Just as the elders said, Angel followed the forested path until he heard the hooting of the owls and could see the embers of fires floating into the air from fireplaces. The village was near, obscured behind a fortress-like wall. Angel crept along the wall until he found an opening and snuck through into the forbidden village. At once, he was struck by a type of magic and fell to the ground unconscious. When he awoke, he found himself imprisoned within a torreon, or circular adobe tower that had been built to protect the original inhabitants from Indian raids. However, the stay wasn't all bad. Angel was well fed with delicious food from a beautiful jailer named Dulubina. Eventually, Angel won over Dulubina's trust well enough for him to be released from the torreon, and a sort of courtship began. The strangest thing to Angel as Dulubina showed him around the village was that it was populated exclusively by beautiful women, all wearing black dresses and black shawls. Like Ursula and her thousands of virgins, there were no men to be found anywhere in the settlement. Even Dulubina's mother, Doña Calada, was beautiful.

Example of a torreon, this one from Lincoln, NM, prior to restoration.

Eventually, Angel asked Dulubina to marry him, and for the wedding, rather than white, she wore a black dress and a black shawl embroidered with black roses. Even her eyes appeared like black marbles that day. At the wedding ceremony, for the first time, Angel saw a man in the form of the priest performing the ceremony. Only the priest had an odd resemblance to a goat, or dare we say the Devil himself, with his upturned eyebrows, goatee, and pointed ears...

The next morning, Angel was surprised to find Dulubina and her mother packing to leave. They wanted to go with him to his village. Though Angel would have been content to stay in Los Voladeros forever, he obliged. His main qualm was transporting Dulubina's rather odd possessions, which included strange, black leather-bound books and potions that Dulubina used to bathe with. Lastly was a heavy headboard carved with beautiful cherubs and other symbols of love. Though he thought it would be too heavy to transport, when Angel went to lift the headboard, it seemed to move with ease. It was almost magical...

Even when Angel returned to his village with his beautiful bride and became ill, he never suspected his wife or her mother of witchcraft. Angel was aware that the food they prepared for him was the cause of his sickness, but so blinded by love was he that he simply assumed they were poor cooks. Not even the odd smell of sulfur here and there raised his hackles. It wasn't until Angel began to notice that his wife went missing in the middle of the night that he finally suspected that something was wrong. Thinking she was having an affair, one night he purposefully did not eat the food that he knew would put him to sleep. He pretended to sleep and felt his wife leave the bed. Quietly, he crept to the door and peered outside. There Dulubina had turned into an old hag along with her mother, now also very ugly. In an instant, the two women turned into owls and took flight. Angel finally realized he had married a witch.

He ran back into the house in horror. Now when he looked at the ornate headboard, he no longer saw angels or hearts, but skulls and cauldrons had taken their place. And where he used to see the number nine, he now saw several sixes. Lastly, the peaceful dove had turned into an ominous owl. Angel knew what he had to do. He dragged the devilish headboard outside, and this time it was incredibly heavy instead of light as it had been when he brought it down the mountain. He tossed the headboard outside, and added the evil spell books and potions on top of it. Then, he set the satanic paraphernalia aflame. To his shock, when it finished burning, there were no traces of any remains. It was as if the evil items had never existed at all. Now he only had to contend with his wife and mother-in-law. Not knowing what else to do, he barricaded himself in the house.

On the first morning, the witches didn't return. But, by nightfall, they came back, still in their owl form. Having burned their potions, presumably they were unable to return to their human form. From that point on, they taunted Angel day and night, as he stayed barricaded in his home. Inside, he fashioned makeshift crosses out of every object he could find, lit candles, and performed exorcisms every day. All the while, the villagers shook their heads. They had warned him not to go to Los Voladeros and had watched him return with two old hags that had bewitched him into thinking they were beautiful women. Aragón doesn't say what happened to poor Angel, and thus ended the tale with him trapped in his home, the owls always outside, always hooting until they drove him mad. If there ever truly was a real village that influenced the folktale of Los Voladeros is unknown, but I did find at least one other mention of it.

In Nasario García's *Tales of Witchcraft and the Supernatural in the Pecos Valley*, he recounted a tale from Pablo Aguilar, who was born in 1913. At one point in his youth, he traveled with his mother and brother on horseback from Villanueva to La Pintada, another village fifty some miles away to the south. Because of the long distance, they had gotten up very early in the morning to hit the trail. In particular, there was a steep slope they had to climb on their way there along the Villanueva trail. Apparently, Los Voladeros was located somewhere in that vicinity. In Aguilar's own words, "When we got to the foot of the trail, Mom looked on up ahead, up towards a place called Los Voladeros. Way up at the peak of the tallest of Los Voladeros, there was this little old lady like so [hunched up], at about five, six o'clock in the morning."[24]

Becoming frightened at the sight of what was surely a witch near the main witch village itself, Aguilar's mother urged her children to hurry up the hill and not look at the old woman. Aguilar noted that the horse he was riding was usually notoriously slow and stubborn when it came to climbing steep trails, but not that day. That day the horse made great haste, and the trio made it La Pintada in record time, arriving there by two in the afternoon. When Aguilar's mother told her father of the incident upon arriving there, he told her that it was indeed a witch they saw.

Even if there's not much to the particular story, it does seem to indicate that there was a belief in a village of witches called Los Voladeros. However, there seems to be a discrepancy in the location between Aragón's tale and Aguilar's. As such, Los Voladeros was probably just a mythical village that could hypothetically be located anywhere in the mountains of New Mexico. As for Aguilar's story, though you can call him superstitious if you want, you have to admit, why would such an old woman be hanging out alone on a high mountain peak so early in the morning? Perhaps she was there to await the dawn and watch the sunrise. Or, maybe she was a witch.

THE VILLAGE IDIOT AND THE WITCHES' SABBAT

Charles Lummis collected one of the best witch sabbat stories in 1880. It concerned Patapalo, the village idiot of San Mateo, who had a witch friend, Jose, invite him to a sabbat where he would be granted intelligence. Being a simpleton, Patapalo agreed. Jose told him, "Come with me tonight and I will make you the wisest man in the world, so that you can play any music, speak any language, and even know what happens a hundred miles away." Telling this story to Lummis firsthand, Patapalo related,

Penitente cross near San Mateo, New Mexico, circa 1898. (George Wharton James)

That night about eight o'clock Jose came for me, and we started walking across the plain. After a half hour we found ten thousand mesquite bushes and on each one hung a rosary. I was often there before but never saw a single mesquite. I said, 'What is this thing?' but Jose replied, 'Keep your tongue to your teeth and come on.' At that moment we came to a great door with an iron lock, and a voice from within called, 'Who's there?' Jose said, 'We are two. One is ignorant.' Then the door opened, and we went into a room, so large I could not see the end of it. There was a bright light and I saw hundreds of people, the men on one side and the women on the other. Many of them I knew from Socorro and other places. In the middle were dozens of musicians with all classes of instruments and when they played very fine music, the men and women danced together.

Such fine dancers I have never seen. Then a very large goat came in and spoke to all, and everybody had to kiss him. And when the goat had gone there was a snake—of larger body than mine—that came in upright. And it moved to every man and wound itself around him and put its tongue in his mouth, and the same to every woman. And when he did so, they talked words that I could not understand. But when he came to me and put his face before mine, my heart left me, and I

183

cried, 'Jesus, Mary, Joseph, save me!' And at that instant I was standing alone in the plain. The snake, Jose, and the people were gone, and there remained only a strong smell of sulphur. I walked home a long way very much alarmed.

Next day I saw Jose and he said, 'Fool! The snake was ready to give you the tongue of wisdom, but you called the holy name and ruined all.' He wanted me to go again, but I was afraid and never did."[25]

Regardless of whether this tale was simply a pastiche created by Patapalo or a real event, it has many of the hallmarks of similar folktales the world over. Journeying to a strange place that would appear to be within another realm is common to fairy encounters of Ireland and even modern alien abduction claims of the modern era. Some researchers call this fairy realm Magonia, others Etheria, and it would seem that Patapalo entered such a realm. The idea of the gigantic snake also tied into distinct New Mexico Native American beliefs connected to Montezuma and his sacred serpent. Some of the pueblo peoples believed that Montezuma appeared to them in the guise of a giant rattlesnake that would offer its tongue for a kiss. If the person the snake appeared to kissed their tongue, it would grant them wisdom, as was the case of Patapalo, who rejected the kiss and performed a quick exorcism of sorts.

A similar snake tale was told to authors Sherry Hansen-Steiger and Brad Steiger, which they published in their book *Montezuma's Serpent and Other Supernatural Tales of the Southwest*. A man identified as Reuben Montoya related that back in 1940 he lived in a New Mexico village with "much talk of witches and devils."[26] He and his grandfather were walking through an arroyo at night when a gigantic rattlesnake materialized in front of them. Like the one from Patapalo's folktale, it was as tall as a man when it reared up and as big around as a large man's thy. It came before Reuben and touched him with his tongue. Though young Reuben was unaware, the serpent was offering its tongue for him to kiss. Eventually the snake disappeared in a puff of smoke, with a smell of "spent shotgun shells" and Reuben's grandfather began to weep. He told the boy that he had rejected an offer of wisdom and power from the serpent of Montezuma. The angry grandfather slapped his grandson and he ran home in tears. The following was presented to Steiger not as a folktale but, like Patapalo's story, as a firsthand experience of the witness.

SAMUEL B. AXTELL
AND THE WITCH TRIAL

Governor Axtell c.1876.

This story, "Whipped for Witchcraft," appeared in the *Santa Fe Daily New Mexican* on October 2, 1882. Notably, it featured the former New Mexico Governor, Samuel B. Axtel, who infamously oversaw the state during the Lincoln County War of 1878, leading to him being replaced by Lew Wallace. Though disgraced when he was removed from his position as governor, in 1882, Axtell was serving as Chief Justice of the Territory.

Persons just returned from Tierra Amarilla, where the Rio Arriba county court was in session last week, advise of a trial before Chief Justice Axtell, which recalls the dark deeds of centuries ago, when torture and even the stake were resorted to as persuasives in cases where confessions were wanted, renunciations of faith were desired, or withheld information was sought to be exhorted. This modern barbarity occurred in Tierra Amarilla in the year of our Lord, 1882. The offender is Felipe Madrid, and his victim was a woman with whom years ago he was intimate. Felipe had broken off relations with his sometime associate, and after years of promiscuous distribution of attention to other females was seized by a loathsome disease. After months of suffering he conceived that he had been bewitched by the woman alluded to, and whose name the writer could not learn. He was encouraged in this by Cipriano Medino, and other associates, and finally determined to free himself of the spell by adopting the only course known to the believers in witchcraft, which course is to make the offending witch cure the patient, and if she refuses, to whip her to death.

Accordingly he sent three men from Tierra Amarilla to Abiquiú with instructions to bring the woman to his house. They obeyed, and when they had brought her to him Madrid tied her up by the hands in his house, and told her if she did not cure him he would whip her to death. She protested her innocence and declared her inability to effect the cure,

185

whereupon Madrid whipped her with a "black snake" until she was very nearly dead. She at last promised to cure him, being willing to promise anything in order to be released.

Madrid let her down intending to renew the whipping if she failed to make her promise good. The woman, to gain time, called for ointments and medicines and finally succeeded in escaping from the house, whence she made her way back to Abiquiú. The matter was brought to the attention of the grand jury and an indictment for assault and battery was the result. The case being tried the prisoner was fined $150 and costs, that being the extent of the law in the case, as the prisoner was in a state of health which would not admit of his being imprisoned.

THE THREE WITCHES OF SAN RAFAEL

"I had the probably unprecedented privilege, a short time ago, of photographing three live witches as they stood in the door of their little adobe house. Antonia Morales and Placida Morales, sisters, and Villa, the daughter of Placida, and not more than seventeen years old."—Charles Lummis, A New Mexico David.[27]

During his travels, Charles Lummis once famously made a photograph of three witches in the village of San Rafael. Of the women, Lummis said, "The town is much in awe of these three lone women. No one dares to refuse when they ask for food or other favors. They will do almost anything rather than incur the displeasure of the brujas, as the witches are called."[28]

186

The witches comprised of Antonia Morales, the eldest, Plácida Morales, and Villa Morales, who was Plácida's 17-year-old daughter. In the photo, Antonia can be identified by the shawl along her shoulders and the ax she carries in her gnarled hands (just out of frame). She is notably not looking at the camera. Plácida, too, has a shawl drawn over her head, which obscures her face, which is looking down at the ground. And then there is Villa, who stared challengingly into the lens. Jack Kutz warned in *Mysteries and Miracles of New Mexico* that "one should not look too long into those haunting eyes"[29] as they once turned a man into a woman. Kutz was also astute enough to point out that Villa's shawl was unique among the three and seemed to be designed with curious symbols.

As to the story of one of the witches turning a man into a woman, Lummis related in *A New Mexico David* that "Any one can tell you direful tales of what befell those who were rash enough to offend them." Lummis went on to tell the tale of Francisco Ansures, "a good-looking young Mexican, whose adobe house is one of the six that constitute the little village of Cerros Cuates…"

As Ansures told Lummis, he "had the misfortune four years ago to offend one of the witches." Lummis said that Ansures was unaware of what he did to draw the ire and wrath of the witches, but knew he had become bewitched when he drank a cup of coffee from one of them.

Lummis related:

> In a few minutes thereafter he was horrified to see that his hair had grown two feet in length, and that his rough overalls had turned to petticoats. Still worse, when he cried out in dismay, his pleasant tenor voice had become a squeaky treble.
>
> In a word, he had been turned into a woman — at least, that is what he says, and what his industrious little wife maintains to this day. They declare that he remained a woman for several months, and recovered his proper sex only by paying a male witch who lived in the Cañon de Juan Tafoya to turn him back again.[30]

DOLORES LA PENCA

In the last house outside of Santa Fe on the road to Agua Fría lived the witch Dolores La Penca. Her last name implied that she was "a stray," or a baby that had been either abandoned by the mother or orphaned with no close relatives to look after her. The girl's foster mother considered Dolores to be quite odd from a young age. Initially, Dolores may have been thought of as more of a curandera who lived on her own in a secluded home. She was known to spend much time in the wild, out collecting various herbs. However, many were afraid to take her herb concoctions for fear that they would be bewitched. Perhaps it was the strange items she kept hanging on the wall of her home, which included the hooves and horns of livestock in addition to many bags of dried herbs and leaves.

Carlota Quintana told folklorist Ruth Laughlin Barker her own tale of Dolores La Penca related to her by her grandmother.[31] "The day before I was to be married, forty-eight years ago, [Dolores] came to bring me a gift," Carlota said, quoting her grandmother. The gift was a perfumed soap Dolores had made. The girl's mother told her not to use it, but it smelled so wonderful that she couldn't resist, and she washed her hair with it that evening.

The next day, the girl's face, arms, and hands had broken out into a horrible red rash. Naturally, it was assumed that the jealous Dolores had bewitched her on the eve of her marriage. Salvation came via her brother, Jesus, and her cousin, Antonio, who were in Silver City with a surveying party. Though she was disappointed they were not home for her wedding, it would turn out to be a blessing in disguise. One night—the very night her wedding was to take place as it turned out—they were sitting around their campfire when Antonio mentioned to Jesus it was a shame they would miss the wedding. Upon mention of his cousin, an owl began to hoot. Immediately, Antonio surmised that the owl must be Dolores la Penca. "She is looking for news to take to Santa Fe," he told Jesus.

Antonio then took out a bullet and etched a cross on it before loading it into his rifle. Carefully taking aim, he shot the owl through the eye, killing it. As he examined the body, he took note of the fact that the left wing was raised and almost torn from the body, while the left foot was doubled up under the torso as well.

"You mark this, Jesus," Antonio said to his cousin. "You can write; so you write what has happened to the owl. We will see when we get back to Santa Fe."

A week later, the duo arrived in Santa Fe to find the bride to be healthy and happy, cured of her affliction when Dolores had died mysteriously. A sheepherder had come to bring her rare herbs from the mountains to trade, as was the common custom with Dolores. The sheepherder found her dead on the floor, in the same position as the owl shot by Antonio. Her eye was shot out, her left arm was raised above her body, and her left foot was doubled up to her chest.

THREE GRAINS OF CORN

"Three Grains of Corn," one of the other stories related by Ruth Laughlin Barker in *Tone the Bell Easy*, told the rare tale of a girl born a witch. Typically, women become witches rather than being born that way (one of the rare exceptions being the Tlahuelpuchi of Mexico). The tale centered around Paulita Barelas, whose siblings claimed that she could make them do things against their will. Paulita's favorite sibling was her brother Jose, and she was jealous of any girl who won his affections. Eventually, Jose became engaged to Maria Baca, who Paulita poisoned with three kernels of popped-corn. When his bride-to-be became ill, Jose took to beating his sister until she cured her. Paulita did so by boiling water over the fire and then stirring a fine powder of an unknown substance into it. After Maria drank it, she vomited three mice from her mouth, and she was cured.

THE TAOS WITCHES

Photo by Donna Blake Birchell.

Similar to an old grave in Las Cruces, said to be the burial spot of an unnamed bruja, is the tale of the three witches of Taos.[32] The alleged witches are interred in three unmarked plots within the Kit Carson Cemetery, near the wrought iron gate at the entrance to Dragoon Lane. Oddly, the unnamed witches are sealed into their graves via blocks of asphalt and concrete. Some view this as either a literal or symbolic sealing-off of the witches from the physical realm. Whether it be their bodies or their spirits, there seems to be a fear of the witches escaping. The jagged tombstones record no names or information of any kind since area lore says that the three witches were so terrible that they either dared not record their names or wished to erase their memory forever. The jagged markers would appear to be fragments of exploded rock. While the assumption was that the tombstones had always been this way, others say that they exploded after the women were buried. One piece of lore alleges that the supernatural vapors of hell itself made the tombstones explode, while the more practical minded think a vandal did it with explosives.

What these women did is recorded in no folktales, so the number of their victims or how they bewitched them is unknown. Considering the cemetery was founded in 1847, that would presumably mean that the witches perished at some point after that date. The only official information on the graves merely lists them as "Three Taos Women" in registers, and that's it.

WITCHCRAFT IN PUERTO DE LUNA

Puerto de Luna (which can be translated as "gateway to the moon") got its name from conquistador Francisco Vázquez de Coronado—or at least that's the story according to legend. Rather than Coronado naming the area while gazing at the rising moon, author Daniel B. Flores says in his book *Puerto de Luna* that the name more likely came from the Luna family that settled the area and that "Puerto" in this case was referring to "mountain pass" as opposed to "door" or "gateway." Whatever the case, it's a beautiful name and the village was formally settled in the early 1860s, about 35 miles north of Fort Sumner. Like that village, it too is greatly associated with Billy the Kid due to the fact that he ate his last Christmas dinner there in 1880 after being captured by Pat Garrett.

Like most Spanish villages in New Mexico, it was also rife with tales of witches and hauntings at one time. Below will be reprinted two of the more popular Puerto de Luna tales of the supernatural.

From an 1888 edition of the *Journal of American Folklore* came the following supernatural tale, which involved a well-known New Mexico citizen, Lorenzo Labadie:

Lorenzo Labadie, a man of prominence in New Mexico, once unknowingly hired a witch as nurse for his baby. He lived in Las Vegas. Some months afterward there was a ball at Puerta de Luna, a couple of hundred miles south, and friends of the family were astonished to see the baby and the nurse there. "Where is Señor Labadie and his family?" they asked. The nurse replied that they were at a house a few miles distant, but too tired to come to the ball. The friends went there the next day and found the Labadies had not been there. Suspecting the nurse to be a witch, they wrote to Don Lorenzo, who only knew that the nurse and his baby were in his house when he went to bed, and there also when he woke up. It being plain, therefore, to the most casual observer, that the woman was a witch, he promptly discharged her.

A few years later, another strange story about Puerto de Luna was printed in the *Sioux Valley News* of Correctionville, Iowa, on April 28, 1892:

HAD THE EVIL EYE
A Strange Story from Puerto de Luna of a Terrible Babe.
Las Vegas, N.M., April 26—A strange story comes from Puerto de Luna, on the Rio Pecos, near Fort Sumner. Two weeks ago the wife of Miguel Terraza became the mother of a girl baby, which had but one eye, located in the center of the forehead. Shortly after the birth of the infant, its mother expired suddenly. Two days later Donna Inez, the baby's nurse, was taken with spasms and died after an illness of an hour. The father and the baby's brother, a boy six years old, were soon afterwards taken with spasms. They are still alive, and hopes are entertained of their recovery. The physician attending them says they all have the symptoms of poisoning. Upon the death of Donna Inez a young woman named Mariana Castono was employed as a nurse to the babe. When the father and brother became ill she fled from the house and declared to her relatives and friends that the babe's single eye was an "evil eye," and that no one could long remain in the babe's presence without becoming dangerously sick. The little one expired from neglect, no one having attended to its wants since the departure of Marianna Castono.

Was this a bizarre made-up tale, as newspapermen were wont to do during the Golden Age of Journalism? Or was a one-eyed baby really born in Puerto de Luna? Only the old-timers would have known for sure.

BURNING THE WITCH'S HEART

Nambé Pueblo.

In December of 1883, about thirty years after the famous witch executions of the 1850s, Adolph Bandelier visited Nambé, where the population had dwindled significantly, many say due to superstition. Bandelier recollected that

> I asked positively about the matter of Nambé and was told that they were in the habit, until 15 years ago, of killing their most intelligent people under the pretext of witchcraft, and that this has greatly contributed toward depopulating the pueblo. Not longer than one year ago, a woman at Nambé was beaten to death by order of the authorities for having been the concubine of a married man. About witchcraft they know of the custom of pricking images, but have no knowledge of that of infanticides.[33]

It's unknown exactly when this story took place, but it was recounted to a historian sometime in the first quarter of the 20th century by an old woman in Nambé, who told of yet another witch hunt. According to the old woman, Nambé was in the midst of a pandemic wherein the little children of the village would come down with a bad cough and eventually die. The village elders met in a kiva to discuss the matter, and one of the poisoning witches brought them food. But, the elders were wise to witches. They each "spit their medicine" at the old woman's food after she left, and it began to bubble. The men determined the meat she had tried to serve them had come from a dead child. The elders had found their witch, or one of them at least.

The witch soon learned that she had been found out and told her sisters about it. The witch sisters, along with a male witch from Tesuque Pueblo, went to work making voodoo dolls of the elders, stuffing their stomachs with chili seeds, rags, and dirt to induce the coughing sickness in them. Notably, the dolls had two faces. One face was to make the coughing sickness, and the other was to kill them. A wise chief observed the witches sneaking about in the forms of cats and dogs, following their tracks to a deep arroyo. Peering down at the witches' gathering, he could see they had resumed human form and were laughing as they stuffed the dolls. Nearby was a simmering cauldron in which the chief presumed to be the flesh of dead children exhumed from the graveyard.

The chief took no action that night, being outnumbered. The next night, he sent several men to arrest the three women and the male witch. In a deserted rectory, now void of its priest, the four witches were bound with rawhide ropes. An old woman began pleading to be able to see her daughter among the witches. When this was refused, she asked that she be given a rosary belonging to her. Suspicious, the chief cracked open the rosary and found between the beads a small bag of seeds of corn and wheat. Also, there was a small stone which represented the witch's heart. The chief threw the cursed items into the fire, and when consumed, the old woman dropped dead. The village officers set about torturing the witches until they vowed to bring no more sickness upon them. The torture was so severe that the male witch died. As for the women, the village elders removed from them more strange bags containing their stone hearts. They burned these bags, and upon doing so, the witches expired.

Were-Witch of Watrous

For a few nights once per month, the denizens of Watrous were terrorized by a black dog. It would slink into town on dark, moonless evenings. There it would target and kill dogs belonging to locals.

After a few nights of terror, it would disappear and not resurface until the following month. Eventually, the townspeople set out to capture the sinister animal. The next time that the moon entered its darker cycle, the townsfolk hid in the shadows to wait for the dog.

Just as they hoped, it sauntered back into town. They sprang on it and beat it with ax handles and chunks of firewood. The dog wasn't killed and ran off into the wild. The next morning, it was business as usual in the village except for one thing: an old woman that lived on the edge of town had yet to be seen. Concerned for their elderly neighbor, several people went to check on her. Inside her home, they found her bruised and beaten nearly beyond recognition.

THE WITCHES OF SAN MATEO

Unlike Spanish villages that had only one witch to contend with, San Mateo reportedly had a whole coven. And the tricks they pulled were the stuff of legend. One witch there, Marcelena, even turned a man to a woman like the witches of San Rafael. (In fact, the two tales are suspiciously similar.) The tale was told firsthand to Charles Lummis and recorded in *A New Mexico David*:

> A witch named Marcelina — a poor, withered little woman about fifty years old — was stoned to death in San Mateo, thirty miles north of San Rafael, in 1887, because she had "turned Don José Patricio Mariño into a woman, and made Señor Montaño very lame."[34]

Montaño is still lame; but not nearly so much so as before he helped to kill poor old Marcelina. That pious act not only relieved his feelings, but soothed his distorted muscles also. Mariño is again a man — and one of very good standing in San Mateo — having hired another witch to re-transform him into a man's shape. [35]

Don Mariño's brother, Nicolas (aka 'Coulas), also encountered a witch once while in an arroyo that ran through the borders of San Mateo. One day while riding through the arroyo, he spied a ball of fire floating through the air. [36] Perhaps not being named Juan and thus unable to draw the magic circle in the dirt, he pursued the ball of fire on horseback. Lummis related,

'Coulas, as he is familiarly called, is a brave man; and though he knew this must be a witch, he started in pursuit. Just as he reached it, the ball of fire turned into a big rat, which ran off through the grass. When he caught up with the rat, it changed to a huge dog, which growled savagely, sprang clear over his head, and disappeared among the willows. [37]

Even though the witch Marcelina had been killed, she had a daughter, Salia, who continued to plague the village, specifically in bewitching a girl named Maria Acacia. The girl's mother, Juana Garcia, went out to collect some healing herbs on the night that Maria suddenly became ill. As she did, she spied an unfamiliar animal hanging around—and as every good New Mexican knew back then, any unfamiliar animal scrounging around at night could be a witch. And, being named Juana, Maria's mother had the witch-catching power of a Juan. Juana snatched up the animal, which immediately transformed into human form, revealing the witch, Salia.

"Cure my daughter," Juana ordered, "or I will have you killed!"

Salia obliged, claiming she would undo the bewitchment, and Juana let her go. However, when morning came, Maria was still ill. Juana marched to Salia's house and yelled, "Why didn't you cure my daughter, like you promised?"

"I don't believe she is still sick," Salia answered indignantly. "I'll go and see."

Swiftly, Salia marched to the house, beating even Juana there. By the time Juana arrived back home, Salia was gone and Maria was up making tortillas as though she had never been ill at all.

"What did she do to you?" Juana asked.

"She just took some ashes from the fireplace, and rubbed them on my arms, and I was well," Maria said.

Group of Penitente in New Mexico by Charles Lummis.

A member of the Penitente brotherhood, Juan Baca, and his wife also had an incident with Salia around this time. When Baca's wife refused a cup of coffee to Salia, the next day a sore formed on Señora Baca's nose and out of it would drop small white pebbles. Señor Baca knew she had been bewitched and angrily confronted Salia.

"Look, you have bewitched my wife. If you don't cure her at once, I will hang you," Juan told her, and out of fear, Salia agreed to cure Señora Baca. As with the previous tale of Maria and Salia, the latter made no effort to cure the former, for when Juan returned home, his wife had gotten even worse. Juan grabbed his trusty lasso and headed for Salia's house.

"I have come to hang you," he said angrily.

"No, don't! I'll come right over!" cried a frightened Salia.

She went home with Juan and he watched as she administered a foreign black powder to Señora Baca's nose. Almost instantly a four-inch sinew came from the sore and the wound was gone.

EYE-COVERED AND THE BONE ARROW

One of the more detailed accounts of Apache witchcraft was collected by Morris E. Opler in his book *Apache Odyssey: A Journey Between Two Worlds*, which recounted the life story of a Mescalero Apache he identified only as Chris to keep his identity secret. When exactly this story occurred is unknown, but since one of the star participants died in 1908, it had to have been prior to that. The star participant I referred to was known as "Eye-Covered" due to the fact that he was a medicine man who had lost an eye while trying to cure Chris's 18 or 19-year-old bewitched half-brother.

The medicine man, not yet called Eye-Covered, was fond of the young man and agreed to try and save him even though he suspected that the witchcraft used on him was strong enough to kill him in the process. It was believed the young man was a victim of shooting sorcery. According to Opler's account, the medicine man stated that "the boy was witched and a strong witch weapon was in him, and whoever took it out was going to die afterward."[38]

He elaborated that the youth had been bewitched out of jealousy of his good looks. He also stated that removing the object from the boy would cause him to lose his own eye. Knowing this, he sang four songs, then proceeded to utilize the sucking way cure on the young man's head, and pulled an accursed object from him. "It was a bone, shaped into an arrow, with the arrowhead painted red. The arrow was blue and it had hair wrapped around it," Opler recorded, and also added, "the bone was a human bone and the four strands of hair were human hair."[39]

The three-inch arrow was taken and burned, and in accordance with Apache witch stories, it made a loud pop like a gunshot when it was destroyed. Unfortunately, there was a second object buried somewhere in the boy that could not be removed. Furthermore, it was later learned that the witch who had perpetrated the deed was already dead. According to some witchcraft lore, when this happens, the witch's spell can no longer be reversed. And so, sadly, the young man died, and four days after having removed the bone arrow, the medicine man's eye burst. Henceforth, he was known as Eye-Covered.

TURN OF THE CENTURY ZUNI WITCHCRAFT

In the late 1880s into the early 1890s, charges of witchcraft were rife at Zuni Pueblo. In August of 1889, amidst a terrible drought,

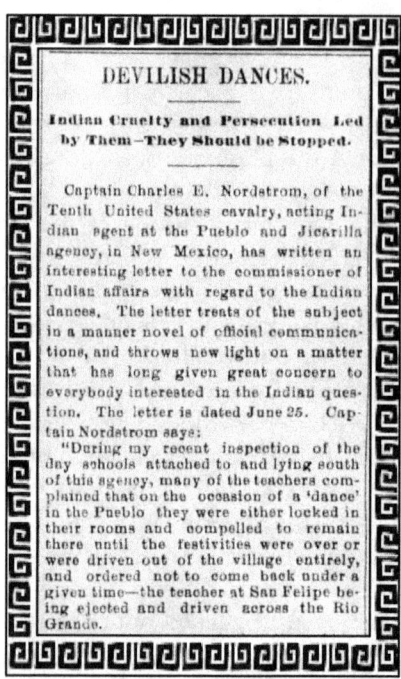

DEVILISH DANCES.

Indian Cruelty and Persecution Led by Them—They Should be Stopped.

Captain Charles E. Nordstrom, of the Tenth United States cavalry, acting Indian agent at the Pueblo and Jicarilla agency, in New Mexico, has written an interesting letter to the commissioner of Indian affairs with regard to the Indian dances. The letter treats of the subject in a manner novel of official communications, and throws new light on a matter that has long given great concern to everybody interested in the Indian question. The letter is dated June 25. Captain Nordstrom says:

"During my recent inspection of the day schools attached to and lying south of this agency, many of the teachers complained that on the occasion of a 'dance' in the Pueblo they were either locked in their rooms and compelled to remain there until the festivities were over or were driven out of the village entirely, and ordered not to come back under a given time—the teacher at San Felipe being ejected and driven across the Rio Grande.

accusations amplified. An old man accused of keeping the rain away was hung up by his wrists with them tied behind his back. The man "confessed," possibly just so that he would be let down, and left the pueblo. But still the drought continued… so, another scapegoat was found. In October the same was done to an old woman who then placed the blame on her 16-year-old nephew. His punishment was even more extreme, possibly because he would not confess. In his case, he was not only hanged by the wrists, but also held underwater and beaten before he finally died. When white settlers observed the boy's dead body hanging by the wrists, they intended to cut the boy down but were stopped from doing so.

An Indian Agent report from 1892 seemed to allude to this event plus other instances of witchcraft, be they real or imagined:

This evil still goes on. The victims are often those who depart from the old pueblo customs and incline to the ways of civilized life. In the estimation of the ruling Zuni, what we call progress is the most criminal of offenses and must be trodden out by the most summary and vindictive tortures. While this report was waiting for the printer, early in December, two Zuni Indians with whom I talked freely last July were seized and subjected to the witch torture methods. They were probably the most progressive of any people in the pueblo. Seized, violently seized, they were strung up by their wrists, beaten with war clubs, and kept hanging all night, all the next day, and until 10 o'clock the second night. They were let down occasionally for a few moments to induce confession but suffered indescribable torture. To end the suffering, they finally confessed that they were witches; and were let off when life was almost gone. Some perish in these tortures. I

198

asked an intelligent gentleman, a resident in this pueblo for twelve years, "How often do these witch cases occur?" He replied:

One nearly every year, either resulting in death or being run off from the pueblo, sometimes followed and killed—some years more than one. Half a dozen Americans have witnessed some cases. No Zuni Indian has been brought to justice and punished for these outrages; but, now three men are arrested for the late offenses and in jail awaiting trial. They are undoubtedly not the guilty parties. The real offenders, men of influence in managing the affairs of the pueblo, turned over to the authorities these three poor men who were unable to help themselves...

Zuni Pueblo c. 1879 (John K. Hillers).

From 1898 to 1899, an epidemic of smallpox was blamed on witchcraft as well. Two young men were blamed for the outbreak and would have been killed if not for the interference of a local schoolteacher. To save them, the teacher called for a detachment of soldiers to come. Though they saved the two boys, a few of the soldiers and their horses later died of poisoning. The year before, in 1897, Captain Charles E. Nordstrom, Indian Agent for the Jicarilla Apache, wrote of Zuni witchcraft goings on in his article "Devilish Dances," which I retrieved from the *Santa Fe Daily New Mexican* of July 26, 1897. Nordstrom heard tales that a Zuni youth who had recently been schooled outside of the village refused to participate in a tribal dance at Zuni when he returned and so was tied to a tree and beaten until he agreed to participate. This story prompted a lengthy discourse on the Zuni from Nordstrom:

> Zuni, it will be recalled, was the scene of the recent hanging of a poor old creature as a witch. While I was there Miss DeSette, the estimable principal of the school, sent for the victim of this revival of the days when our New England forefathers piously devoted their neighbors to the stake, and bared her poor, old arms to my inspection. There was no difficulty in discerning the scars made by the cruel cords, which had cut the flesh through to the bone. This poor old woman is at least 76 or 80 years old... As this lady, her voice trembling with indignant emotion, described the circumstances of this unspeakable horror, my own cheek blushed that 86 years of my life had been spent in the service of a government under which such things could be done.

It was only by the year 1925 that the final witchcraft trial was held in Zuni, though belief in witches still persisted for many years, just sans the beatings and executions.

SKINWALKER SLAIN NEAR CHACO CANYON

As stated earlier, Navajo witchcraft often formed the backbone of the mysteries presented in Tony Hillerman's beloved Joe Leaphorn-Jim Chee novels, such as *Coyote Waits*. Hillerman typically used real New Mexico locales of note, such as Chaco Canyon. Hillerman surely would have been fascinated by this story, as it featured the killing of a Navajo witch at Chaco Canyon. *The Santa Fe Daily New Mexican* of May 23, 1895, reported:

A few days ago a foul murder was committed among the Navajos at or near the Hendricks' cow camp on the Chaco. An old Navajo man was accused of being a witch, as it is alleged by the Indians that he made their children sick every time he came around. When finally they captured him, one buck held him while the squaws stoned him to death. The old Navajo's sons are on the war path, and trouble is expected among the Indians, as several of them have been trying to borrow guns and ammunition.

Juan Chavez and Chata

Another of New Mexico's renowned witch wranglers was Juan Chavez, albeit a more sympathetic one. Chavez lived in Tome and one story of his witch-thwarting prowess is said to have occurred in 1897. Chaves was riding his horse from Tome to Casa, Colorado, to pick up a milk cow a friend was giving to him. As he rode along, he spied a ball of fire leaping across the countryside. Knowing it must be a witch, he dismounted his horse, picked up a stick, and drew a circle in the earth. As was customary, the ball of light bounded into the circle and disappeared, thus trapping the witch for the night. Juan rode on to his friend's home, stayed the night, and then returned the next morning with his milk cow. There he found a friendly local woman, Chata, who had the reputation of being a witch. Rather than mocking her or threatening to kill her, he indulged her in pleasant conversation and a slight bit of teasing before extending his hand and thus releasing her from the circle's grasp. Chata then followed him back to Tome, and that was that.

Los Lunas Were-Witch

Wesley R. Hurt Jr. collected the following tale from a buffalo hunter from Manzano. He told of a poor sheepherder, Manuel Lujan, from a long time ago who worked in the area of present-day

Elephant Butte Dam. One day the man's boss sent Lujan and an unnamed companion to deliver some sheep to Valencia County, north of them and near Los Lunas. The men should have been wary, for that was the land of witches—or so they claimed.

One night, while camped at a river crossing at Valverde, Lujan's companion woke up to a strange noise. He looked through the darkness and spied a small animal gnawing upon a piece of meat left over from their dinner. The man swiftly grabbed his rifle, shot at the small predator, and it fled. The next morning the two men continued their journey north and came across footprints in the wild. This was strange, for no one lived in the area apart from the Navajo, who would have ridden horses across this particular terrain. Thinking that perhaps someone was in need of assistance, they followed the trail of footprints until they led to a pool of blood. Perhaps an Indian massacre had occurred? The footprints continued into the river and to the other side leading to a wooded area. It was decided that the companion would stay with the sheep, and Lujan would cross the river to see who may be in the bosque. Lujan crossed the river and into the trees to find a frail old woman huddled against a tree. Her shoulder was bleeding badly. "Were you attacked by Indians?" Lujan asked.

"No," she replied angrily, "You shot me!"

"I shot you? But I haven't shotten anyone on the whole trip," Lujan rebutted.

"If not you, then it was your companion last night," the old woman answered.

In a moment of horror, Lujan realized that the little woman was a witch who had shapeshifted into a coyote or other predator in the night. Out of fear of bewitchment, Lujan offered to take the woman to Los Lunas to get medical attention, and she agreed. After leaving her in Las Lunas, Lujan hoped never to see her again, and apparently, he didn't, for no sequels exist of Lujan suffering the wrath of a witch.

PÁNFILO AND THE CAT-EYED WITCHES

Once upon a time, according to the witch chapter in *Tone the Bell Easy*, lived a man called Uncle Pánfilo.[40] A lonely widower, the highlight of his week was going to visit two inseparable sisters. One of them he was attracted to and wished he could marry, that being the younger of the two, Pilar. However, he knew if he married Pilar, he would, in essence, also be married to her sister, Fefe, since they were practically joined at the hip. Both were older and beyond their child-bearing years, which was just fine with Pánfilo who was no spring chicken himself. Pilar, it was said, had tea-colored eyes with flecks of green and gold, while Fefe's eyes were the color of coffee. Both had dark circles under their eyes, as though they didn't sleep at night. This, naturally, implied that they must be witches. Despite the whisperings and warnings of his fellow villagers, Pánfilo never feared visiting or playing the gambling game of Canoncito with the two sisters. Though Pánfilo would be content to play the game all night, every evening at dusk, the sisters would bid him farewell as though they had other things to do. Pánfilo would sometimes stare at their abode from a distance, waiting to see where they went, but never did he see them depart their home. If he peered through the windows, the house was dark and lifeless apart from two cats, whose eyes glittered in the darkness and who became agitated if he came too close. Although he knew the sisters didn't leave the previous night, the next day they would gossip about events in the village the night before, events that inexplicably ended up being true. It was as though they had witnessed them firsthand...

Knowing that they must be witches, one night Pánfilo decided to make up an excuse to barge into their home after dark. When he went inside, the home was empty. Not even the cats were there. But, on the hearth of the blazing fireplace, a glitter caught his eye. He approached to see four orbs resting there—no, they were eyes! He recognized them immediately as the eyes of the two sisters. Surely Pánfilo should have known that witches removed their eyes at night and switched them with those of an animal. Rather than leaving them where they sat, he became disturbed and tossed them into the fire. Instead of burning up at once, they floated around and seemed to dance in an effort to escape the flames. Perhaps regretting what he had done, Pánfilo scooped the eyes out of the fire. But it was too late. They were burned and ruined like blackened walnuts. About then, the two cats came running into the room, their sockets devoid of eyes. As the cats mewed and cried, Pánfilo made the sign of the cross and ran away. With much guilt and trepidation, he approached the sisters' home the afternoon of the next day. He boasted and spoke loudly as guilty men do, and was answered by a tired-sounding Pilar, who bid him entry. As he walked inside, the two sisters were not their usual selves and kept their faces turned away from him. When they moved about, it was as though their eyes were no longer accustomed to the daylight. "We are busy, amigo. We cannot play Caiioncito again," Pilar said sadly.

When Pánfilo looked at her, he saw that her usual tea-colored eyes were gone, replaced by those of a cat's. The same was true of Fefe. Then, the two cats crept into the room and began hissing at Pánfilo. They had no eyes at all in their sockets. Knowing what he had done, and that he could no longer be friends with the sisters like in the old days, he left. Nor did he go out after dark again for fear that the witches might seek retribution, and he kept all his doors and windows locked. This, of course, was just a pastiche of similar tales, no doubt, but it is undoubtedly the best example of the tale of witches with cat's eyes.

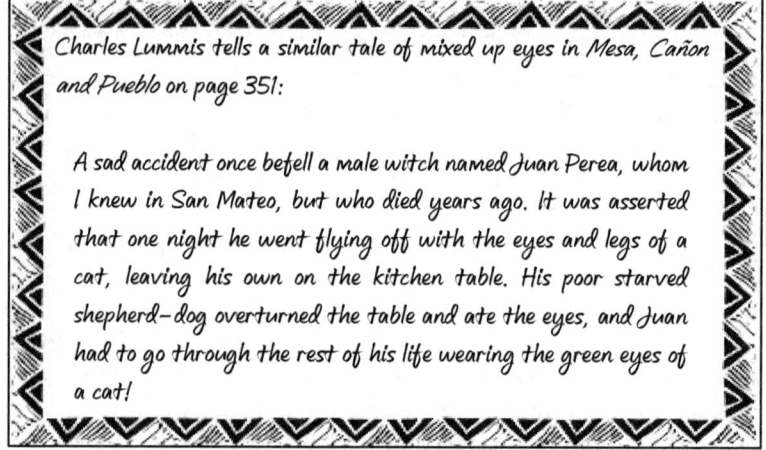

Charles Lummis tells a similar tale of mixed up eyes in Mesa, Cañon and Pueblo on page 351:

A sad accident once befell a male witch named Juan Perea, whom I knew in San Mateo, but who died years ago. It was asserted that one night he went flying off with the eyes and legs of a cat, leaving his own on the kitchen table. His poor starved shepherd-dog overturned the table and ate the eyes, and Juan had to go through the rest of his life wearing the green eyes of a cat!

JUAN CATCHES A WITCH IN THE SANDIAS

In *The Sandia (New Mexico) Story* by F. Stanley, the author wrote that Sandia was "backward in many ways especially witchcraft."[41] Stanley also noted that Sandia, "like Salem, brought its witches to execution. This scare and horror of witches and witchcraft has not been stamped out to this day…" This day, in Stanley's case, meaning the publication of his booklet in 1968. Stanley continued that there had been no-known executions for the last several years, noting, "no known deaths take place mostly in fear of action by government authorities."[42]

This little vignette, set within the village of La Madera in the northern foothills of the Sandia Mountains concerned yet another man named Juan thwarting a witch. The tale was told in the 1930s and presumably took place in the previous century sometime. In the "La Cita de las Brujas" by Rumaldita Gurule, the following was recorded:

When a witch cast an evil spell upon any of us, we set a Juan to catch her. He would go out into the night and watch for her. By and by, he would see the witch because she could never sense the presence of a Juan. When he saw her coming, he jerked off his shirt, turned it wrong side out and flung it in her path. There was no way a witch could see this shirt, and she got tangled in it, sprawled on the ground, and was unable to move. Early in the morning, the townspeople would come and take her to the houses of persons she had hexed. They made her cure them and threatened her with death if she worked her magic again. Then everyone seized switches and lashed the witch out of the village.

THE FLYING GOAT

You've heard of friends loaning each other a car, but what about a flying goat? One story had a man in Colorado pining to return home to Villanueva for a dance. A witch helped him out by having him ride a flying goat there, just so long as he returned it by midnight. The man said the unholy incantation—"Without God and the Virgin Mary"—and took flight to Villanueva, attended the dance, repeated the process and was back to the witch in Colorado by 11:30. Isidora

M. Flores related this story in *Tales of Witchcraft and the Supernatural in the Pecos Valley* on page 45. The same story was repeated in the book by Josephine M. Gallegos, also of Villanueva, so it was apparently a popular tale there.

TESTING A WITCH

"There is another sure way to find out if a person is really a witch, for witches are afraid of the cross."— *Ruth Laughlin Barker,* Tone the Bell Easy[43]

In the same way that *Tone the Bell Easy* presented the quintessential tale of a witch's disembodied eyes being destroyed in the night, "The Way to Find Witches" is also the best rendition of a family inviting a suspected witch into their home to test them. The suspected witch was Doña Refugio, who was coming to the unnamed family's house that afternoon for a visit. "Get me four needles," the father said.

The father made a cross out of the needles and placed them under the *saleas*, a sheep-skinned liner placed under the doorway to block the cold wind leading into the kitchen. After Doña Refugio arrived, the father then placed the other needle-made cross under the saleas she had just entered. Now the front and back doors were essentially boobytrapped.

When the time was right, the father cried out, "Doña Refugio! Doña Refugio! Come quickly. Your house is on fire." This was a lie, though, and simply a ruse to get the witch to try and run outside. According to the story, when she set her foot to the salea to rush outside, she jumped back as though she had been burned. So, she ran to the other door, and the same thing happened. In a frenzy, she ran through the home, peering through the windows, trying to get a glimpse of her home.

"Take that salea away," she cried to the daughter. "It's dirty. I cannot step on it."

To diffuse the situation, the father came to the door and said, "Never mind, Doña Refugio. Your house is all right. I went to see. It was only the smoke in the chimney."

Then, he kicked the salea away as Doña Refugio had requested and pointed out that his wife had lost two needles under the salea. This way, it seemed like an innocent mistake rather than a ruse, and he would thus avoid the witch's wrath for outing her.

Doña Refugio ran away to her home, while the father said to his family, "Ah, ha! Now we know you for the old bruja that you are."

SIERRA COUNTY WITCHCRAFT

Our next tale recounts a rare instance of witchcraft in southwestern New Mexico in Sierra County, of which Truth or Consequences is the county seat. Mrs. Benito A Baca told the tale to a WPA writer in the 1930s in Albuquerque and said it happened to her when she was a child of seven or eight in a little village in Sierra County.

One day while she was playing outside, she stated that she observed four "little balls of fire" roll by on the road in front of the family home. The orbs of light stopped there and the little girl ran inside to get her mother. Together they watched the glowing orbs roll down the road and out of sight. The mother told her daughter that the balls of light were brujas sent by their neighbors to bewitch them. However, the bewitchment didn't occur until a few years later. It was coming up on Easter, and an old woman came up to the house asking to borrow some candles. The mother truthfully told her they had none and needed to go to the store to buy some. The old woman didn't believe her and cursed at her as she departed. The mother went back to sweeping the house. "While she was sweeping one of us children called to her about something and mother turned her head to answer and when she tried to turn her head back, she couldn't do it! Mother began to cry and said that she had been 'witched' and that she would have to go around with a twisted neck for the rest of her life, and all us children began to cry," Mrs. Baca said.[44]

When the father came home and heard what happened, he immediately suspected it must have been the old woman who had cursed at her earlier. He picked up a cactus stick, sometimes used on witches and marched over to her home. Banging loudly on the door, he never received any answer, and so forced his way inside. The family saw no sign of the witch, only a big, black cat resting on her bed. Either out of instinct or anger, the father struck the cat with the cactus needle, and it let out a human scream before it fled. When the family returned home, the mother was well again, and all surmised that the witch had transformed herself into a black cat to hide.

A WITCH'S MAGIC USED AGAINST HER

In the little village of Cieneguilla just a ways south of Santa Fe came a story of a witch's magic being deflected back onto her. A woman named Doña Vicenta Lopez suddenly became sick, and no herb was able to cure her. At first, only a small red spot had appeared on her cheek, and then began to spread until it seemed as if her whole face might rot away. Señor Lopez hitched up his wagon and took his wife to better doctors in nearby Santa Fe. But, like the herbalists of the village, they could do nothing and poor Señora Lopez went home to die.

A few days later, a crippled Indian man mysteriously showed up at the couple's doorstep, asking for lodging. Lopez told the man of their unfortunate circumstances and how there was no room due to their children having come home to bid farewell to their mother. The man offered to try his own methods in curing the woman. "Let me stay three days, for in that time I can heal her," said the mysterious man, who added, "But you must watch the house, patron, for someone will come in these days who has put this sickness upon her."

Three days later, a neighbor woman came to the house, perhaps to pay Señora Lopez one last visit. Strangely, it seemed as though she could not step foot on their property, stopping at the gate and then turning back. Not coincidentally, Señora Lopez began to get better, and the neighbor woman died. The old Indian had known that the witch would come calling and had somehow turned her own spell against her.

THE WITCH NURSE

In 1938, 67-year-old Rumaldita Gurule of Placitas told a story involving her grandmother, Quiteria, back in her days as a midwife. Quiteria was working for a couple named Narciso and Margarita, pregnant and soon to give birth to her fifth child. Before Quiteria, the couple had used the old witch nurse Doña Tomasa. They had called on Quiteria because she was younger and lived nearer, but this had apparently offended Doña Tomasa. Whether Doña Tomasa was causing the difficult pregnancy was unclear, but it was certainly an arduous affair, and Quiteria had done everything she could. Narciso decided to call upon Doña Tomasa and rode to her home in the mountains four miles away. He found her in a state of anger at having been replaced, refusing his request to come and help. "My wife, she will die," Narciso explained, and then threatened, "You will go or I will lasso you and drag you behind my horse to my house!"

At that, Doña Tomasa relented and told him, "You go. I will follow you."

However, when Narciso arrived home, Doña Tomasa was already there. Narciso was not entirely surprised. She was a witch, after all, who was always "suddenly appearing or disappearing."[45] What did surprise him was that she was sitting by the fire, warming her hands and rolling cigarettes as Margarita cried in agony. For hours it seemed, both Quiteria and Narciso begged Doña Tomasa to help. Finally, Doña Tomasa walked over to Margarita and said sternly, "Give me your hand, you coward!"

Margarita did so, and the moment their hands met, it was said that the baby's cry sounded in the room. It was as if it had magically materialized out of the womb. "Doña Tomasa gave them all a look of triumph—Margarita's baby had come as she willed."[46]

POISONING IN SAN CRISTOBAL

San Cristobal, a remote hamlet about four miles from Arroyo Hondo, suffered an epidemic of herbal magic in the form of peyote-laced cigarettes. It was customary in those days for women to share tobacco with one another at dances, and at times, a jealous woman would slip in the loco-berry-laced tobacco. The afflicted woman would be forced to seek the aid of a curandero, in those parts called a medico. At that time, the local curandero was Don Benerito, who profited so much from curing people suffering from this malady, some wondered if he was also providing the problem to get to profit from the solution. (In other words, it was he who was sneaking in the bad tobacco.)

THE BEWITCHED TREASURE

"I've seen lights myself in those homes. Of course when one gets close to them, they go out, but as soon as you walk away, they light up again… People say that there's hidden treasure or something."—Damiano Romero, Brujerías: Stories of Witchcraft and the Supernatural in the American Southwest and Beyond[47]

The following is a rather unique tale connecting bewitchment to lost treasures in New Mexico. Simply titled "Treasure" and compiled by Ramitos Montoya, the relevant bits will be presented below:

Time and time again I have heard stories about hidden treasures in New Mexico. Years ago when New Mexico was still a plain with wild Indians running all over it, there was much gold in this region. The Indians had possession of this

209

gold. Many of them practiced witchcraft; by some magical power they enchanted much of the gold. A treasure that is enchanted is not easy to discover. In fact, many say that only those practicing witchcraft are able to get the treasure.

The following stories were told me by my old uncle.

There was a certain house at Roy, a small village, where many strange things happened. One night while the family enjoyed their supper they heard the galloping of a horse. The sound came nearer and nearer. The head of the house went outside to inform himself about the rider. Instead of seeing anyone he heard only a voice crying for help.

At another time, laughing and loud talking, murmuring, the crying of women, and singing were heard. The people never knew the reason for such strange happenings.

One night, when the family was returning from a baile, they were very much surprised to see a light in the house. As they looked through the windows, they saw a strange sight. In the middle of the room was a table full of lighted candles. As they entered, the table disappeared.

On still another occasion the family was sound asleep. They were abruptly awakened by the clanking of heavy chains. They offered prayers and had the priest bless the house. The house, however, seemed to be bewitched. It is claimed that in this house there was a hidden treasure enchanted by the Indians, and that for this reason strange things happened. The people searched for the enchanted treasure but were never able to find it.[48]

THE LIBERTY WITCH KILLING

The Bell Ranch near Liberty, NM, c. 1914.

You've no doubt heard of the famous Bell Witch of Tennessee, but how about the Witch of the Bell Ranch? The Bell Ranch was overseen by Geroge Ellis from 1946 to 1970. His wife collected local folklore from the Liberty area, one of which was a witch tale from many years previous. F. Stanley wrote about it in *The Liberty (New Mexico) Story*:

> The ranch has its legend and stories. There is the story of the bruja that sheepherders blamed for lack of rain. Her feet were tied together and she was dragged to death. She was buried in an unmarked grave near La Loma. No one mentions whether the rains came after her death. Her body was discovered by a musician from La Cinta who was on his way possibly to Liberty to play for a dance. He was kind enough to give her a decent burial.[49]

THE BLACK MARE

One of the rarer instances of a witch taking the form of a horse can be found in the tale of "The Black Mare" wherein Ute Indians stumbled across a herd of horses that they recognized as belonging to a friend of theirs, Felipe Lucero. There was a beautiful black mare among the herd, though, that they knew didn't belong to Lucero. When they went to collect the mare, it ran way from the herd and into a thicket. In the brush they found Dolores, a "very dark-skinned woman whom all suspected of being a witch." Sweating profusely and out of breath, it was clear that Dolores had just transformed from the black mare into human form. There was talk of killing her, but since she had a large family, the Utes let her go after they threatened her not to take the form of the black mare again. There are several variations of this tale amongst different tribes.

A BEWITCHED WOMAN BECOMES A CURANDERA

Jesusita was a beautiful redhead of French descent who lived in Corrales sometime in the late 19th century. One day a wealthy stockman named Eugenio came along and became so smitten with Jesusita that he left his own wife for her. The only problem was his old wife knew the ways of witchcraft. Years later, when Jesusita was 25 years of age, the ex-wife came for a visit; only Jesusita did not know what the woman looked like, so she could not recognize her. The woman came calling when Jesusita found herself in a state of exhaustion, and so the seemingly friendly woman offered to fix her a cup of coffee. The tired Jesusita gladly accepted the offer from the stranger. However, the woman claimed she suddenly had to leave and left Jesusita alone to drink her coffee. Upon finishing it, Jesusita suddenly went mad, screaming and tearing off her clothes.

The family eventually deduced she had been bewitched by the scornful ex-wife. Eugenio nearly went bankrupt trying to cure his wife's condition, but no one seemed to be able to help. Jesusita's parents eventually took her to a curandero in the Sandia Mountains in the vicinity of what is today Bear Canyon. The secluded spot was said to be the rendezvous of witches in the form of owls, but the old curandero feared them not. Not surprisingly, his name was Juan (remember, Juans had power over witches) and his wife was Josefeta. There the husband and wife team cured many afflicted by witchcraft. The couple placed a *cachana* charm necklace on Jesusita for protection against witches in general, while for Indian witches, they fastened *osha* roots to her body.[50] They also forbade her to speak of her illness for the entire two-month period that she stayed with them. Instead, they told her to proclaim in faith that she was better.

Each day Juan mixed for her the heart of a chili pod with sal de Zuni, burned it, and then distributed the ashes into a glass of water for her to drink for purification purposes. The couple also held a wake over her on Thursdays and Fridays (the latter perhaps not coincidentally being the day of the week that witches were at their most powerful). It was also impressed on Jesusita's mind that on one these days she would be cured.

One Friday, Juan took Jesusita to a secluded pool in the mountains and had her look at her reflection in it. Juan stuck his knife into the waters and told Jesusita that in time she would see a face appear. This face would be of the one who bewitched her, and when she saw it, she would be cleared. Several hours had passed, and Jesusita saw the face of the woman who had given her the coffee that day. Her mind had been restored to her.

Jesusita never sought revenge on Eugenio's bruja of an ex-wife. Instead, when she and Eugenio began a new life in the vicinity of Placitas, Jesusita became a curandera herself out to cure fellow victims of bewitchment.[51] The old FWP document that this story derives from recorded that,

> From Juan and Josefeta she learned much of curealls, where to obtain them, and how to use them. But her yerbas and other cures were second to her faith in God and in her own mind. Many were the healings she made with a cup of cold, clear water, which she gave them to drink with the words, "*En*

el nombre de Dios te voy a curar." (In the name of God I shall cure you). But never did a patient know that the cup contained no yerba.[52]

THE WITCH QUEEN OF ARROYO HONDO

One of the more detailed FWP accounts of brujería is that of "The Witch of Arroyo Hondo," which started by stating, "Even at the beginning of the 20th century superstition was rampant among the inhabitants of the smaller New Mexican villages."

The document chronicled the decade of the 1890s, with accounts of a ball of light seen flying out of the chimney of Toña Trujillo in Arroyo Hondo in between Taos and Red River. Many nights at midnight, observers claimed to see the ball of fire fly from her chimney, presumably on its way to a witch gathering somewhere in the mountains. Formerly known as Tia Toña, she was about sixty years of age, and quite lively despite her frail, aged appearance. She had "matty disheveled hair" and "small, wasp-like eyes half-hidden by her abnormally wrinkled face and a complexion that indicated a scanty acquaintance with soap and water," the document said.[53] Though her appearance was witchy, she was said to be very welcoming. But that didn't stop children and the more superstitious-minded from being afraid of her. And, one couldn't discount the mysterious balls of flame coming to and from her home.

These flights of fancy were said to occur at midnight once a month, and the ball would always be seen flying in an easterly direction. Curious onlookers would peek through the windows and find Toña to be gone. "Many a time, in conversation at home she would allude to some happening that conveyed the idea that she did attend meetings of witches," the document reported.[54] And indeed, Toña did have many houseguests in the form of gamblers who used her home as their nightly rendezvous. Her home was conveniently located at the end of a long row of houses on a wide stretch of road within the village in the upper valley. In Toña's home would be played games of monte and poker late into the night hours. As far as witches went, Toña was quite popular. If you'll recall, most of the more superstitious folk wouldn't dare eat a dish prepared by a witch, but that's just how Toña made her living: cooking for the gamblers. One even affectionately, if not somewhat disrespectfully, referred to her as his *vieja*, or "old woman." A great time was had at her home by all, without a hint of supernatural evil.

However, Toña wasn't the only bruja in town. There was also a brujo by the name of Pedro Barela. People whispered that when "he stripped for the purpose of bathing or to change his under garments, that a flame could be distinctly seen inside of his chest." It was also said that "on some dark nights the glow would penetrate through his clothing like a visible aura."[55]

One night in November of 1895, Barela got into an altercation with Marcos Valdez, the one who lovingly called Toña "mi vieja." Barela had several altercations with Valdez in the past, but this one was apparently the last straw as he cried out, "You fleeced me this time, but I will fleece you later when you least expect it."

A few nights later, at about midnight, Valdez was leaving one of the usual gatherings at Toña's place. Riding his horse on a lonely stretch of road, it suddenly became spooked. In the distance, Valdez spied a long ghostly white veil snaking its way through the air close to the ground. "It approached him—passing under his horse, swishing about its legs in rapid motion, then rising in front and continuing its motion in the shape of a vertical elongated figure eight. Swish! Swish!"[56]

The ghostly veil made a show of itself in front of the horse and its rider taking on various shapes until it finally snaked up Valdez's body and tightened about his neck. Valdez flung off the ghostly veil easily and began to tear it to pieces. However, the pieces drifted in the air and reformed themselves into their original shape. The veil flew up the road towards the village with Valdez in hot pursuit. He reached town just in time to see it disappear at the door of Pedro Barela, the brujo who had threatened him.

As Valdez trepidly approached the house, he spied through the window what he at first took to be a flickering candle being carried about the room. Peering closer through the window, he saw what he had thought was a long white veil, but in reality was "the white fleece of a sheep, twisted and disheveled upon the covers of a bed, a strange, flickering radiance emanating from it that illuminated the whole room."[57] Valdez watched as it slowly assumed a human form and transformed back into Pedro Barela. Astounded at what he had seen, Valdez returned home to ponder the night's events.

Though Valdez had never been a believer in the supernatural, he was now. Wanting to learn more about witches so that he could get back at Barela, he decided to spy on his friend Toña's house on one of the nights she didn't allow visitors. Along with Valdez was a younger companion three or four years his junior, Erineo Martinez.

The duo found a vantage point on the Cuchilla, a ridge overlooking the Hondo River.

Bar at Arroyo Hondo, c. December 1941, by Irving Rusinow. Perhaps a few witch tales of the old days were told in this bar, and possibly a few current ones, too.

"At about the hour of midnight they saw the mysterious ball of fire arise from the chimney of Tia Toña's house," the FWP report stated. "Higher and higher, it arose, and increased momentum as it floated eastward, passing high over the heads of the two observers who immediately followed it at breakneck speed on their horses over the road along the edge of the hill."[58]

The two witch-hunters followed the ball to the nearby village of Valdez, which the FWP report identified as the "Witch Town." The men watched with great awe and wonder as the ball of light circled the town multiple times, as if to signal something. They watched in further amazement as a "multitude of balls of fire arose from the houses of the village" to join Tia Toña in the air—no wonder they called it the Witch Town! The flock of brujas and brujos headed north for *Canada Escondida* (Hidden Canyon) at the foot of the mountains about one half-mile away. The two men swiftly followed the procession, and what they witnessed in the canyon is better left un-paraphrased:

There a strange celebration was in progress. From a vantage point the two observers could see a merry dancing party in an open space in the canyon. The fantastic figures of the dancers, were gayly dressed, strangely semi-transparent and the group illuminated by a diffused, light from some unseen source. Not a sound or a noise of any sort could be heard, but the varying expressions on the dancers faces and their rhythmic movements of body clearly indicated that jollity, laughter and music was the order. Opposite the dancers, on what appeared to be a throne, sat Tia Toña, as queen and master of ceremonies. But not as the old disheveled hag usually seen at the gambling joint, for now she was a woman of refined appearance, attired in elegant, flowing gown and sparkling jewels.

The village of Valdez, from which the two men watched the witch balls rise and take flight. The photo was taken in 1941 by Irving Rusinow.

Marcos Valdez and Erineo Martinez watched the witches' celebration in bizarre fascination 'til the dawn, when the revelers faded away with each increasing ray of sunlight until nothing remained. "Por Dios! Mi Vieja," Valdez exclaimed. "I do believe in witches now." Valdez and his companion rode away, now apparently too afraid to exact any revenge on old Pedro Barela. If Valdez ever returned to see his "old woman" is unknown as the story ends at this point. And who told it according to the FWP report? None other than Marcos Valdez himself.

LA CINTA WITCH KILLING

A rarely discussed killing of an alleged witch was reported in newspapers across the country in the year 1897. This particular account was retrieved from the *Meeker Herald* of July 17, 1897. In the little village of La Cinta, not too far from Las Vegas, lived a young man 22 years of age named Teodoe Tafoya whose younger sister was suffering a mysterious illness. As was often the case back then, their mother believed the sickness was inflicted by a witch, who she suspected of being 80-year-old Teodore Salas. Mrs. Tafoya instructed her son and a friend, 18-year-old Antonio Lucero, to go after the old woman. The young men tracked her on horseback to a spot about three miles outside of San Lorenzo. There they intimidated her to get on Lucero's horse with him, the intent being to take the suspected witch back to La Cinta and make her cure the ill girl. Something must have transpired between the trio because, for no reason listed in the article, Tafoya suddenly became violent with the woman.

The paper reported, "After going a short distance Tafoya pulled his pistol and killed the old woman's dog, remarking that he had gotten rid of one 'bruha.'" (This was done, of course, due to the belief that witches could shapeshift, and the men thought the dog was simply a transformed witch.) The article continued that Tafoya lassoed the old woman and yanked her from her horse. "He then instructed Lucero to attach his lasso to her feet and the two, starting their horses on the run, dragged the woman to death, not a vestige of clothing being found on the body when discovered. The murderers disappeared."

When the police came calling at the residence of Tafoya's mother, she told the officers matter-of-factly that she had told her son to kill the woman because she was a witch. She was then arrested, and that's where the paper trail ends on this particular story.

THE WITCHES AND THE FLYING PUMPKIN

The efforts of the Federal Writer's Project unearthed a dearth of witch stories in the 1930s, among them this one from the Peñasco region in Taos County. In 1937, Emilia Pacheco told Manuel Berg about a childhood reminiscence from her school days in Peñasco. One of her school friends, Vicenta Chacon, told Emilia that her grandmother, Luz Chacon, was a bruja. One afternoon in her home, she had been hosting a bruja's gathering. "Each of the brujas came to this meeting with a black cat and a pumpkin," Vicenta said.[59] Vicenta's grandmother put her to bed, but naturally Vicenta couldn't resist peeking from under the covers to spy on the witches. At first it was no different from any other gathering, with the women eating fine food and singing songs. But, as the hour grew late, still singing, each of the brujas plucked out their eyeballs. They then picked up their black cats, plucked out their eyes in turn, and swapped them. (This, of course, was a common belief by now that witches took the eyes of cats—presumably so they could see in the dark—for their nightly prowls.)

Peñasco Ranger Station Group, c. 1932 by W. G. Koogler.

Next, the witches gathered their pumpkins to determine which of them was the largest. When this was decided, they began to hollow it out. Vicenta explained, "Then making themselves as small as possible, about the size of a duende (dwarf), they took a stick and all climbed into the pumpkin."[60] When they were all inside, one of the witches shouted a variation of the typical witch phrase: "Con Dios y sin Santa Maria!" or "With God and without the Virgin Mary!" (The teller of the tale may have been misremembering things, since typically the phrase was "Without God and without the Virgin Mary.")

Like a flying saucer, the pumpkin lit up and emitted sparks as it levitated into the air. Vicenta got out of bed and watched in amazement as the pumpkin flew out the door and into the night skies. The bruja-filled pumpkin returned at about four or five o'clock in the morning, with Vicenta hiding under the covers. She watched as the witches switched their eyes back from the cats. However, Luz, Vicenta's grand-mother, saw the girl peeking and refused to put her eyes back in and began cursing at the girl.

"Afterward the old grandmother could no longer see very good even in the daytime," Emilia began to conclude the tale. "In fact she was almost blind and she would curse Vicenta all the time." Emilia then went on to say that over time Vicenta became thin and seemed to wither away until finally she became so "weak and thin that she finally died because of the things she had seen!"[61]

Algodones, a little village north of Albuquerque, was supposedly the hub of male witches according to Bencés Gabaldón in *Brujerías: Stories of Witchcraft and the Supernatural in the American Southwest and Beyond.* She claimed that many years ago, as several men were clearing a ditch, they found a pumpkin with suspicious holes carved in it. The superstitious wanted to break it up and destroy it, as they suspected it to be a means of witch travel. The witches had been flying the night before but had to stop at dawn when the ability of flight was rendered powerless at sunrise they suspected. A member of the group warned against destroying it, and the next day when they returned, the pumpkin was gone. Of course, an animal could have gotten it, but those in the know said that not only had the witches come in the night to take flight, but also that the man who stopped them from destroying the pumpkin might be a witch himself.[62]

THE WITCH FABIANA

Agua Fria c. 1900.

Though it is not said where the following story took place, it was taken from Juliana Martinez in Agua Fria in 1941. She began the tale by simply stating that one day "in a little village" a mysterious, middle-aged woman appeared. She was "very dark and ugly" and essentially a beggar, as all she did was wander from house to house, asking for food. When asked for her name, she gave it as Fabiana. Eventually, she wandered to the home of a kindly couple who had no children. Having the space, they offered to take the woman in. However, Fabiana never seemed terribly grateful for this, nor did she offer to help with any of the housework. Eventually, the wife complained about this to the husband and Fabiana overheard.

Unbeknownst to the woman, Fabiana was a witch. Deceptively, Fabiana asked if she might borrow the woman's hairbrush for a moment, to which she obliged. Fabiana secretly snatched some of the woman's hair so that she could work a bewitchment, then told her hosts that she was leaving to stay with another family on the other side of the village.

The wife was relieved to be free of the lazy, thankless Fabiana until her arm was stricken with a sudden pain. Soon it began to swell, so she called for a curandera, who was unable to help. The woman's husband decided to take her to the Hot Springs in hopes that a soak would do her well. But, if you remember some of the witch lore from this tome's introduction, when the woman tried to enter the springs, the water would boil unnaturally. Now they knew that she had been bewitched. On their way home from the springs, they stayed the night at a small ranch and told the family there what had happened. They advised the couple that there was an old Indian woman in a nearby pueblo that could cure *maleficio*.

They went to see the old Indian woman who administered a cure in the form of curious green water to be consumed at sunrise. The

220

mysterious remedy worked, and the wife was well again. But their troubles weren't over yet. Fabiana next bewitched some cattle belonging to the husband, making their heads swell so intensely that they could not lift them. As such, they were not eating or drinking.

The man stormed over to Fabiana's house. Whereas before they were willing to let the old witch go, now he was ready to murder her for what she had done. He confronted Fabiana as she stood beneath a cottonwood tree near the acequia. "He had no sooner spoken, when, in the place where Fabiana had stood, there was a big owl, which flew up into the tree," said the story.[63] Enraged, the man cast a stone at the owl and hit it square in the head. It fell from the tree, and soon there was Fabiana dead with a wound to the head. "The village people all said they were glad he had killed the witch," the story ended simply.[64]

No. 106. Looking up Caliente Rio, at the Hot Springs. D. B. Chase, Photographer, Santa Fe, New Mexico

"Looking up the Caliente Rio at the Hot Springs"
by D.B. Chase (date unknown).

WITCH FOR A WIFE

Another witch tale, albeit lacking an exact date and location, was collected by Lorin W. Brown from a Cordova woman named Guadalupe Martínez. She told Brown of an estranged grandfather who had left New Mexico for old Mexico, vowing never to return for fear of a witchy wife. She told of how her grandmother had died and her grandfather unknowingly remarried to a woman who was a witch. Her name was Salomé Baca, and according to Guadalupe, she had sold her soul to the Devil. Guadalupe crossed herself as she told

Brown how Baca would cast a spell on her grandfather so that he would not awaken "on the nights when she wished to go to a witches' gathering or to go on some wicked errand for the devil, her master."[65]

One morning, after coming out of one of these spells, the grandfather could not hear his wife stirring around in the kitchen as usual. When he went into the kitchen to investigate, he knew something was wrong as his wife hadn't even started a fire. He walked through the house until he found his wife lying beside the fireplace as though she were dead. She appeared to be wounded on the shoulder as it was bleeding. There was also blood up in the fireplace, and the ashes were swept aside as if from a bird's wings. The grandfather went to get help in the form of two neighbor women and his godfather. While the women nursed Salomé back to consciousness, the grandfather and his godfather went onto the roof to take a better look at the chimney. There they found blood and owl feathers, which all but confirmed that his wife was a witch who had been wounded while in owl form.

The man confronted his wife about her nocturnal deeds, and though she swore to give up her witchy ways, deep down, he knew she wouldn't. One day upon returning home, he found the front door locked mysteriously. He broke it open and marched inside, looking for his wife, only to find her gone. Oddly, an earthen pot sat unattended by the fireplace. Usually, dough for tortillas could be found inside. When he opened the pot, sitting atop the dough was a toad. Knowing some bewitchment was at hand, the man decided to leave his home and never return, hence why he now stayed in old Mexico.

Though it sounds like another folktale, to Guadalupe Martinez, it was a true story.

CURED BY THE WITCHDOCTOR

Sometime in the late 1800s, near Cerillos, lived a young man by the name of Juan José Gonzáles, who had been cursed by a Navajo servant belonging to his family named María. Juan José had just returned from a trip from Albuquerque when María, who usually had a sullen attitude, surprised him by being quite congenial and offered him some apricots. Soon after eating them, Juan José became very ill and María was nowhere to be found, having fled. Juan José hadn't just been poisoned by her; he had become bewitched. In the night, he was accosted with horrible visions of "apparitions." Some had horns, he told Lorin W. Brown, while others had "eyes like the flames of hell."[66]

One of the ranch hands, identified as Pedro, was sent at once for a healer by the name of Don Secundino—not a curandero in this case, but a known witchdoctor. Upon arriving at the man's home, his wife told him that Don Secundino was already aware of Juan José's condition via a premonition and had left to gather the necessary herbs. Upon Pedro's return to the ranch and the relay of this information, Don Secundino suddenly showed up on the doorstep. "How he arrived, nobody knew; there was no horse or mule to be seen," Juan José told Lorin W. Brown. "These folks must have some alliance with Satan or else how can they do the wonderful things they do?"[67]

Don Secundino used his dark arts to somehow heal Juan José, as no one knew exactly what he did to cure the young man, but a strong smell of sulfur was left in the room after he did so. Juan José had no recollection of what the witchdoctor did either, and concluded, "It is not wise to try and find out too much about those things. It is enough to take advantage of their knowledge of those hidden things for well-being, because acts of the devil have to be fought by those who have an understanding with him."[68]

As for the bruja María, she was never seen again, but Juan José kept his revolver loaded with crucifix-etched bullets on him at all times, just in case…

BLOODSUCKING WITCHES OF ARROYO HONDO

Once upon a time in Arroyo Hondo was a young boy named Carpio, suffering from what Cleofas Jaramillo only called "strange ailments" in her book *Shadows of the Past*. Presumably, these strange ailments were similar to anemia, as Carpio was beset upon by bloodsucking witches whenever he was left alone at home.[69] When Carpio's mother would return home, she would find her son crouched in a corner. He claimed that women dressed in black shawls had entered the house and pricked him with "long cactus needles." After piercing his skin, they would suck his blood, throw him in a corner, and then leave.

Carpio's mother decided to take him to another witch, Librada, to seek a cure.[70] Librada obliged but stressed that this must be kept secret, for she could not have the same witches attacking her. She instructed Carpio's father, Don Pedro, to bring her the largest sunflower he could get his hands on, a new copper kettle, and to leave Carpio in her care for three days. Librada took the sunflower and threw it into the copper kettle along with some unidentified herbs to boil in water over the fireplace. Every night, she gave Carpio a cup of the special herbal potion and sent him to bed. For protection, she placed a statue of San Cirilo, the saint who wards off witches and witchcraft, inside the hearth of her chimney. That night, as Librada suspected, the witches plaguing Carpio came as owls. However, they could not gain ingress through the fireplace as planned with the statue of San Cirilo standing guard.

Jaramillo related the tale's conclusion thusly,

> Late in the night [Carpio] heard noises at the door and window, as if someone were trying to enter; then he heard hooting and flapping of wings on the chimney top. A loud downpour of water came through the chimney. Carpio sat up, lighted a candle, and looked into the fireplace. The statue stood undisturbed inside the fireplace and everything was quiet, so he went back to bed. The same thing happened the second night, but the witches could not get in, for San Cirilo was guarding the only opening. On the third day, Don Pedro took his son home cured.[71]

LIBRADA AS A WITCH

While Librada acted in the role of a curandera of sorts in the previous account, yet another Arroyo Hondo tale painted her in a more negative light. Assuming this was indeed the same Librada, though. In any case, Cleofas Jaramillo said the following story was told by her father's foreman, identified only as Matias.

Matias told an oft-repeated tale of riding along late at night when he spotted a dance occurring in an old vacant house. In this case, it was on the outskirts of the village of Arroyo Seco, about twelve miles from Arroyo Hondo. Matias said that though the house was in ruins, he could clearly make out a light inside and people dancing. However, whenever he approached it, the light vanished, and so did the people. Feeling afraid, he quickly rode away. When he looked behind him, the dancing had resumed, and the building was lit once again.

Matias made his way to Arroyo Seco where he stopped for shelter at the home of Doña Librada. The old woman got a mattress for Matias to sleep on in the main room. He had not slept for long when he was awoken by a strange noise. Opening his eyes, he watched in astonishment as sparks began to swirl from the fireplace. "Then there was a scraping sound in the chimney, and out of the fireplace flew a large pumpkin," Matias said. More pumpkins flew from out of the chimney, and from out of them stepped women in their best clothes. "They stood around the table, rouging and powdering their faces and admiring themselves in small pieces of broken mirrors," Matias related.[72]

Librada soon entered and, clearly familiar with the women, asked them where they were going, to which they responded, "To the dance at the old *sala*." This confirmed for Matias that not only had he witnessed a dance of witches earlier, but that Librada was herself likely a witch. Soon after, the women crawled back into their pumpkins and flew out the chimney on their way. Matias then spied Librada remove her eyes as witches did, placing them on a saucer above the fireplace. Matias claimed to have gotten up after Librada left to throw the eyes into a simmering pot and then went back to sleep. The next morning, he found Librada in the kitchen. Disturbed, she covered her face with one arm while she picked up a pair of eyes sitting on the table and plopped them into her sockets as slyly as she could. She offered Matias some coffee before he left, but fearing it would naturally be bewitched, he declined and made his way out the door. On his way out, he stumbled across an old blind dog missing its eyes from its sockets. Obviously, the night before, the dog had been Librada's animal of choice and now she would forever be stuck with the eyes of the dog.

LA CHON

Another famous witch of Arroyo Hondo was La Chon. In *Shadows of the Past*, Cleofas Jaramillo began her description of her in this way:

Old women who lived alone were often suspected of being witches. La Chon was one of these women in our village. She was usually found sitting on a sheepskin in the corner of her fireplace, smoking a *cigarrito* and poking the fire with a stick to keep her pot of beans boiling. A low door, always kept covered with a ragged patch quilt, led into her storeroom. No one was allowed to enter this secret room, where bunches of dried herbs hung from the rafters of the ceiling and a pile of ripe pumpkins stood in the corner. From the pumpkin rinds, Chon made *guejas*, into which she crawled and sailed through the air to places she wanted to visit.[73]

Supposedly, two girls once went to La Chon's house to see her. When she could not be found, they entered the forbidden room and found her sitting atop a pumpkin with both her eyes removed. Her eyes were placed on a cushion on her lap, and presumably she planned to switch them with an animal's eyes as witches did. In any case, the terrified girls couldn't stand the sight of La Chon's dark, eye-less sockets and fled the house.

MORE ARROYO HONDO WITCHES

Another witch of the Arroyo Hondo region was a goat owner well-known for making delicious cheese named Candelaria. One night, a young man named Marcos became suspicious of an owl hooting in a nearby tree in the distance and shot it in the leg. It tumbled to the ground, but when Marcos got close enough to see it for himself, he found Candelaria sitting under the tree. When she stood, she had a bad limp and claimed she had hurt her leg recently. A bit later, when some cheese was procured from Candelaria, Marcos's mother was wise enough not to eat it suspecting it was bewitched. Knowing that the evil spell was always in the first slice, she cut it off and slipped it into her pocket. Later, she fed it to the dog, which became sick with worms soon after.

One tale told of how La Chon was encountered walking through the park in Santa Fe by another woman. Recognizing La Chon as being from Arroyo Hondo, she asked if La Chon could take a package home with her to deliver to her mother. La Chon obliged, and the woman received the package the very next morning, even though in those days it took three days to travel from Santa Fe to Arroyo Hondo.

"The Black Cat" by Lionel Lindsay (1922).

La Chon accomplished this like any witch by use of flight, whether it was in the form of a ball of light or an owl. La Chon was notorious for turning into animals, and another popular tale had her encountered in the form of a dog. According to the story, the dog was seen hanging around the yard of a sick woman, rumored to have been bewitched. Whether the woman's husband suspected that the dog was a witch in animal form or not, he took to beating it with a stick. The next day, La Chon was found bedridden herself, her body black and blue with bruises. A similar story had La Chon accosted by a group of boys while she was in the form of a black cat. For reasons unknown, the boys caught the cat and proceeded to torture it by sewing its eyes shut. They then tied its legs together and strung it from a ladder. The next morning, La Chon was seen with swollen red eyes when a neighbor went over to borrow a coal from her. La Chon claimed that she had been stirring a pot of boiling corn gruel when some shot into her eyes. However, the boys knew better.[74]

The idea of a witch taking the form of a fleece or shawl, as La Chon will soon do, is also known as "The Evil Hour". This concept was written about extensively by folklorist Aurelio M. Espinosa in his piece "New-Mexican Spanish Folk-Lore," appearing in *The Journal of American Folklore* Vol. 23, No. 90 (Oct. - Dec., 1910), pp. 395-418:

The myth about the evil one, *la malora* (*mala hora*), also pronounced *malogra* (literally, "the evil hour"), is indeed interesting, both from the purely folk-lore side as well as from the philological side. How *mala hora*, the evil hour, ill fate, bad luck, came to be thought of as a definite concrete idea of an individual wicked spirit, is interesting from more than one point of view. This myth is a well-known one. *La malora* is an evil spirit which wanders about in the darkness of the night at the cross-roads and other places. It terrorizes the unfortunate ones who wander alone at night, and has usually the form of a large lock of wool or the whole fleece of wool of a sheep (*un vellón de lana*). Sometimes it takes a human form, but this is rare; and the New Mexicans say that when it has been seen in human form, it presages ill fate, death, or the like. When it appears on dark nights in the shape of a fleece of wool, it diminishes and increases in size in the very presence of the unfortunate one who sees it. It is also generally believed that a person who sees la malora, like one who sees a ghost (*un difunto*), forever remains senseless. When asked for detailed information about this myth, the New Mexicans give the general reply, "It is an evil thing" (*es cosa mala*).

One last La Chon tale sounds quite similar to another tale from Arroyo Hondo wherein a man was attacked by a brujo in the form of a white fleece. La Chon was said to take the form of a black fleece to attack at least one traveler on horseback. Jaramillo wrote that "A horseman who often rode into town on dark nights was bothered at times by different objects appearing in the middle of the road. Sometimes a black sheep fleece rolled and rolled before his horse for miles, then it would turn into a bright spark of fire, skipping before him."[75] One night, the horseman was attacked by a black shadow that kept swarming about the head of his horse, causing it to panic. The man prodded his horse along, trying to outrun the specter, but it always kept pace. The man plucked the shadow from the air and found an empty black shawl. Whatever spirit that had been compelling it now departed.[76] As the man entered Arroyo Hondo, he saw the same black shadow against the house of La Chon. He rode towards it and found the shadow to be La Chon herself, panting and out of breath. Knowing she had been caught, she begged the man not to hurt her and promised not to bother him again.

THE WIZARD OF GUADALUPE COUNTY

A story appeared on the newswires in 1906 telling of a somewhat more comical witchcraft tale involving what sounded to be more of a snake oil salesman. Entitled "Fakir Practiced Witchcraft in New Mexico," it ran in the *Prescott Weekly Arizona Journal Miner* on July 4, 1906. The story originally ran in the *Santa Rosa Sun* and was paraphrased by other outlets. The article began by comparing New Mexico to Salem, Massachusetts, 300 years prior, and then delved into the finer details of the case.

Apparently a man named Juan Gonzales of Mexico was wandering northern New Mexico proclaiming himself to be a 32nd Degree Wizard.[77] Residents did not take kindly to his antics. "After being driven away from Anton Chico and various other settlements by outraged citizens, he drifted into Pintada Canyon." There he found a bedridden superstitious old woman afflicted with rheumatism who hired him to cure her. "After much mummery, spells and incantations, he pronounced her bewitched and picked two poor weak-minded old women in the vicinity as the ones who had bewitched her." In an odd turn of events, the self-proclaimed wizard took the two "witches" with him before a justice of the peace, and via what the paper called Gonzales's "glib, persuasive tongue," got the judge to place the two witches under Gonzales's charge! The two women were then charged to "obey the wizard in all things."

The article explained, "The wizard and his two assistants proceeded to cure the old woman. They rigged up a manikin of rags with a series of strings, which they could pull and make this doll take the bent shape of the patient, and used many kinds of forms and spells, all with no perceptible effect." Furthermore, Gonzales was abusive to the two old women he called witches in his care. He would often beat them and threaten them with their lives by taking them out to a tree and threatening to hang them. Witnessing this, the people of the area appealed to officials at Santa Rosa for help. The so-called wizard was arrested (it doesn't say what happened to the two old women) and was taken before Judge Morse in Santa Rosa who "bound him over on three charges to await the investigation of the grand jury."

The article concluded with the following: "The climate of Guadalupe county does not agree with wizards, and the others had better hunt a more congenial dime in old Mexico."

SKELETON WITCHES OF PUYÉ

H 3507   PREHISTORIC CLIFF DWELLINGS, PUEBLO OF PUYÉ, NEAR SANTA FE, NEW MEXICO

In 1907 Edgar Hewett began excavations at the Puyé cliff-dwellings with the Southwest Society of the Archeological Institute of America. It is thought that between 900 and 1580 A.D., around 1500 people lived in the cliff dwellings before abandoning them. To carry out the diggings, members of San Ildefonso Pueblo were hired. As they began their excavations and began removing some of the dead buried there, the skeletons were said to come back to life.

Elsie C. Parsons related the incident in her work, *The Social Organization of the Tewa of New Mexico*, published in 1929:

Sickness or death may be caused by death scare. A story was told of how when the men were excavating at Puyé the foot of a digger was caught by one of the dead who said, "Don't take me from this ground." The digger got scared, he jumped out and said, "I don't know who is talking to me underground." He got sick and died. "This is not a story," added Rosita, "this the truth." She went on to say that white people had paid a lot to San Ildefonso men to take out dead people at Puyé. The bones talked to them, "Don't take me out," they would say. That is why they have been dying at San Ildefonso.[78]

"EL CHIVATO"

In the introduction was mentioned a cave in the vicinity of Pena Blanca where the Devil himself was said to teach a witch's school. This story, too, takes place in that vicinity and concerns a boy named Guadalupe, raised by a reputed witch called Nana Pabla. Eventually, she gave her son permission to go with a brujo friend to a witch's meeting. As per many stories, Guadalupe climbed on the brujo's back. The man told him to keep his eyes closed and not to open them until he was told. If he opened them, they would both die, he claimed. With the usual blasphemous exclamation, the brujo took flight, and off they went. Guadalupe kept his eyes closed as told and did not open them until instructed.

When they landed, Guadalupe saw before him a beautiful house with many people inside going about happily. Before he could enter, Guadalupe had to hang his rosary on a cedar tree nearby. Inside, Guadalupe danced with the others, and then eventually, they all sat down to have supper. All was well until Guadalupe bit down on something hard in his food. At first, he thought it was a bone, but when he spit it out, he saw it was a human fingernail.

Soon after, a goat, the titular El Chivato, came prancing into the room and Guadalupe watched as all the witches kissed its tail, and he did the same when his turn came. However, next slithered in a snake. It wrapped around each of the witch's bodies and then stuck its tongue in their mouths. When it came time for it to be Guadalupe's turn, it was too much for him and he cried out, "Jesus, Maria y Jose!" In an instant, the house and the witches disappeared, leaving Guadalupe in a barren plain. When Guadalupe returned home to his witch mother after three days of wandering, she was greatly disappointed in him.

However, Guadalupe was fortunate, for he had enacted only two out of the three main rituals of the witches' sabbat. Had he enacted all three, he may have sold his soul. In reverse from most witches' sabbats, in this case the cannibal feast took place first instead of last, which was odd. Otherwise, all three rituals were present and accounted for in the tale... if it had any truth at all. And perhaps it did. In 1950, when Lois Bartlett Harpham wrote her thesis entitled "Witches and Witchcraft in the Hispanic Folklore of New Mexico," she questioned the collector of the tale, Dr. Juan B. Rael, about its veracity. In a footnote related to the story, Harpham recorded that "Dr. Rael told the writer of this thesis that the narrator who had told him the above tale sincerely believed it and told it to him as the truth."[79]

THE GHOST WITCH OF MOGOLLON

Old Mogollon, NM, postcard.

In southwestern New Mexico, in Mogollon, lived a fortune teller called Erlinda. A practitioner of witchcraft, she also used monos that she would stick with pins or cactus needles to inflict pain upon whoever she was targeting. These weren't personal vendettas on her part, but services rendered to others for money. Unlike most witches that were unmarried elderly women, Erlinda was married and only 65 when she died. On her deathbed, her husband finally learned of her secret practices in witchcraft and proclaimed that he would never forgive her.

After this, when the man remarried, he found that his house was haunted. He called for the local pastor, who searched the house and cleansed it of items left over from the days of his dead wife's witchery. These items included hidden monos, plus the pins she had used to stick them with and the bodies of dead frogs. The pastor burned the items, but still the house was plagued by strange noises so the man and his new wife moved away. Neighbors claimed they could see a ghostly woman on a black horse ride into the house during the day and ride out again at night. Eventually, the house was demolished due to its reputation.

BASILIO ARAGÓN'S SPECIAL LASSO

José D. Chávez told a short but unique tale in Nasario García's *Brujerías: Stories of Witchcraft and the Supernatural in the American Southwest and Beyond* of a man named Basilio Aragón who had a special lasso that he used to catch witches. The lasso had been treated with *oshá*, a special medicinal root that could also be used against rattlesnakes. (Supposedly, if one chewed up a piece of *oshá* then spit it into a handkerchief, then tied it into a knot, you could throw it at a rattlesnake and it would go to sleep.)

One night, Aragón came across a gathering of witches, or what Chávez called a "flock of women," atop a small mountain used as a school for witches. Aragón then used his special lasso to rope the women and bind them in place. What Aragón did with the witches once he roped them, Chávez unfortunately neglected to say. But, if nothing else, it provided another unique New Mexico method of rendering witches powerless. Notably, Aragón was spoken of by Chávez as though he was a real individual who had passed away rather than the fictional star of a folktale…

233

THE GOVERNOR AND THE WITCHES BALL

Most of northern New Mexico's villages have distinct tales of witchcraft, and one such place is La Manga, located south of Las Vegas. An FWP interview conducted there on February 10, 1939, with Mary Elba, unearthed an interesting variation of the witches' sabbat, here called the "witch ball." In it, a shepherd by the name of Don Juan was approached by a stranger one night and invited to attend the ritual. Normally a simple variation would not bear repeating, but this one had some intriguing flourishes. Don Juan followed the stranger to the witches' ball just over the hill and was instructed to take off his rosary before entering, which he did. He was also advised that when the snake entered the room, he should take the invitation to kiss its tail. (Usually, one kissed the goat's tail and the snake's tongue.) He was also told that when invited to eat at the banquet table, under no circumstances was he to ask for salt, as salt represented purity and the salt of the earth was deadly to witches.

Upon entering the room, Don Juan was shocked to see the governor of New Mexico himself present along with other prominent New Mexican politicians. However, it was stated these men had been taken in their dreams and were not aware that they were present. Don Juan sat at the great banquet table with the important people, and, wouldn't you know it, he asked for some salt. Upon the simple mention of the word salt, he found himself suddenly alone outside, the building he had previously occupied mysteriously vanished. This, of course, was another odd variation, as usually it was the mention of God or the saints that did the trick. Not only was this an alteration of the usual Witches' sabbat tale, but also of a folktale from Mexico wherein someone would enter an enchanted cave, often inhabited by the Devil, and attend a luxurious banquet with them. In any case, it's interesting to see an old Spanish folktale where government officials are in league with the Devil.

BEWITCHED WEDDING

In the little community of La Madera in the Sandias lived a beautiful witch named Refrigia. Featured in the WPA story "The Enigma" (*El Misterio*) recounted by Catalina Gurulé, of Refrigia, it was said:

Refrigia lived at the edge of La Madera with her old mother. She was very pretty and had large eyes and long lashes that hid them, and she put her hair high upon her head and made herself look very beautiful. Who would ever have thought that she was a witch? But none of them ever saw her eyes when she thought of Quita. Then they were balls of fire like cats' eyes and her fingers reached out like cats' claws that wanted to tear the flesh of someone.[80]

Refrigia hated Quita because she had won the affection of the handsome man she admired, Felipe. One night, Refrigia confessed her love to Felipe, who very gently broke the news to her that he loved Quita and would wed her soon. On the day of Quita and Felipe's wedding, the groom suddenly began acting childlike. The story related:

[Felipe] ran around Quita and laughed and pulled at the wedding veil as a child would do. When they came home, he cried at the wedding feast and would not eat of it, but asked for a tinaja (bowl of pottery) of atole (a drink made from milk and roasted and ground blue or pueblo corn) just as a child might do. All the wedding guests thought the handsome bridegroom was making a clown of himself for their amusement.[81]

Felipe never snapped out of his strange, child-like condition. In fact, the village even built him a crib to lie in. Not only that, he was besieged with a pain in his head. And poor Quita stayed faithfully by his side, though it took a toll on her youthful beauty. As for Refrigia, she had become a hermit. Quita decided to confront Refrigia in her home, but was rebuked and sent away swiftly.

But the story eventually concluded with a happy ending:

Then one day Felipe suddenly became himself again. Quita, too, looked as she did on that fateful wedding day. What of Refrigia? They ran to her house. There on her floor she lay dying and beside her was her witch doll and in her fingers was the big thorn she had pulled from its head. She had relented when death struck her and freed Felipe from the spell she had cast upon him.[82]

THE NIGHT WATCHMAN AND THE WITCH

Jack Kutz recounted a unique, Las Cruces-based witch-tale I have yet to see anywhere else. In *Mysteries & Miracles of New Mexico*, Kutz

235

told the tale of a night watchman in Las Cruces "at an unspecified time in the town's early history."[83] The site of the story was also a bit nebulous, as it was identified only as a "local lumber mill." Anyhow, on with the tale.

Old Las Cruces in the 1890s. (Palace of the Governors Photo Archives, NMHM/DC. Neg.#009395)

The Las Cruces Lumber Mill had been plagued with a case of two deceased night watchmen. Both men had been found dead one after the other each morning when the foreman came to work. He could never figure out how they had died. They seemed to have simply dropped dead. Naturally, job applicants were hard to find under the macabre circumstances. However, a rather portly man showed up and applied, and though he wasn't as fit as the previous two guards, the foreman's choices were limited. The man got the job, and on his nightly rounds he heard something unexpected. From a keyhole through the main door, he heard a seductive female voice whispering to him. "His fat cheeks blushed red as she described the ecstasy they would share if he permitted her to come in," Kutz wrote.[84]

However, this watchman learned from the mistakes of his predecessors. The woman's offer sounded too good to be true, and this must've been what led to their demise. Cleverly, the watchman cracked the door open and asked the young woman to extend her hand. As she did, he made the sign of the cross on it. The woman let out a hellish shriek, and the watchman now knew he was dealing with a witch. He slammed the door against her wrist, and then took his ax. He swung and chopped off the witch's hand. Though the witch made great haste in departing, the severed hand flopped

236

around on the ground as though it had a life of its own. The watchman kicked and stomped at it until it finally shriveled into a balled-up fist. After the story got out, residents whispered that the witch must have wished to procure the corpulent man for a witch's feast somewhere.

THE WITCHING OF NOGAL CANYON

Old mail route through Nogal Canyon.

Nogal Canyon is located in the rolling hills of Lincoln County, not too far from the Mescalero Apache Reservation. In the old days, it was the home and stomping grounds of quite a few Mescalero Apache. And it was also witched.[85]

"They say Nogal Canyon was witched," the narrator called Chris told author Morris Opler in his book *Apache Odyssey.*[86] Chris described how many people suffered accidents in the canyon, like his father, who fell and broke his leg, as did another girl he knew there. "Swinging-Lance fell on a cornstalk, and it went up his nose and nearly killed him," Chris said of another bizarre accident there. After listing a few more strange incidents to Opler, Chris told how several area medicine men set out to find the cause of the bewitchment. They pinpointed it to the dead child of a Lipan Apache.[87]

This Lipan Apache man became angry when his child died in the canyon and claimed that many more would die there as well. "Only one tree at the south end would live," claimed the Lipan Apache according to the story. From Chris's perspective, this all came true as he claimed that "Now only that tree is sticking up there among those Indian fields." Chris also claimed that many families that remained in the valley died, and those that didn't moved away. (Those were just the Apache, he claimed that some Mexican families stayed there.) Next, Chris had a prophetic dream of Nogal Canyon catching fire and "popping" as bewitched items do in the Mescalero belief. As proof of his prophetic dream, Chris told Opler, "This was just before rations were being given out. Now it is true. The place is deserted."[88]

Apart from the bewitching from the Lipan Apache man, a witch who could take the form of a grasshopper was also said to frequent Nogal, where she poisoned springs and fruit crops in the area. Specifically, Chris said, "She lived at Nogal... from there she rode out and witched four springs, each in a different direction. Then for four days she took the form of a grasshopper and did her witching."[89] She was also accused of shooting sorcery in a few instances. The witch met her end when the shooting sorcery she performed on a man with stronger power than hers reflected back to her, and she became sick and died. When she did, the springs she bewitched became pure again.

DEVIL OF SEVEN RIVERS

"A few times in the early morning hours, I have seen his twisted old body roaming the banks of the Pecos River—even after these many years."
—Old Sheepherder, "The Devil Never Sleeps"

Over 100 years ago, in the vicinity of present-day Carlsbad and Seven Rivers, lived a man known simply as Chappo. However, a more ominous name given to the old-timer was El Diablo. Why was this? According to an article published in *Old West* in the early 1970s, called "The Devil Never Sleeps" by Monk Lofton, Chappo was a badly deformed and crippled hermit who lived alone in the hills. One night, a young sheepherder was attacked by something "inhuman" in the darkness. Presuming it to be Chappo in his diablo form, he hacked the old man to pieces with an ax in a truly brutal murder. As it was, Chappo was the scapegoat for any misfortune or strange event among sheepherders in the area. An old herder said of Chappo, "I knew and hated and feared Chappo. As to what form the devil takes in the early morning, I do not know; but I do know he becomes evil and inhuman."[90]

Even the famed lawman Dee Harkey (*Mean as Hell: The Life of a New Mexico Lawman*) had heard of Chappo and his sensational death. Harkey told Lofton in the 1950s that Chappo was murdered sometime after midnight. The young sheepherders had all just gathered at what Harkey called "a party of some sort" at Chappo's shack. When most of them had left, and only Chappo and one other herder remained, the young man murdered him. The sheepherder was found the next morning clutching a bloodied ax and mumbling "El Diablo!" over and over again.

Harkey pointed Lofton in the direction of another old herder named Winston Shillito, who said that many people were relieved when Chappo was murdered, even if they could concede that it was a gruesome deed. Shillito could only pinpoint the year of the murder as occurring sometime between 1902 and 1910. Though Shillito never used the term brujo, some witchy elements were ascribed to Chappo by him. Chappo was incredibly wise, for instance, and was known to mysteriously procure replacement sheepherders when they were needed. "Just what method Chappo used to make these youths always available to the ranchers, perhaps no one ever knew," Shilito said.[91] Also, like some brujos and curanderas, Chappo dealt in drugs as well.

Seven Rivers ruins. Courtesy Southeastern New Mexico Historical Society/ Near Lovings Bend.

Lofton next interviewed an unnamed elderly relative of Chappo's living in Loving. The man began to shake merely at the mention of Chappo's name and was reluctant to discuss him at all. When pressed

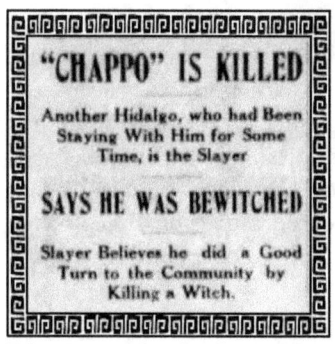

"CHAPPO" IS KILLED

Another Hidalgo, who had Been Staying With Him for Some Time, is the Slayer

SAYS HE WAS BEWITCHED

Slayer Believes he did a Good Turn to the Community by Killing a Witch.

for details about Chappo's true identity and what he really did, the man told Lofton that "Chappo had no name. He came from nowhere. He did nothing for a living. He lived on evil—people made evil by his influence. Perhaps he was all the bad that comes from a century?"[92]

Afterward, Chappo's ghost was seen and for a time he was the Seven Rivers area's de facto boogeyman. However, that was the story according to the *Old West* article, but newspaper accounts of the time told a very different story of Chappo. While some whispered he had no name, the papers listed it as Francisco Sanchez. And while he was indeed murdered in October of 1909, the killing didn't occur off in the mountains, and nor was it committed with an ax.

The *Carlsbad Current Argus* of October 15, 1909, identified the killer as a 21-year-old named Rosilio Rubalcao.[93] The killing, it said, occurred in a Carlsbad slum within Chappo's "little shack on Greene street" at about midnight. The account in the *Current Argus* painted a completely different picture of Chappo, who they described as "quiet" and "generally liked among his own people and also among the whites." In yet another passage, he was called a "quiet harmless and faithful old soul." Stranger yet, Rubalcao, the killer, was described as a friend of Chappo's.

If this is so, why then did the man murder Chappo? Was he mentally disturbed or under the influence? Oddly enough, Rubalcao was deemed by the authorities to have been completely sober when he killed Chappo. Nor was he considered psychotic, as Rubalcao was described by the authorities as appearing to be "intelligent," "sane," "intellectual," and "rational" in the paper. Despite being effectively homeless, he was also described as "neat" and "well-groomed."

Why, then, did he kill his friend Chappo? According to the article, Rubalcao considered it a mercy killing of sorts because Chappo had become bewitched. The *Current Argus* related that:

> [Rubalcao] says he does not know what time it was when he went to bed, but after he had been asleep he discovered that Chappo was "bewitched." He said he saw cats and dogs and indefinite forms of all kinds before his (Chappo's) door and that he called to him to come. Then he attempted to go inside and as the door was locked he tried to force an entrance. He

240

used a big rock which would probably weigh ten pounds to batter in the door, after which he killed his bewitched friend with his knife.

That was another big difference between the story Lofton dug up in the 1950s and the newspaper account of the time: Chappo had not been hacked to death by an ax but by a knife. It was a very violent affair, and a young man who witnessed the crime described seeing Rubalcao stabbing Chappo in the head with the knife, which had broken in two during the fight. After the police collected Rubalcao, Chappo remained conscious for an unspecified amount of time before expiring. Notably, though he was able to respond to questions, he never revealed what caused the fight.

According to a court interpreter, Rubalcao considered this either a mercy killing or an honor killing—it's a bit unclear. Whether Chappo was willingly entertaining the Devil or was unwillingly possessed by the Devil, Rubalcao apparently felt it his duty to kill Chappo and put him out of his misery. The paper reported:

> Through Mr. Carlisle [the interpreter], who has spent many years as a missionary in Mexico and is thoroughly conversant with Mexicans and their customs, it was learned that in the republic when any one of their number is believed to be bewitched they are set upon by their brothers and killed and [Rubalcao] was simply following the laws and customs of his home country by doing what he has been taught to believe is right and proper.
>
> [Rubalcao] is a peculiar specimen of a human being. He converses in an intelligent manner and seems to be rational and sane except for the hallucination relative to the witches which he asserts most positively he saw issuing from the door of his victim's shack and also many other indefinite and indescribable forms which were floating in the air before the door...

Could we assume that Chappo's legend, as reprinted in the *Old West* article, grew out of this tragic misunderstanding? Did Rubalcao murder Chappo for other reasons and thought that perhaps the witchcraft excuse would get him acquitted? Or did Rubalcao really see demons—real or imagined—floating about poor Chappo's shack? At this point, we will never know, but Rubalcao was sentenced to 99 years in prison for his deed.

Section Notes

[1] Stanley, *The Zia (New Mexico) Story*, p.22.
[2] Kluckhohn, *Nahao Witchcraft*, p.114.
[3] Ibid, p.34. Kluckhohn added, "Some informants mention Mexicans as the source, others, Pueblo Indians."
[4] Birmingham, "The Navajo at the Bosque Redondo," *New Mexico Historical Review* (Vol. 60, #4, 1985), p.408.
[5] Brown, *Hispano Folklore*, p.82.
[6] Ibid, p.83.
[7] Blue, *Indian Trader*, p.9.
[8] Ibid.
[9] This likely wasn't due to Hubbell sharing that belief so much as he knew the Navajo held that belief and would no longer frequent his post.
[10] Blue, *Indian Trader*, pp.8-9.
[11] Ibid, p.9.
[12] Ibid, pp.9-10.
[13] Ibid, p.11.
[14] Ibid.
[15] Reportedly, even Mucho participated in the killing despite his earlier protests. However, he later feared that due to his "serious transgression, the killing of a relative" that he would suffer retaliation of some sort.
[16] It is unknown if these letters were written before or after the killing of Hastiin Biwosi.
[17] It's possible that either this witch or simply another Lincoln County witch was mentioned in *Tone the Bell Easy*. A witch identified as Doña Paulita was discussed who lived in Alto, presumably the same Alto of Lincoln County high in the mountains. It was said that she sent a big dish of cheese, called a *requesda*, to a family who was rightly weary of it. They let it sit for three days, after which it turned into worms.
[18] Perrone, Krueger & Stockel, *Medicine Women*, p.179.
[19] It should be noted that the family had yet to settle in Seven Rivers yet and was living closer to the Ruidoso area at the time this story took place.
[20] Ball, *Ma'am Jones*, p.34.
[21] Kutz, *Mysteries and Miracles of New Mexico*, p.94.
[22] Lummis, *A New Mexico David*, p.128.
[23] Aragón, *Enchanted Legends and Lore*, p.23.
[24] García, *Tales of Witchcraft*, p.25.
[25] Lummis, *A Tramp Across the Continent*, pp.196-98.
[26] Steiger, *Montezuma's Serpent*, p.1.
[27] Lummis, *A New Mexico David*, p.125.
[28] Ibid, p.126.
[29] Kutz, *Mysteries & Miracles of New Mexico*, p.95.
[30] Lummis, *A New Mexico David*, p.127.

[31] Considering the tale was first published in the 1930s, and that the witness was speaking of her grandmother, we can presume the story took place in the mid-1800s.

[32] In addition to being called the Three Witches, they have even been called the three La Lloronas. And indeed, sighting of La Llorona are fairly frequent in nearby Rio Lucero.

[33] Lange and Riley, *Journals of Bandelier*, p. 173.

[34] According to the July 1888 edition of the *Journal of American Folklore,* she wasn't stoned but beaten to death by clubs.

[35] Lummis, *A New Mexico David*, p.127.

[36] Jack Kutz presented a variation of this tale in *Mysteries and Miracles of New Mexico*, setting it in the vicinity of Mount Taylor though still starring Nicolas Marino. According to Kutz, Marino observed a fireball come down from the sky and then "curve gracefully up through an arroyo" [p.98]. Marino cautiously gave chase and actually managed to come face to face with the glowing orb, out of which sprang a snarling dog. The animal pounced on him, but soon ran away after knocking him over in that version.

[37] Lummis, *A New Mexico David*, p.129.

[38] Opler, *Apache Odyssey*, p.72.

[39] Ibid.

[40] It was said he died two years before the stories in that chapter were recorded.

[41] Stanley, *The Sandia (New Mexico) Story*, p.5.

[42] Ibid.

[43] Barker, "New Mexico Witch Tales," *Tone the Bell Easy*, p.62.

[44] Berg, "The Twisted Neck and the Black Cat," 5-5-18 #3, WPA New Mexico Collection, Fray Angélico Chávez History Library, Santa Fe, New Mexico, U.S.A.

[45] Batchen, "Doña Tomasa – The Witch Nurse," 5-5-49 #'s 29 to 33. WPA New Mexico Collection, Fray Angélico Chávez History Library, Santa Fe, New Mexico, U.S.A.

[46] Ibid.

[47] García, *Brujerías*, p.94.

[48] Montoya, "Treasure," *Lost Treasures and Old Mines*, pp.62-63.

[49] Stanley, *The Liberty (New Mexico) Story*, p.19.

[50] There is a whole folktale, "Ricardo's Deer," devoted to cachana being used as a charm against witches. It involved a man, Ricardo, who went hunting in the mountains without his cachana root. He came across a small deer sleeping in the woods. When he reached out to grab it, it "grew to huge size" and kicked him so hard he became unconscious. When he awakened, he found himself face to face with the witch Dona Euphemia, who offered him his rifle back. Without his cachana, Ricardo was fearful of touching the gun and ran away.

When he returned to his cabin, he found his rifle propped against the door waiting for him, but chose not to touch it until his cachana charm was safely on his person again.

[51] Jesusita appeared in at least one other FWP account titled "La Curandera" from August 5, 1940. It was for certain the same Jesusita, as she was listed as living in Placitas where the other story had her settle. Still she clutched the cachana root given to her in the other story. So, it would appear that whether the story was true or not, Jesusita was for certain a real curandera in the Placitas area.

[52] Batchen, "The Story of La Curandera," 5-5-31WPA. New Mexico Collection, Fray Angélico Chávez History Library, Santa Fe, New Mexico, U.S.A.

[53] Martinez, "The Witch of Arroyo Hondo," 5-5-60 #8. WPA New Mexico Collection, Fray Angélico Chávez History Library, Santa Fe, New Mexico, U.S.A.

[54] Ibid.

[55] Ibid.

[56] Ibid.

[57] Ibid.

[58] Ibid.

[59] Berg, "The Flying Brujas," WPA 5-5-60 #1. New Mexico Collection, Fray Angélico Chávez History Library, Santa Fe, New Mexico, U.S.A.

[60] Ibid.

[61] Ibid.

[62] García, *Brujerías*, p.22.

[63] Thorp, "Fabiana – Witch Story," 5-5-52 #69. WPA New Mexico Collection, Fray Angélico Chávez History Library, Santa Fe, New Mexico, U.S.A.

[64] Ibid.

[65] Brown, *Hispano Folklife*, p.87.

[66] Ibid, p.51.

[67] Ibid, p.52.

[68] Ibid.

[69] While I was tempted to lump this in with tales of Tlaxcala's Tlahuelpuchi, these bloodsucking brujas were only quasi-similar to the Tlahuelpuchi in the sense that they turned into birds and went after a young boy for his blood.

[70] Specifically, Jaramillo referred to her not as a curandera, but an *ambularia*, which in Arroyo Hondo terms referred to graduates of witchcraft.

[71] Jaramillo, *Shadows of the Past*, p.101.

[72] Ibid, p.102.

[73] Ibid, p.99.

[74] Unfortunately, Cleofas Jaramillo wasn't clear in *Shadows of the Past* if La Chon's attackers suspected the animals of being witches or if the perpetrators were inflicting random acts of animal cruelty.

[75] Jaramillo, *Shadows of the Past*, p.100.

[76] I have to wonder if this was simply a variation of the other floating fleece story from Arroyo Hondo, as that seems to be the only area where I've seen tales of witches assuming that form.

[77] Perhaps he was inferring in some way he was one step shy of being a 33rd Degree Mason?

[78] Parsons, *Social Organization of the Tewa*, pp.62-63.

[79] Harpham, "Witches and Witchcraft," p.24.

[80] *Women's Tales from the New Mexico WPA: La Diabla a Pie* (Kindle Edition).

[81] Ibid.

[82] Ibid.

[83] Kutz, *Mysteries & Miracles of New Mexico*, p.102.

[84] Ibid.

[85] Even the canyon's namesake was allegedly a witch. In *Apache Odyssey*, Chris spoke frequently of an elder called Old Nogal, so it would make sense the region was named for him. Old Nogal was a professed witch himself, and towards the end of Old Nogal's days he boasted of his witch ways to a large crowd according to Chris.

[86] Opler, *Apache Odyssey*, p.95.

[87] Opler noted that the Lipan had relocated to Mescalero in 1903 and were regarded as being strange by the Apache, and accused some of them of witchcraft due to having different customs.

[88] Opler, *Apache Odyssey*, p.96.

[89] Ibid, p. 194.

[90] Lofton, "The Devil Never Sleeps," *Old West* (Winter 1972), p.30

[91] Ibid, p.46.

[92] Ibid, p.47.

[93] A later issue of the paper gave the last name as Rucabo.

Special Section

LA LECHUZA

"The owl is associated with death and is believed to be the form assumed by the spirits of dead witches." –Morris E. Opler, Apache Odyssey[1]

Like the Navajo skinwalker, the Lechuza is another distinctive type of witch said to inhabit the Southwest to this day. Not to be confused with witches who simply take the form of owls for their nightly prowls, the Lechuza is more of a were-owl. Or, that is to say, the Lechuza is a gigantic owl with humanoid features. The Lechuza can be quite large, sometimes standing as tall as seven feet with a fifteen-foot wingspan.[2] Some even claim that the larger Lechuzas have run cars off the road. And naturally, like all owls, they are seen mostly at night but not always.

Though usually fixated on children, the Lechuza preyed upon drunks as well. That said, I would imagine that the owl witch going after drunks was a recent addition to the legend, and the witch's true origins lie in that of child death like many other vampiric figures. For instance, other variations on the whims of the Lechuza—and there are many—claimed that the owl witch specifically craved the blood of unbaptized babies. As such, the Lechuza served as an impetus to get one's child baptized at once.

Like a skinwalker, a Lechuza could emulate the cries of an infant to lure victims out into the open. And like La Llorona, hearing the Lechuza's cry was considered a bad omen, perhaps foreshadowing that you or someone you know might be about to die. (Dreaming of the Lechuza was an equally bad sign.) As killers of infants, La Lechuza and La Llorona are vaguely similar, just with different attributes. Likewise, they probably descend from a common legend. Like La Llorona, La Lechuza has an origin story involving the death of a child. In this case, some think that the original La Lechuza had a child that was wrongly killed by people in her village, while others specify that her child was killed by a drunk and so therefore she attacks drunkards. Some folktales also claimed that the first Lechuza was a murdered witch who came back as a gigantic owl and no child death figures into the legend.

247

But, as stated before, anyone could be at risk of being carried away by La Lechuza, not just children and drunks. For instance, it is said that if you whistle three times at night, you may summon a Lechuza to attack you.[3] And, if so much as a feather of the Lechuza touches you, even if you escaped its clutches, you will later die. At best, you might only find scratches on your door or windowsill where the Lechuza had tried to gain ingress the night before. Some pour salt along their windowsill to keep a Lechuza out, while another superstition will see someone hang a rope with seven knots tied into it over their door. This won't abhor the Lechuza in this case, and it will take it as a sign of respect.

Driving away a Lechuza is no different than any other witch, as spiritual rebukes or simply throwing salt at them is said to suffice. However, other sources state that salt alone will not do, and it needs to be a special combination of salt and chili powder. More specific rituals include saying the *Magnifica*, a prayer from the gospel of Saint Luke, recited in Spanish forwards and backwards.[4] Like other witches, a crucifix-etched bullet could be used to shoot and kill the Lechuza. However, if you shot at the Lechuza and didn't kill it or missed, you would die instead. If you hit the witch, the body of the giant owl would not revert back to that of a woman's until sunrise.

The Lechuza isn't a thing of the past, either, and if anything appears to be becoming more prominent as opposed to being forgotten. In 2014, a video surfaced of people in rural Mexico burning a large owl alive as they were certain it was actually a Lechuza. Why the hate and fear for this particular witch? As alluded to earlier, the main reason is that it is said to crave the blood of children.

"I believe that you can find the owl in Mexican folklore and I believe that it's aligned with vampires," said Eileen Dolores Treviño Villarreal in *Brujerías: Stories of Witchcraft and the Supernatural in the American Southwest and Beyond*.[5] And indeed, if one correlates this to legends of the demon spirit Lillith and the vampiric Tlahuelpuchi of Mexico, both of which prey upon children and are associated with owls, this seems to be true.

248

Lillith, for those unaware, was Adam's rebellious first wife from Jewish folklore and Biblical apocrypha. Whereas Eve was created from Adam's rib, in Jewish myth, Lillith was created in the same manner as Adam from the same dust of the earth. As such, she saw herself as Adam's equal and would not submit, and so she was banished from Eden to the ends of the earth. Out of jealousy, she then preyed upon the offspring of Adam and Eve, thus making her the first she-demon and one of the premiere specters to prey specifically upon

Lillith, Carl Poellath (1886).

children. While mostly apocryphal, Lillith is actually mentioned canonically in the Book of Isaiah, where she is compared to the screech owl.[6] And as you already know, the owl is the animal most associated with the witches of New Mexico.

Lillith was also said to be the mother of demons and had underlings called Lilitu, whose demonic aspirations centered on the destruction of the family unit in some way or another. Usually, this was done in the form of killing an infant in the night or by seducing a wayward husband away from his wife. The Lilitu were occasionally depicted as bird-footed night demons that subsisted on the blood of infants and their mothers.[7] As such, there's an undeniable link to female vampires that prey upon children and birds. And again, in many cases, Lillith is associated with the screech owl.

Of course, Lillith hailed from Sumer, which is a long way from Santa Fe, so we'll relocate to a place a little closer in the form of Mexico. Notably, the Aztecs had female deities that weren't terribly dissimilar to Lillith in the form of Cihuacoatl, the goddess of motherhood. While this might sound nice, the name Cihuacoatl translates to snake woman. And, in the same way that the Lilitu were the devotees of Lilith, the cihuateteo were the servants of Cihuacoatl. Specifically, the cihuateteos were the spirits of mothers who had died in childbirth. The cihuateteo also had macabre bird-like characteristics, as they were depicted with skeletal faces and eagle claws for their hands. Like the Lilitu, they were believed to abduct or kill children, seduce men to adultery, and induce madness and seizures (a common sign of possession).

249

THE LEGEND OF MU PITZ

In addition to ancient Sumer and Mexico, Native Americans of North America also had equivalents of the Lechuza. (Some even gave La Lechuza properties of the Native American Thunderbird, such as the ability to control thunderstorms.) The Mescalero Apache had tales of a similar giant, evil bird that they simply called Big Owl. The Jicarilla Apache to the north also had Big Owl, who in their stories would often paralyze people just by looking at them. After this, it would swallow the victim whole. Commanche lore, too, spoke of what some called a "great cannibal owl." This was an interesting choice of words, as it implied that it either ate other owls or, more likely, was a witch in owl form that ate human flesh, thus making it a cannibal. A notable example was the cannibal giant Mu Pitz of Cherokee belief, which resembled a humanoid owl. Mu Pitz could be considered the male equivalent of La Lechuza as he, too, singled out children for the most part. In *Fossil Legends of the First Americans*, Adrienne Mayor wrote of the creature: "According to anthropologist Daniel Gelo, Piamupits or Mu Pitz was a terrifying, cave dwelling ogre, sometimes visualized as a giant owl-man with a beak, who preyed on humans, especially children. Gelo pointed out that large owls were a 'source of fascination and dread' among Comanche traditionalists. Owls' nocturnal stealth contributes to the idea that they are really ghosts."[8] Likewise, in 1972, the Comanche medicine woman Sanapia described Mu Pitz as a very tall, hairy giant with bird feet.

Another legend that linked the Lechuza to Mesoamerica stemmed from ancient Teotihuacan. For the Aztecs, the owl was associated with the god of rain, but despite this was still considered a bad omen. If a woman was born on the day of *Ce-Ehecatl* ("one-rain") she would develop supernatural abilities and be known as a *Mometzcopinqui*. These women had the ability to remove their limbs and then turn into birds, specifically owls or turkeys. In their bird-like forms, they would go out to feed on the blood of newborns.

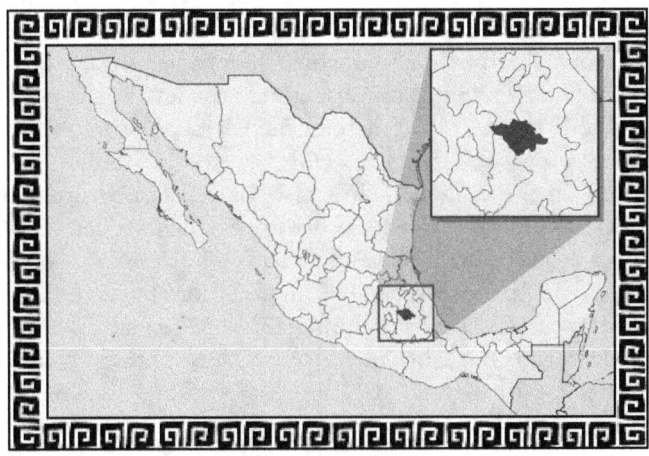

Tlaxcala region.

While these blood-drinking bird-footed she demons might seem like the stuff of legend, they actually had a 20th century equivalent called the Tlahuelpuchi. In the mid-1950s, rural Mexico was beset by a very unusual epidemic of infant deaths in the region of Tlaxcala. In fact, so many death certificates were turned in listing the cause of death as "*chupado por la bruja*" or "sucked by the witch," that it prompted a government investigation. The infants in question almost always died at night and were found with severe bruising or discoloration on their upper bodies. However, no autopsies were ever done on the children to determine if they had been drained of blood for those wondering, and the government simply chalked up the cases to careless mothers.

As with the aforementioned Mometzcopinqui, female Tlahuelpuchi[9] were born that way—there was no occult ritual or vampire bite to transform them. The curse of the Tlahuelpuchi was said to be irreversible and one would not even know that they were a vampire until puberty. Upon the tragic realization, the girl's soul would be lost for several days as she became infused with special

251

powers. These powers mostly included the ability to shapeshift into various animals. Oddly, out of all the forms they could take, they chose that of the turkey. However, like New Mexico witches, the Tlahuelpuchi transformed into fireballs and owls in addition to a multitude of other animals.

To keep the parents or older siblings asleep, the vampire witch was said to emit a supernatural mist that made certain they would not awaken as she fed. As she approached the baby, she would turn back from bird into woman. Others said that she retained her bird form during the act, and sucked the blood through a long, needle-like tongue. When she finished, she would often leave the body outside of the crib or away from the sleeping mat, usually near the door.

The witch's method of transformation was quite elaborate. You might recall a few of the witches in this book had the ability to detach their limbs. In the Tlahuelpuchi's case, on the last Saturday of the month, she would build a fire of dry zoapotl leaves, capulin wood, copal, and agave roots in her kitchen. While chanting, she would walk across the fire in reverence of the four corners of the wind in a north-south/east-west direction three times before sitting on the fire facing north, which enabled her to enact the transformation. To reduce her size to that of the animal she wished to emulate, she would remove her legs.[10] Or, in the case of the similar Mometzcopinqui, the witch would replace her legs with those of a large bird like a turkey.

Anyhow, when she separated from her legs, the witch turned into a bird and flew away while her legs sat in the kitchen. If a witch hunter came upon their disembodied limbs and tossed them into the fire, this would signal the vampire witch's demise. Or, if the Tlahuelpuchi did not feed by daybreak when in their shapeshifted form, they would die. But usually they would return, reattach their legs, and resume a normal life.

Warding off a Tlahuelpuchi was not dissimilar to the methods used to confront witches in New Mexico. Adorning a child's crib with Christian iconography and symbols was an obvious choice, and the use of a cross made of needles or clothespins was popular. Actually, as it stands, the Tlahuelpuchi was said to abhor any type of metal. In fact, they said the best repellent was a pair of scissors, a knife, a needle, or any other type of sharp metal left under the crib.

As to how one immobilized a Tlahuelpuchi, it was similar to the practices of the Juans of New Mexico. Whether named Juan or not, an individual could take off their pants, turn one leg inside out, and then throw the pants at the Tlahuelpuchi. The other method was to place a rock within a white handkerchief and throw it at her. Lastly, if one was wearing a hat, they could remove it and place it upside down on the floor and then drive a knife through it. Any of these three methods would immobilize the creature, and afterward, it could be dispatched permanently. When it came down to actually destroying a Tlahuelpuchi, a stake through the heart or decapitation would suffice as with a normal vampire.[11]

So, as you can tell, while the Tlahuelpuchi wasn't a dead-ringer for a Lechuza, the similarities are still noteworthy. Actually, during the Tlahuelpuchi's reign of terror in 1950s Tlaxcala, a Lechuza supposedly haunted the border town of Nuevo Laredo. According to Mexico Unexplained and several other sources, the owl witch was confronted there at an unspecified date in the 1950s. Similar to many witch tales of the previous century, it had the locals luring the Lechuza out of the trees with a young child as bait. When the giant bird-like being appeared, the townsfolk opened fire on it but only managed to hit it in the claw before it got away. The next day, an accused witch living in the town was seen with a crutch and a bandaged leg.

In *Cryptozoology and the Investigation of Lesser-Known Mystery Animals*, New Mexico journalist Jerry A. Padilla told of a Taos woman's sighting of a four-and-a-half-foot tall owl. More specifically, it took place close to the New Mexico-Colorado state line in the late 1950s or early 1960s when the witness, Rosa M. Lucero, was a little girl. Lucero saw the creature in the company of her grandmother, Elena Bustos Lucero, and said that the animal wandered silently from a cluster of red willows lining their irrigation ditch. She said the bird had feathers atop its head that resembled horns in a way. The owl walked up to within a few feet of the two women, where it paced back and forth while they both frantically made the Sign of the Cross. The owl seemed unafraid of the grandmother even when she waved a large block of firewood at it. To Lucero's memory, at times it almost seemed as if the owl was challenging or taunting her grandmother, but it eventually wandered back into the reeds and was never seen again. "My grandmother was convinced it was a nagual, someone taking the form of an owl, because she herself said that in all her long life she'd never encountered an owl so large and unafraid of people," said Lucero.[12]

One of the most prominent waves of Lechuza sightings may have occurred in Texas between 1975 and 1977, where a "Big Bird" was frequently spotted in the Rio Grande region. In more recent years, paranormal researchers have come to categorize the case in the realm of remnant dinosaurs, as in many cases the big bird looked like a pterodactyl. But it didn't start out that way. To be clear, the media frenzy over the Big Bird began in January of 1976, but the creature had been sighted the previous year. And those particular sightings sound much more like La Lechuza.

The photo printed above was taken by Murray Judson, and shows Detective Daivd Esquivel of the Robstown, Texas, police force with what is more or less a Lechuza effigy constructed by some youths as a prank, or so they say. Reports of a large, bird-like creature with a human face (alternately reported as a man or a woman) began to circulate around Robstown in the Autumn of 1975. The *Corpus Christi Times* of January 22, 1976, ran a story with the above photo, which contained a quote from the Robstown Police Department stating that back in November of 1975, "A bunch of kids fixed them up a dummy of this big bird and hung it in a tree and then called police. We went out there and got it and brought it to the police station." When the sightings jumped into high gear in January of 1976, the Robstown Police Department invited a photographer to see the bird effigy for themselves as though it somehow explained the recent sightings, though it certainly did not. Furthermore, were the police merely assuming this effigy was a prank? It's possible that this Lechuza effigy was, in fact, a serious attempt at either conjuring the witch-monster or perhaps an effort to ward it off.

In addition to blood, some say La Lechuza is a psychic or energy vampire that feeds on negative emotions, though it should be noted that this is a trait of demons and evil spirits in general. It is said that La Lechuza likes to lurk outside of homes during domestic disputes in the hope that one of the participants may wander outside to get away from their spouse and she might grab them. Though there was no mention of domestic strife, a notable instance of this may have occurred during the Big Bird flap. On the night of January 14, 1976, 26-year-old Armando Grimaldo of Raymondville was attacked by a flying creature when he went outside his mother-in-law's home to smoke a cigarette. In the backyard, Grimaldo suddenly heard a flapping of great wings along with a strange whistle (remember, the Lechuza is said to whistle). Soon he was accosted by the nightmarish flying creature that attempted to carry him away. Its wingspan he estimated somewhere in the range of ten to fifteen feet. He described the creature's head as looking like a monkey's or a bat's with no discernable beak. Afterward, he was transported to the Willacy County Hospital in a state of shock.

The only problem with lumping Grimaldo's account in with other Lechuza sightings is that this one was hairless, its wings described as leathery like a bat's. Plus, there were many witnesses of the creature that described it as being like a pterodactyl with a beak. But still, the similarities to a Lechuza account are worth noting, and had Grimaldo's account come about 100 years earlier, there would have been no talk of remnant dinosaurs, only witches and devil monsters.

A report on the sightings, published in the *Rosenberg Herald Coaster* on March 2, 1976, described past Big Bird accounts and noted that sometimes the creature had the face of a bat, monkey, or a human. This article was printed after the most notable sighting of all occurred when several schoolteachers sighted the creature from their car. Though they picked out a pterodactyl as the most likely candidate for what they saw, in reality, the teachers never got a good look at the creature's head.

Mexico Unexplained also related that a Lechuza was seen in Texas the following year in 1977. The incident occurred in Santa Rosa, which is also situated near the border. A woman there claimed to see a huge bird in a tree with a face like an old woman's. It flew down to attack her, but she slammed her door shut, and the creature took to scratching around outside her home. Neighborhood dogs came to the rescue to chase the big bird away. However, the next morning, all of the poor dogs were found dead. Could this Lechuza have been related to the "Big Bird" seen earlier?

Houston Residents Sight 'Batman' On Tree Perch In Yard

HOUSTON, June 18—UP—Five persons, all of whom live in the same house, complained to police they saw a combination of superman and Captain Midnight perched in an oak tree outside their home early Thursday and said he disappeared in the light of a mysterious "rocket" and a second aerial display.

Police said they were "investigating" the stories but admitted they were not equipped to handle such phenomena as the five persons described.

Mrs. Hilda Walker, 23, accompanied by her husband Lloyd, was the first to report the affair to authorities.

As it stands, winged supernatural specters have haunted Texas in the past. The oldest known one was the Texas "Death Bird" of the Old West, considered to be a harbinger of doom or impending death, similar to how Mothman was thought to foreshadow the Silver Bridge collapse in West Virginia. Actually, years before Mothman debuted, Texas had a similar winged fiend code-named the Bat Man sighted in Brownsville in mid-June of 1953. Brownsville was perhaps not coincidentally the setting of a significant "Big Bird" sighting by one Alverco Guajardo in 1976. Guajardo described his "Big Bird" as being otherworldly looking and having red eyes. In the case of the 1953 sighting, the witnesses comprised of the Walker family and some friends out visiting on their front porch at 2:30 in the morning. Hilda Walker saw it first, describing it as looking like the figure of a giant moth. Later, all the witnesses concurred they had seen a humanoid figure with wings perched in a tree. Stranger yet, the figure had a luminous, otherworldly aura about it. (Though I didn't mention it, a glowing aura was associated with the Tlahuelpuchi as well.) For half a minute, they observed the strange being, which eventually shot into the sky without flapping its wings. Was it perhaps a Lechuza?

More recently in Mexico was reported what might be another related entity. Four schoolteachers were driving down a lonely road outside of La Rumorosa in December of 2020 when they sighted a gigantic bird-like creature fly around their vehicle. The creature was definitely humanoid, not only with a body the height of a man but with a human-like face also. There was no beak, but it did possess feathers and clawed feet. The highly publicized sighting encouraged others to step forward, creating what was dubbed the *Hombre Pájaro*, or Bird Man. Stalin Valle Osuna, a paranormal researcher based out of Mexicali, thought that the bird man might be a creation of black magic. He also theorized it was an energy being that fed off the rocks in the desert. This would explain why the creature could emit light from its body, he said. Going back to Osuna's comments on black magic, the Lechuza would be a good candidate for the Hombre Pájaro.

In Janet Smith Kromer's "Witchcraft in Ranchos de Albuquerque," submitted on July 8, 1938, an account was included that sounded tangent to the Lechuza: "I think [the witch] turns into a bird at night... If you hear a bird crying like a baby at midnight, that is a [witch]." The same informant also warned that these bird witches were known to bite and make people sick. The man said the bite would be tiny, like a mosquito bite and only appear later. He then launched into an alteration of the popular Juan account, stating that if you didn't have a Juan of your own to at least borrow the coat or shirt of a man named Juan and turn it inside out. Then draw the circle in your house, summon the bird witch, somehow get it into your oven, roast it alive, and the witch in human form would die elsewhere from the burns.

With so many sightings in neighboring territories—namely Texas and Mexico—it seems rather strange that New Mexico doesn't have more stories about La Lechuza. However, that could simply be because almost all witches in New Mexico could be considered "owl witches" in one way or another...

Section Notes

[1] Opler, *Apache Odyssey*, p.62.

[2] Mark A. Hall, noted cryptozoologist and author of *Thunderbirds: America's Living Legends of Giant Birds*, believes the creatures are real animals as opposed to witches, possibly in the form of the thought to be extinct *Ornimegalonyx oteroi*, a three-foot-tall owl that lived in Cuba up 8,000 years ago.

[3] Whistling after dark is considered a superstitious no-no among many cultures though, and isn't unique to the Lechuza.

[4] Specifically, it was the prayer where the Virgin Mary was praising the power of God and is therefore also known as the Canticle of Mary.

[5] Garcia, *Brujerías*, p.67.

[6] Isaiah 34: "There shall the Lilith repose, and find for herself a place to rest. There the hoot owl shall nest and lay eggs, hatch them out and gather them in her shadow…" One Bible translation even switched "owl" for "vampire". How interesting that Lillith, the first female demon, witch, or succubi—take your choice—was associated with both owls and vampires. (Succubi, by the way, were also said to occasionally have clawed, bird-like feet.)

[7] The Greeks had a very similar female vampire called the Lamia. It had a penchant for preying exclusively on children at night, and like the Tlahuelpuchi, also liked to transform into birds. Having the body of a crow most of the time, it was later incorporated into Roman mythology as a strix, a blood drinking nocturnal bird.

[8] Mayor, *Fossil Legends of the First Americans*, p.196.

[9] There can also be male Tlahuelpuchi but they are very rare.

[10] Actually, that's perhaps more of a practical interpretation of the act. Folklore says that they do this because by removing their legs and losing the ability to walk upright, they lose what makes them human— perhaps drawing a parallel to the serpent in the garden forced to crawl upon its belly after tempting Adam and Eve.

[11] All that said, the only reported executions of a Tlahuelpuchi that we know of didn't utilize any of these methods and consisted of the accused witch being stoned or clubbed to death like a normal human being. Afterward, their corpse was tossed into a ravine. Alternate reports indicate that other accused Tlahuelpuchis were lynched, and their fingers and other sensory organs were cut off after death. The body would then be buried somewhere far away from the village. According to Mexico Unexplained, "many women in Tlaxcala have been killed for being suspected Tlahuelpuchis." The last known execution of a tlahuelpuchi occurred in 1973.

[12] Padilla, "Crypto New Mexico," *Cryptozoology*, p.108.

Part III
Sorcery After Statehood

Even in the time of statehood, New Mexico still had her witches. Though New Mexico Territory had long been neglected by the U.S. government, as evidenced by the Nambé witch trials of the mid-19th century, by the onset of the 20th century, the federal government began to feel pressure to cease the area's barbaric ways. The number of witches executed at the pueblos went down drastically, and those that did happen may have been kept secret. The witch-plagued village of Nambé, for instance, had shrunk to a population of only 88 people by the 20th century, it is thought, due to fear of witchcraft.

The stories of witchcraft in the 20th century could be considered of particular interest because they can't be brushed off as folktales. Notably, many of them exist as factual newspaper accounts, such as the infamous case of the "Frog Man" of Mora County. The story became a mini sensation when the news broke that an accused brujo had turned himself into a frog and attacked his wife and her cousin. That isn't to say, of course, that the man really did turn into a frog, but he did get taken to court over the matter in the early 1940s.

The next decade, the *Albuquerque Journal* of June 8, 1955, reported that in Las Cruces, the police answered a call from a hysterical woman who feared she had been targeted by a witch. As proof, she pointed to a pile of sulfur on the doorstep of her apartment. Along with it was a burnt match pointing towards the door, plus two packets of needles with one needle laid across the rest to make an "X." This had been preceded by an incident involving the woman's former business partner, who threatened to hex her and had used a white powder to form a cross on the ground. A week after that happened, an unknown attacker broke into her apartment and beat her. Though the police swept away the hex material, the woman chose not to sleep in her apartment that night.

Many years later, while writing their book *Medicine Women, Curanderas, and Woman Doctors,* the authors interviewed Las Vegas physician Eileen Lujan, M.D. Lujan told the authors that she still received numerous calls asking her to treat ailments caused by witchcraft into the 1980s, proving that even nearing the end of the 20th century, belief in witchcraft was still as strong as ever.

THE WITCH AND THE HELLHOUND

New Mexicans also believe that a witch may take the form of a black dog. A black dog, however, may represent the Devil or some other evil spirit. A certain woman in Santa Fe was often beaten in her bed by a black dog that no one but herself could see. This was supposed to be a witch; and her neighbors say that it was a witch, the wife of a man with whom the woman who was beaten had had illicit relations.—Aurelio Espinosa, "New Mexican-Spanish Folk-Lore."[1]

Admittedly, the following tale is a pastiche written by folklorist Lorin W. Brown based upon the real exploits of his grandmother, Doña Juanita Montoya de Martínez, a curandera in Taos County. It's unknown when this story would have taken place, but Brown was born in 1900, and in his youth accompanied his grandmother around Taos and heard many fantastic stories. Though fictionalized to some degree, this story still has kernels of truth in it somewhere, and so shall still be recounted.

The tale involved a man named Guillermo, who, in his youth, had been flirtatious with two cousins, Ignacita and Gertrudes. Ultimately, he chose Ignacita, and Gertrudes was embittered about it from then on. Many years later, Guillermo visited Gertrudes as an old friend and made the mistake of drinking a cup of wine given to him. From that day forward, Guillermo became paranoid toward his friends and family, especially his wife. Fearing he had been bewitched by her jealous cousin, Ignacita sought out Doña Juanita, who told her she had heard that Gertrudes and her mother alike were brujas who had sold their souls to the Devil long ago. Doña Juanita advised Ignacita to take her husband to a curandero in Española right away, but Guillermo could not be persuaded. Soon he was bedridden, and, odder yet, a big black dog with green eyes began hanging around their home at odd hours, trying to get inside. It was unceasing, always returning once it had been driven away. Brown related, in the alleged words of his grandmother, "And what an ugly dog, black with ugly green eyes! I know because I saw it more than once, *Madre de Dios*, I have dreamed of its devilish green eyes many times since."[2]

As Guillermo's condition worsened, Ignacia forced him to go to a witch doctor in another village. At the house, the witchdoctor told Ignacita he would mail her a special medicine with instructions to heal Guillermo. As the couple left the man's house, they saw the same black dog slinking around as though it was spying on them. Ignacia crossed herself and decided that when she got home, she would task her brother with shooting the animal. Ominously, when they returned home, the dog had beaten them there. "How could it have come so soon unless it was one of the devil's own, and the form which the bruja took when she was on her wicked errands?" Doña Juanita mused.[3]

The Spanish and the Mexican peoples have their own version of the hellhound called the Cadejo. Sometimes these spectral black dogs are incorporeal visitors from the spirit world that might whisk you away to Hell, while other times they are evil physically incarnated in the flesh. However, unlike other parts of the world, the Mexican people also believe in a heavenly hound from above called the White Cadejo which will sometimes fight and kill its opposite number in black.

A few days later, the medicine was intercepted at the post office by the hellish black dog, which snatched away the package and absconded with it to parts unknown. Then, every night, the black dog would sit outside Guillermo's window and howl from midnight until the first rooster crowed. Unable to rest or get the medicine he needed, Guillermo died. But the story wasn't over.

At Guillermo's wake, the big black dog burst into the room in front of the horrified mourners. According to Doña Juanita, they had just finished praying the rosary, and everything was silent when "a black shape came in through the back door which was open. It trotted over to the coffin and, raising its forepaws to the side of the coffin, looked in at the corpse."[4] Then, the dog smiled "a wicked smile as I have never seen before and I hope to never see again."[5]

Was this dog one of the hellhounds of legend? As it stands, the conclusion of the story bears a slight resemblance to the best-known hellhound story of all time, that of Black Shuck. Black Shuck made his debut during a strange thunderstorm in Suffolk on August 4, 1577. The hellish hound burst through the doors of a church, ran down the aisle, and killed a man and a boy. Where his paws had tread seemed to be burnt as if by fire. Though Brown's story is by no means as fantastic, the similarities of a black dog disrupting a religious ceremony are there all the same. And, though it was mostly assumed that the dog was Gertrudes in

animal form, Doña Juanita wondered if the dog was a servant of Gertrudes rather than the witch herself. Could the witch have had a pet Cadejo, mentioned in the photo caption earlier? Though I couldn't find any New Mexico Cadejo tales, I did find one story of a witch summoning a Cadejo to do her bidding in Mexico, so perhaps it was the same case in this story.

DON LEANDRO AND THE BLACK CAT

Very similar to the tale of Guillermo and the Black Dog was the tale of Don Leandro and the Black Cat in La Manga. Don Leandro was very ill, near death, and the cause was thought to be a mysterious black cat that entered the house at midnight. Whenever Don Leandro's family tried to catch the bewitched feline, it would escape. Finally, someone carved a cross onto a rifle—which is unique considering usually the cross was carved onto the bullets—and shot the cat. The next morning, the witch next door was found dead of a gunshot wound. As for Don Leandro, he made a not-so-mysterious recovery.

The Witch Serafina

Like all little New Mexico villages, Tajique, located smack dab in the middle of the state, had theirs as well. The bruja was written about in 1940 by Wesley R. Hurt Jr. in an issue of *El Palacio*. Since she had been active in recent years, Hurt changed her name to Serafina. The old witch was said to be fat and possessed an unfortunate mustache. Residents whispered that she created monos of certain villagers out of rags. Like a voodoo doll, she would stick the monos with pins to inflict sickness.

The most interesting story of her exploits was told to Hurt by the son of a woman afflicted by Serafina. She was suffering a mysterious illness and had Serafina brought before the local alcalde. As witness, a woman came in who claimed to have snooped around Serafina's abode one day while she was away. A curious pile of old rags caught her eye. Thinking the rags must be concealing something, she removed them and found a large rock with a cross atop it. (This in itself was strange, as witches usually abhorred crosses.[6]) She removed the rock and, to her horror, found a "mass of serpents,"[7] as Hurt put it. These serpents, if they existed at all, could have perhaps been used in rituals like the one spoken of in folktales involving goats and snakes.[8] (It should also be noted that many Pueblo Indians kept what were called sacred snakes, usually rattlesnakes.)

The woman promptly placed the rock back over the snake hole and fled. She also told of another instance where she had accompanied Serafina to Manzano Lake. There, for reasons not explained, Serafina transformed herself into a dog, began barking, and then ran away on all fours. As no hard evidence was presented against Serafina, she was let go, and no charges were filed. According to area lore, in 1926, Serafina was captured by a group of nuns who took her away to their convent and burned her alive!

A Witch at Sky City

"Sky City" atop Acoma Mesa is the oldest continually inhabited village in North America—it also suffered an alleged witchcraft epidemic in the early 20th century. Like the old story of Nambé with the witch-induced coughing sickness, a whooping cough broke out at Acoma. A witch was suspected when a man could be heard walking the streets late at night, all the while beating a drum that sounded a great deal like a person coughing. Medicine men met swiftly, and erected a special altar on which they placed a *ma-caiyoyo*, a type of rock crystal that they believed gave them second sight. Via the *ma-caiyoyo* they found the witch. Arming themselves with flint knives and bear paws, they journeyed from the mesa to find their witch. Their second sight led them to a horse hitched about three miles away from the pueblo. They recognized it as Bessie, a mare belonging to a boy they knew who was attending the Indian School in Albuquerque. Along with the horse, they found an old man they knew to be a witch.

"Witch Rocks" of Acoma Mesa as photographed by Frederik Monsen.

They seized him and carried him back to the mesa to be dealt with. The medicine men pushed the old man headfirst into a special kiva as the Acomans watched with great interest. The witch transformed into a rat and scurried about the kiva, with the medicine men trying to stamp him out before he could escape. They killed the rat and threw it into the fireplace. The next morning, an Indian agent informed Acoma Pueblo that the boy who had been at school (the one that the horse belonged to) had committed suicide that night by jumping out of the third-story window of his dorm. This confirmed to the Acomans that the boy was the real witch. However, this is also where the story gets a bit confusing considering the Acoma medicine men arrested what appeared to be an older male witch. What was the connection between the old man and the boy? Did the boy possess the old man who was brought to the pueblo as a witch? Or was the old man an accomplice of the younger witch? Perhaps something was lost in translation, but whatever the case, the boy was not allowed burial in the cemetery of San Esteban.

VOODOO DOLL OF VILLANUEVA

Once in Villanueva there was a cursed doll made of hair that had bewitched a man. The doll had been buried under the spot where he parked his truck by an unidentified witch. It was discovered when a folk healer was called in to help the sick man. Somehow the curandero knew that outside, buried in the earth was a cursed object. He dug up a small jar, within which was a very well-made doll with hands, feet, etc., representing an old woman and comprised of a woman's long hair and sewn together with leather shoe-strings. The curandero instructed the afflicted and his friends to burn the doll, and when they did, they discovered a tiny skeleton within it, possibly that of a mouse or a bird. After this, the man was cured.[9]

CORPSE POWDER AT THE DANCE

Though corpse powder is typically associated with skinwalkers, at least one report from the FWP found mention of Spanish witches using corpse powder. In Janet Smith Kromer's "Witchcraft in Ranchos de Albuquerque," submitted on July 8, 1938, an episode was recounted where several Mexican men described an incident at a dance the previous evening. There two women got into a fight, and one tried to spray the other with a strange powder. "My godmother—she know that powder made from the bones of dead people," the man said. These men also claimed this woman "had the devil on her back" because her varicose veins seemed to resemble the devil!

MONTEZUMA'S GHOST, BEWITCHED SAND, AND OTHER HAUNTED TREASURES OF PECOS PUEBLO

Amongst lost treasure lore, there is a strange subset pertaining to magic and witchcraft. For instance, one way of using magic to guard one's treasure was to murder a man at the spot of the treasure so that his ghost would guard it. Or, if not murdered there, a man who died at the spot of the treasure might become its guardian ghost and so on. That's why some treasure hunters, including Mormon founder Joseph Smith, would sometimes make blood offerings at alleged treasure sites to appease the treasure guardian. As discussed in earlier portions of this book, ghosts were a very touchy subject for the Apache and the Navajo. Ghosts were a bit less dramatic for the

Pecos people, though, which is why they didn't appear to fear the treasure guardian of a gold cache near the church of Pecos Pueblo. That treasure guardian was naturally Montezuma.

Just as there were many variations of how Montezuma left Pecos for Mexico, there were also tales to the contrary that he had stayed there and died. In the case of this story, he became a treasure guardian, or what the Spanish called the *patrón*. This particular tale was unearthed by famous folklorist J. Frank Dobie, who heard it from José Vaca, a resident of Pecos in the early 20th century.[10] According to Vaca in *Coronado's Children*, the *patrón* was "the dead man who guards the treasure. All these peoples long time ago who hide great treasure been careful to have *patrón*."[11]

Vaca told Dobie of a Pecos Indian who had been jailed in Las Vegas on a rape charge. As the Pecos Indians' execution method for a rape crime was to strip the accused naked and tie them down over an ant den to be picked clean, the sheriff agreed to let the man get away in the night. Out of gratitude, the Pecos man told the sheriff of Montezuma's lost gold buried under Pecos Church.

In this variation, Montezuma was a half-Spanish half-Pueblo Indian chief who loved the Indian side of his lineage more so than the Spanish. Never mind that the historical Montezuma would have had no Spanish blood in him or live in New Mexico during the rule of the Spanish. And yet, somehow this Montezuma still possessed a great horde of gold like his Aztec namesake. This gold he wished to remain hidden until the Spanish had been driven from the land, similar to the legend of the upside-down tree at Pecos featured earlier in this book. The prisoner told the sheriff that the treasure was the "great secret of all the Indians of the Pecos Country."[12]

The story went that when Montezuma was dying, he instructed his people to dig a big hole next to his pueblo and place his gold down in it. Next, the weakened old chief ordered his people to place him in the hole, so that his ghost could guard the treasure. Or in other words, Montezuma was buried alive with the gold to await death. His last words were that the gold was not to be unearthed until the Spanish had vacated the Indian's land.

The prisoner told the sheriff that if he journeyed to the church at Pecos, off to the side of the road, he should find a distinct white rock. Within the rock he would find a small wooden cross wedged into one of the cracks. This signified the spot of the treasure, which was next to a black rock sitting over a cave. The instructions were to dig beneath the white rock, under which he would find the grave of Montezuma himself. Then, seven feet beneath Montezuma would be the treasure horde. However, the treasure was watched over not only by the great chief's ghost, but by secretive pueblo men as well. If the sheriff were to dig up the gold, he had best go at night with a car ready to speed away with the gold at once.

The sheriff rounded up his friend, José Vaca, and was ready to go dig for the treasure, but the sheriff's wife was too afraid of the treasure curse and begged her husband not to go. Vaca himself searched for the white rock on his own but could never find it, blaming Montezuma's ghost. "I cannot understand this *patrón*," he told Dobie. "I am strong man. [Montezuma] is dead, but he keep me off. I wish I know when he sleep."[13]

Dobie also collected a tale concerning bewitched sand at Pecos Pueblo from Vaca, who told how many years ago his grandfather had bought a piece of land at Pecos from an Indian. "You have here now more wealth than is in the world elsewhere," the Indian told Vaca's grandfather.[14]

When Vaca's grandfather asked what he meant, the Indian took him to the land and began collecting what appeared to be ordinary sand from the creek. They loaded it onto a mule and took it to sell. Inside the sand was $25 worth of gold. After the Indian had moved away as planned, Vaca's grandfather returned to the spot and collected several more bags of sand, loading them onto two burros. However, this time when he went to sell them, no gold was found in the sand whatsoever.

Vaca told Dobie that maybe the Indian "was un brujo [a wizard]. Maybe the sand was *embrujada* [bewitched]."[15] Vaca surmised "I know when the Indian is here the sand has gold. I know when the Indian is gone the gold is all gone too."[16]

Vaca had one more bewitched treasure tale for Dobie. Supposedly a treasure cave was located in the Tecolote Mountains overlooking Pecos Pueblo. Vaca at one point even had the assistance of a Mexican treasure hunter of some note in possession of a special witching rod fashioned from the scapula of some animal. (If you'll recall, the bones of dead animals were quite taboo for some tribes in the territory). A glass knob was fitted to the top of the witching rod, and in it were threaded holes that a screw could be fitted into. But the holes were not for screws, but for either shavings of silver or gold. When either metal was placed into the holes, the witching rod would go to work, pulling in the direction of the treasure—and it had never pulled so hard as in the vicinity of the Tecolote Mountains.[17] Holding the rod transported Vaca into a form of "ecstasy" he claimed.

However, this witching rod never led directly to the treasure and Vaca sought the services of a well-known brujo/fortune teller in Santa Fe named Nicolas. The wizard agreed that Vaca was on the right track and was even willing to invest in the endeavor himself. However, a short while later, Nicolas located a treasure in an old Santa Fe home "and as a result he at once bought a fine automobile and left the country."[18]

Vaca never did find the treasure, but did find a large white rock that used to have a wooden cross embedded in it in the area, so perhaps the story of Montezuma's grave from earlier had become conflated with this alleged treasure cave.

Old José Vaca did at least have one treasure hunting venture that paid off in the form of a haunted house in Pecos owned by a Frenchman. Strange lights and noises emanated from the home, causing the man to vacate it. He later consulted Vaca and another old Pecos resident, who was too afraid to approach the house and its strange lights. One night Vaca accompanied the Frenchman. He watched and listened as the Frenchman conversed with someone inside, presumably the spirit or patron as it was called, in a language he could not identify as either Spanish, French, or English. The Frenchman came out and told Vaca that they could return the next night to retrieve the treasure. They did, and breaking into one of the adobe walls found $125 in unspecified currency.

PUEBLO WITCHCRAFT IN THE 20TH CENTURY

Zuni Pueblo had always been one of the more notorious hot spots for witchcraft in New Mexico Territory, and this trend continued into the era of statehood. Elsie Clews Parsons collected quite a few accounts of witchcraft from that era which she published in the June 1927 issue of *Man* in her article "Witchcraft Among the Pueblos: Indian or Spanish?" The article related that in 1903 a witch named Philip was accused of sending a horde of grasshoppers to devastate the crops of the Zuni farming community of Nutria. A few years prior to that, the same brujo had bewitched some fruit trees in the region as well. During that same period (exact date not given), there was also a case of shooting sorcery, and the sucking way cure resulted in a caterpillar and a worm being pulled from a man's body, along with candy of all things. (The candy was implanted within him to feed the insects, it was said.)

In 1906, a female witch named Tsatsi was executed. Long suspected of being a witch, the final straw was the discovery of a wolfskin hanging from a beam in her home. The witness noted that the paws were arranged like moccasins "with tie strings in front." In 1917, a young woman who was being courted by two different men died after her father burned one of the suitor's gifts. As such, the suitor was suspected of being a brujo.

Witchcraft was alive and well at Nambé in the early 20th century as well. When a Nambé man died there under somewhat mysterious circumstances (his foot and leg swelled until he died), witchcraft was blamed. A little while before that, according to the man's widow, a bright light had been observed floating through the air and landing at their home. In later years, such a sight would have been lumped in with UFOs, but as they still had not yet come to prominence, a witch in flight was blamed. However, rather than the man being a victim of witchcraft in the traditional sense, others whispered that he himself was a witch. It was thought that the man had himself bewitched someone, and his magic had been turned back against him. According to Parsons in *The Social Organization of the Tewa of New Mexico*, the man's relatives had been accused of causing an epidemic sometime in the past as well. Supposedly they were "caught making dolls, packing their stomachs with chili seeds, dirt, and rags to make the people cough." And, as with other witches, it was said that they transformed into "cats and dogs to go to their nefarious factory where they retransformed into human beings. They also boiled the flesh of the children they had killed after exhuming them from their graves."[19]

THE BOOTLEGGING BRUJA

In Albuquerque, during the prohibition, there was even a bruja who served liquor named Doña Luisa. Actually, that she was a bootlegger was fairly common knowledge; that she was a witch was only whispered. Two men went to her home to procure some liquor, and as Doña Luisa went to the basement to get it, they secretly followed her. In the basement, they were shocked to see witchcraft paraphernalia of all kinds, including strange herbs and monos, the distinctive New Mexico variety of voodoo dolls. Doña Luisa caught the men and was furious. She told them if they ever revealed to a single soul that she was a witch, they would pay a price. Years later, one of the men, identified as Pedro, was sitting around a campfire listening to his compatriots belt out tall tales as men around campfires did. Wanting to one-up them with the truth, he told of his encounter with Doña Luisa. He was immediately stricken with an epileptic seizure. He suffered from epilepsy for another three years before he and some friends confronted Doña Luisa and beat her until she agreed to remove the spell. She did, and Pedro never suffered a seizure again.

FELICIA AND THE HALF-WITCH

In the late 1870s, Ojo de La Casa, a rural community near Placitas, received a new family in the area. The mother was named Felicia, and the father Roque, though the children's names have been lost to the sands of time. The family moved into a small one room adobe home at the foot of a mountain on the east end of Las Huertas Canyon. At first, they seemed like any other family aside from Roque making strange midnight forays worthy of gossip. But then, one day, a woman named Maria de Las Angeles Gallegos came to call on Felicia. Hanging behind her door, Maria spied a witch doll that Felicia had failed to hide. Maria hastily departed the home and spread the word. From that moment on, everyone in the vicinity of Placitas knew the newcomers were witches.

No effort was made to drive them away. Locals were too afraid. And so, when their children wanted to play with Felicia's children, they let them. And, when Felicia offered food, outwardly they gladly accepted it and reciprocated with food offerings of their own. But, privately, any food given by Felicia was promptly disposed of for fear that it was bewitched with strange herbs and poison. Eventually, Felicia became wise to this and turned to deception. A neighbor woman named Ignacita had become ill recently. In anger, Felicia called for a neighbor boy to take some bewitched goat's milk to Ignacita. She told the boy to tell Ignacita that his mother had sent it and to drink it at once while it still had warmth. It would cure her, she said, and fearfully the boy obeyed.

Call her a hero or call her a busybody, Maria Gallegos just happened to be watching as the boy left Felicia's home and followed him to Ignacita's. Bursting inside just as Ignacita was about to take the fatal first sip, Maria seized the cursed milk from her hands and threw it into the fireplace. At once, supernatural sounds of hissing and moaning emanated from the fire in addition to a white foam. The white foam rose until it lifted a pot cooking over the fire into the air before setting it back. This process repeated itself several times before the women fled from the house.

Felicia's next target was an old woman named Sarita who lived alone with her little dog. One cold winter night, more than anything, Sarita wished for a warm slice of goat's meat. Lo and behold, a knocking came from her front door. When she opened it, there was a mysterious little girl offering her a plate of goat's meat despite it

271

being the dead of winter. Sarita took the offering, and the girl disappeared. Now more suspicious than ever, and despite her great temptation, she could not bring herself to eat the meat. She also could not bring herself to throw it away and left it out all night. When she awoke the next morning, she found the meat gone and her little dog was dead. Not only was it dead, but it was in an advanced state of decay. It had eaten the bewitched meat in the night. Obviously, this was Felicia's doing and the villagers were more weary of her than ever.

As the years passed, Felicia was said to grow uglier and uglier and bolder in her evil deeds. More and more people complained of mysterious ailments, which they supposed must have come from witch dolls stuck with cactus needles. One person who was not afraid of Felicia was a selfish, temperamental woman named Juanita who had turned most of her friends and family against her. Juanita asked Felicia if she might be her apprentice and she obliged. The original WPA story reported that

> [Felicia] helped her make the many little bags and stuff them with the hair of every different animal and of people, which she must fasten inside her petticoat and wear at all times, to save her from the power of other witches. She taught Julianita how to make and use a witch doll. It, too, was filled with hair from every living thing they could find.[20]

For her next lesson, Felicia was going to teach Juanita to fly, or "go forth into the night like the wind," as she put it. Felicia told Juanita of the usual incantation, that being to hold up her arms and cry out, "I go without God or the Holy Virgin!" Felicia did so, drawing Juanita into the air with her. Not yet flying under her own power, when it came time for Juanita to do the profane chant, she couldn't bring herself to do so, crying instead "I go with God and the Holy Virgin." Juanita dropped to the earth and found herself in a strange place surrounded by cats eyes in the darkness. In the background was an unholy, wailing wind. Juanita then began her long journey back to La Placitas.

But that wasn't the last of Juanita's witchy ways. After some time had passed, she came to call on Felicia again and found that she herself had been bewitched. Over the fall, Felicia had raised an abundant crop of chili. However, none of her neighbors would help her harvest it, and so she had to secure some Indian laborers from San Felipe. Three men had come to harvest her crop under the condition that Felicia would share some of it with them. As Felicia gazed upon the beautiful red chili ristras recently hung on her porch to dry, she could not bring herself to part with them and so paid the Indian men in pees instead. Felicia should have known that many Indians knew witchcraft, and the men formerly under her employ cursed her. Felicia soon began to feel the odd sensation of pees being emptied into her stomach, making her heavy and weighed down. One day, she felt a weight in her stomach so heavy that she surmised a metate, a heavy stone used for grounding corn, had materialized inside of her. She died soon after in the year 1925.

D-21   Chili (Red Pepper) Drying in Front of an Adobe Home

Despite Juanita's reluctance to utter the profane rite and take flight, she still wished to bewitch those around her. She had taken over for Felicia, supplying her friends and neighbors with food that not even the dogs were given to eat. And so, Juanita switched to making wine. Her wine was so irresistible that people drank it in spite of where it came from, "for they had not the power of mind to refuse the clear, purple liquid she sent them," it was said.[21]

Juanita had a daughter named Petra, who eventually fell in love with a young man who was the only heir to his uncle's estate. The uncle, Miguel, owned land and houses in Tecolote, and he was wary of Petra as Juanita's daughter. He sent his nephew away, hoping he would find another girl. In retribution, Juanita prepared a bewitched bowl of pezole, a type of corn dish, for Miguel. Knowing Miguel would not accept it from her, she used an old trick of Felicia's and asked a friend named Teresa to deliver it. Why Teresa agreed to even

273

entertain the offer is unknown, but she set out on her way to deliver the pezole. Eventually, her conscience got the best of her. Juanita had the reputation of a witch. The dish could be dangerous. Teresa decided to try a trick of her own. She made her own dish of pezole and mixed it in with Juanita's and took it back to her. She claimed it was a thank you gift from Miguel, who wanted her to try his pezole.

Juanita ate it and soon became ill. Teresa had been right, and had in turn used the witch's magic against her. Juanita withered away for the next three years until she finally succumbed on San Antonio Day in 1939. The village of Placitas strangely felt sorry for what they called the half-way witch (seeing as she could not bring herself to renounce God) and buried her with every crucifix, rosary, and image of Santo Nino that they could find. "These would protect her from the witches who would otherwise enter her casket and eat her away bit by bit."[22]

THE MORA FROG MAN

"People always said that [the witches] would head for Mora. I don't know why, but Mora was a kind of place where they fulfilled their wishes. Stories floated constantly about the fact that there were many witches in Mora."—
Filimón Montoya, Brujerías: Stories of Witchcraft and the Supernatural in the American Southwest and Beyond[23]

Murphy's Canyon is a tiny mountain community southeast of Mora in the Sangre de Cristo Mountains. Being isolated from modern society, it was perhaps the perfect locale for one of New Mexico's last major tales of witchcraft that sounded almost like a folktale. The Mora region was steeped in folklore and what might be called religious intrigue. For instance, in 1860, a local priest by the name of Father E.M. Avel was murdered when he drank poisoned altar wine. And, the ghost of La Llorona haunted the ditches and streams, naturally. Actually, on the note of water, the village's name is believed to come from a tale that a French trapper found a skeleton in the stream and called the place *L'eau des Morts* (Water of the Dead), which became *Lo de Mora* in Spanish, eventually shortened to Mora.

Well into the 20th century tales of witchcraft persisted there. Enter a man by the name of Avelino Espinoza, who the locals whispered was not only a sorcerer but an immortal one at that. And stranger still, they said he had the ability to transform into a frog.[24] According to some sensationalized newspaper accounts from 1940, he was even called "The Frog Man" by locals, though this may have just been an exaggeration on the part of the newspapers, who loved a weird story

WITCH SCARE STIRS HAMLET

New Mexico Police Quiz 'Frog Man'

Mora, N. M.—(AP)—A witch scare inflamed this little Sangre De Cristo mountain hamlet.

Sporadic fears of the Spanish-speaking folk have reached the courts and state police were ordered to investigate a weird story accusing Evelino Espinosa, known locally as "The Frog Man," of witchcraft.

Crowds of mountain people thronged the courtyard while Espinosa was arraigned. He was held for preliminary hearing January 8 on charges of mayhem. Acquaintances quickly provided him $1,000 bond.

such as this. People in the little community lived in fear of Espinoza, lest they cross him and he turn them into "frogs or donkeys or birds."[25] Whether or not Espinoza actually transformed into a frog, accusations against the man were enough to draw a state police investigation in 1940.

It was said that on Christmas night of 1939, Espinoza began acting strangely around his wife and her cousin, Mrs. Amadeo Sisneros. They claimed he began hexing them by drawing strange signs on the floor by the women's beds. After that, he left, and they locked the door in fear. According to one account, the next morning, the wife saw a frog in her room. She later told the court, "There was a frog in the room, but it disappeared when I called my husband and he entered by another door." However, according to another article, shortly after an argument with his wife, a "few minutes later [Espinoza] disappeared and a frog appeared. And the frog was so very angry that it bit [Mrs. Espinoza]."[26] Mrs. Espinoza went to the authorities and showed them scratches and bruises along her body that she claimed came from the attack. So, too, did her cousin, who appeared battered and was missing two teeth from the attack.

WEIRD WITCH SCARE INFLAMES TOWN IN NEW MEXICO

By January 8th, "Avelino Espinoza, a wizened 95-pounder," was being held for a preliminary hearing for the charges brought against

275

him by his wife and her cousin, with the trial slated to take place on the 11th. An article entitled "State Probes Story of Man Able to Take Form of Frog, Bewitch People," published in the *Boone News Republican* on January 11, 1940, reported the following:

> Superstitious Spanish-American residents of the almost primitive mountain settlement gazed fearfully at the wizened little man, who may be about 60 years old, and gave him a wide berth. They accuse him of having 'bewitched' the villagers seven times in the last six years. Each time, they charge, a murder has followed.

Espinoza, his wife, and a few witnesses from Murphy's Canyon were escorted by the state police to the courthouse in Mora, the county seat, around January 8th. According to the papers, "Crowds of mountain people thronged the courtyard" while Espinoza was arraigned. In front of the Spanish-speaking court, Mrs. Espinoza told of the events of that night and also that her husband conversed with the Devil whenever he pleased. She also claimed that he had put the "evil eye" on her with the promise to turn her into a frog. Ominously, Avelino Espinoza never denied her allegations; he only "smiled blandly through her recital"[27] during the hearing. Likewise, when questioned, Espinoza would not answer and kept the same smile. Present during the proceedings was R.E. Cooper, the Assistant District Attorney, who noted that the wife's fingers were indeed injured. More disturbing was how he described the cousin, Mrs. Sisneros, whose face "looked as if someone had chewed it."[28]

The then-current Mora courthouse built in 1939.

During the trial, the police brought up yet another curious incident from Christmas Day of 1938. On that day, the couple's 19-year-old

276

son had mysteriously died. Before he expired, the young man cried out to his father, "You made me this way. You put witch powders in my candy." However, the papers reported that an autopsy on the youth revealed no traces of poison, though it still didn't say what exactly killed him. Notably, another article described the 19-year-old as being "child-like" in appearance, so perhaps he had pre-existing health conditions that led to an early death. However, that still didn't explain the fact that over the past six years, seven murders had occurred in the mountain region where Espinoza lived. All residents whispered that he was the cause, though, when questioned about these accusations by the State Police, residents were too frightened to come forward.

Though Mrs. Espinoza had brought up charges of "mayhem" and "witchcraft" against her husband, according to Herbert O. Brayer, a former Santa Fe archivist in 1943, "The trial judge changed the charge to 'disorderly conduct' but went ahead and tried the man on his wife's testimony that he had turned into a frog." In other words, it would appear that the judge took the allegation seriously. Espinoza was informed that he would have to produce $1,000 bail immediately or go to jail. To everyone's shock, he produced that exact amount in cash on the spot. "This caused some surprise because Espinoza had been receiving relief for more than a year. Relief authorities were investigating that angle of his case," reported the papers.[29] As it turned out, this money was provided by locals out of fear that Espinoza would bewitch them if they didn't pay his bail! Captain Roy Vermillion of the New Mexico State Police told papers that "residents of the community revealed they have been paying heavy tribute to Espinoza not to bewitch them or their families."[30] Or, in other words, much in the same way that the mob would collect a

277

"protection fee" from businesses, it seemed that Espinoza was doing the same under the agreement not to hex residents. The same article concluded with this statement from Vermillion: "The whole village fears Espinoza. Witchcraft is as rampant there as it ever was centuries ago anywhere in the world."

The trial then ended with Espinoza assuring his wife he would not turn her nor himself into a frog and the couple returned to Murphy's Canyon.[31] Though there is likely more to the story, that is where it ends. When, or even if, Espinoza eventually died is a mystery...

THE "HEX MURDERS" OF FARMINGTON

Just a few years after the Mora County Frog Man trial, a much more macabre example of witchcraft-related hysteria occurred in the Farmington region. Because it involved a young boy who appeared to be suffering from tuberculosis, the story has some similarities to the famous Exeter, Rhode Island, vampire case of 1892. In that instance, people dying of consumption were thought to be the victims of vampires. No one was killed in that case, as dead bodies were exhumed to check for signs of vampirism and folk cures were implemented (unsuccessfully) from remnants of the dead.

At Farmington in 1942, the young son of Custer Badoni was suffering an ailment now thought to be tuberculosis. However, at the time, Badoni had consulted a mystic known for dealing peyote from Huerfano to ask her who had bewitched his son. The woman named the daughter of a man called Grey Horse and her husband as

278

those who had bewitched Badoni's son. A bit later, Badoni was home with his son while his wife was away at a Squaw Dance and the boy died. Badoni went off and decided to kill the accused witch family of Grey Horse and grabbed a pistol.

On September 18, 1942, the *Farmington Times Hustler* summarized the account thusly in their article "Custer Badoni Slays Three Navajos, Then Shoots Self Monday on Fruitland Project":

Grim tragedy stalked the old farming section of Navajo Indians on the lower Fruitland Project west of Farmington early Monday morning when a "hex" murderer took the lives of a young Navajo man and wife, and fatally wounded an elderly Navajo man, then blew off the top of his own head.

During the dance, Badoni marched to the home of Grey Horse's daughter at two in the morning and barged into the couple's bedroom, fatally shooting both. (According to Clyde Kluckhohn in *Navaho Witchcraft*, all the names were changed in the article, which identified the murdered couple as Mr. and Mrs. George Nice.) Afterward, Badoni went to the home of Gray Horse, spoke to him for a while, and then shot him. After that, Badoni wandered to a tent out in the wilderness and shot himself in the head.

The article reported that before the death of the son that night, two of Badoni's other children had died previously, though it didn't specify if for certain they also perished of tuberculosis. It also revealed that the Nices didn't die immediately and lived long enough to tell Mrs. Nice's sister that they had been shot by Badoni. It was also revealed that Mrs. Nice was expecting a baby herself at the time. The article concluded by stating "Navajo Indian police are working on the hexing angle of the case."[32]

The tragedy left several mysteries and unanswered questions in its wake. Did the mystic from Huerfano, herself an accused witch, manipulate the situation to some evil end, pinpointing the Nices as the hexers for some reason? Did the Nices actually bewitch the children of Badoni? Or was it all a tragic example of tuberculosis being blamed on black magic? As it stands, even the 1892 Rhode Island case was considered sensational in that people at the close of the 19th century would believe in such things. Perhaps because it didn't involve any talk of vampires, this case never generated the same sensationalism that the Exeter case did, but it was certainly more tragic.

CAVE OF THE SNAKE PEOPLE

Guadalupe Peak, c.1940.

(National Parks Service)

Hidden away in a bewitched cave in the Guadalupe Mountains, which span lower southeastern New Mexico and western Texas, is said to live a giant rattlesnake in association with a sinister tribe known as the Snake People.[33] Similar to the skinwalkers feared by the Navajo, the Snake People possess a powerful, dark medicine, and many Native Americans are reluctant to speak of them. Supposedly these Snake People could even breed with rattlesnakes and turn themselves into snakes.

Mescalero Apache often talked of sheep mysteriously disappearing in the vicinity of the Guadalupes, while other sheep found dead had so much rattlesnake venom in their systems that their insides were nearly dissolved. One Apache man in the1940s was working with two other sheepherders when a large rattlesnake slithered into their camp. He told his comrades it was a warning from the Snake People to move their herd elsewhere. They only laughed at him and killed the snake. Two weeks later, they were dead by snakebite.

An Apache man identified as Mahlan told author Earl Murray a unique tale of the Snake People for his book *Ghosts of the Old West*. In 1982, Mahlan was going to visit his sister, who had married a rancher in Dog Canyon.[34] While exiting his vehicle to open the gate to his in-law's property, he claimed to see two huge, viper-like eyes illuminated in the darkness of night. From the illumination of the eyes, he could also make out a fork-like tongue darting from a huge mouth. He didn't just see the creature; he could also smell something that reminded him of a viper den. As if it were merely a vision, it eventually disappeared. When the man told his sister of the encounter, she admitted that she knew that the cave of the Snake People was nearby. To keep her family safe, she offered up their livestock to the Snake People on various occasions. She claimed that their grandfather had taken her to the opening of the evil cave when she was a girl and told her to be careful of the area. She saw no snakes, only a dark bottomless pit. When she tossed a rock into it, she heard what sounded like the buzzing of a thousand rattlesnakes, while an alternate account stated that the woman was forced to witness one of the sacrifices to the giant snake.

Mahlan's sister also told him that back in the 1940s, tales of the Snake People and their dark powers reached the government, which sent two anthropologists to investigate. The two men were lowered into the cave where the mysterious tribe supposedly still practiced via ropes operated by several ranchers and cowhands. The men above heard a great deal of screaming coming from below, as well as loud buzzing rattles, and tried to hoist the men back up. Only one of the men was pulled back out that day. He was dead and had an extremely high amount of rattlesnake venom in his system. One version of the story said his entire torso was in the process of being dissolved it had so much venom in it. The story concluded weeks later when the government sealed up the entrance to the cave with several tons of rock. Two weeks later, a new entrance was clearly visible, with the appearance that something pushed its way out from the cave.

THE GHOST OF DOÑA LETICIA

This story, recounted by Alberto Serano in *Adobe Angels: Ghost Stories of O'Keeffe Country* by Antonio R. Garcez, took place in a little village three miles northeast of Santa Fe in the mid-1950s. The narrator was a young man at the time, and his family had inherited the home from his grandfather. At the age of 15, Alberto was warned to be wary of their neighbor to the east, Doña Leticia, as she was a witch. Doña Leticia was adept at casting the evil eye, but most of the time to work her magic, she did so by use of a mysterious accursed animal that she kept in a wooden box. Serano related that she "fed the animal a concoction of herbs, threads from an intended victim's clothes or strands of hair, and drops of her own blood."[35]

Not long after hearing of the witch, Doña Leticia suffered an accident and died when her cart tipped over on the way to Albuquerque. The accident broke her back and she died a day later. Her home was subsequently sold to the Serano family at a reduced price. As they went through it, Alberto found the mysterious wooden box hidden beneath a floorboard. He said that it was so old that a faded green patina had covered it. Inside, the box was lined with red cloth. On it he found the tiny animal, which he described as a "black, coiled shriveled worm."[36]

Alberto showed the creature to his mother, who reacted by crossing herself in fear and instructing him to take it outside. Alberto and his father gathered some wood for a fire and placed the box and the creature it contained within the flames. Though it didn't pop or explode in some dramatic way, Serano noted that he "watched the passion of the fire consume the green box and its twisted, black contents."[37]

Afterward, the house became haunted. Wanting to see a return on their investment, the Seranos began renting the house. The first couple to live there complained of horrible nightmares and so they left. One night, Alberto and some relatives heard the cries of a baby coming from somewhere within the home. Alberto walked down the hall to find the source of the noise and encountered three monstrous shadows, which he described as "three, tall, cat-like creatures" that were standing upright. As he came closer, the shadows glided across the wall and began to argue in the voices of women.

When Alberto told his father of the incident, he decided to spend the night in the home with two other men. Later, Alberto was awakened by the sounds of his father and the three men returning home. They couldn't stand to stay in the house either after their own ghostly encounter with the witch.

According to Alberto's father, they heard what they assumed to be a large dog scratching at the front door. When he went to investigate, he saw nothing and so opened the door. At that moment, "something streaked into the house,"[38] and the three men glimpsed a "flash of black"[39] dart through the hall towards the bedroom. In the bedroom, the shadowy figure of a woman materialized and yelled at them to leave her house while a cold wind blew upon them. After that night, the family only went inside the home in the daylight hours. They still attempted to rent the home, but always the renters complained of ghostly happenings. A medicine man from San Juan was called to perform a blessing ceremony on the home. Not long after, the Seranos sold the home to the highway department, which bulldozed it to the ground.

Apparently the witch may still haunt the neighborhood in some way. In the early 1990s Alberto returned to his old neighborhood and spotted a big, black raven perched atop a boulder. It cawed at him several times and flew away. "I know it was just that old witch letting me know she's still around—to this very day!" he told Garcez.[40]

282

RANCH OF THE WITCHES

Ghost Ranch as depicted in an old postcard.

Since the 1940's, the 21,000 acre Ghost Ranch has been synonymous with beloved artist Georgia O'Keeffe. However, most people don't know that not only is Ghost Ranch within the vicinity of Abiquiú but that the name of the ranch was originally translated as Ranch of the Witches. (The old Spanish name of the ranch was literally *Rancho de los Brujos.*) But, just as ghosts are synonymous with witches for some, Ranch of the Witches became anglicized to become Ghost Ranch.

It was called Ranch of the Witches not because of its proximity to Abiquiú but because of stealthy cattle rustlers and a murderous pair of brothers. The unnamed rustlers were so good at what they did in the early days that area residents thought them to be phantoms. It was said that when they herded their stolen cattle into the box canyon at the ranch, no one dared to venture into it to find them. Tales abounded of witch balls of fire, ghost horses, and the sounds of phantom gunfights constantly echoing from the canyon walls.

The ranch may have hosted a pair of serial killers in the form of the Archuleta brothers, who settled the area in the late 1800s. As their homestead was the lone source of shelter and water for a great distance, travelers would often ask to stay the night. The Archuletas would kindly oblige and then murder them in the night, taking their possessions for their own, or so the stories go. Others say that the Archuletas purposely led people on to believe that their ranch was haunted to keep people away and went so far as to hang dummies from trees. Eventually, one brother killed the other over a gold dispute. After this, locals rode to the ranch to reclaim it by hanging the remaining brother. A bit later, in 1928, the name was changed from Ranch of the Witches to Ghost Ranch.

Truthfully, there aren't a lot of witchcraft tales at Ghost Ranch, and it's more tangent to the tales of Pecos Pueblo, as it, too, allegedly harbored a titanic serpent. Actually, the ranch hosted several monsters. In later years, an unnamed daughter of one of the deceased Archuleta brothers claimed to have seen six-foot-tall sasquatch-like creatures at the ranch in her youth. They were covered in red hair and would literally crawl out of the sand as they emitted screams that sounded like children in pain, which is why she called them Earth Babies. Her father claimed to see a flying cow with wings which was a witch in disguise as well.

However, the most famous monster is still the 30-foot snake of Huerfano Mesa, a sacred spot for the Navajo. Within the tunnels of the mountain was the demonic rattlesnake called Vivaron. Every night at sunset, it would emerge from the tunnels to hunt for children to eat. Maybe it was the Pecos Pueblo rattler relocated?

Perhaps not coincidentally, Ghost Ranch is also the spot of several unique fossil finds. In 2016, a distant relative of the modern-day crocodile, a species of *rauisuchid*, was found and given the name of Vivaron in honor of the Ghost Ranch's ghost snake. The Guinness World Records even made Vivaron the world's 'Oldest Ghost' after the discovery. Though I can find no specific ghost snake stories from the region, according to cryptidz.fandom's entry on the creature: "Throughout the years, people have reported seeing a strange, snake-like apparition in Ghost Ranch."[41]

EVE BALL AND THE BRUJO?

There was perhaps no more respected historian in the Ruidoso region than Eve Ball. Born in 1890, as an adult, she moved to the mountain village of Ruidoso in southeastern New Mexico where she worked as a teacher. In the 1940s, she began collecting the history of the Mescalero Apache at a time when the tribe was shown little academic interest. As such, much of her work serves as a primary source for academic material on the Apache to this day. Her sources were firsthand, and the most famous was undoubtedly Asa Daklugie, nephew of Geronimo and son of Juh. Some even whispered that Daklugie was a powerful witch.

In addition to being accused of witchcraft, Daklugie also told a story from his youth about he and a friend of his being on the run trying to escape witchcraft themselves. One night, in the wilderness, he heard the ominous hooting of an owl but could not place its location. He told Ball he was fearful of falling asleep, for he felt the owl was hunting him and if he slept it would work its spell on him. "Suddenly I realized that something—something big—was sitting beside me, and that it was dark and menacing," he recalled.[42] Daklugie's companion sensed it too, and both young men packed up their camp as quickly as they could and rode off into the night, in the opposite direction of the owl. (Daklugie noted that owls were often harbingers of ghosts and spirits, so rather than a witch in owl form, Daklugie implied the unseen presence he felt was likely a ghost heralded by the owl.)

Before going any further, it should be reiterated that in the Apache culture there is a thin line between one being a medicine man and a witch, as both use the Power, an invisible spiritual force that guides individuals and sometimes gives them unique abilities.

As Eugene Chihuahua explained it to Ball,

Witchcraft is just the wrong use of Power. Like a gun or knife, it can do good or harm. I know that there are witches. People are afraid to oppose them, so they become dictators. They dominate everybody—except White Eyes. If they could do that there wouldn't be any White Eyes.[43]

Though Chihuahua was a distinguished member of the tribe, of all of Ball's interview subjects, Daklugie was her favorite. He was also the most cantankerous and difficult of the bunch, as he had an extreme dislike of the "White Eyes."[44] Even some of Daklugie's own people were fearful of him, claiming he was more than a medicine man; he was a witch.

This rumor was whispered often. What gave it away, according to an Apache who worked for Ball from time to time, was the fact that Daklugie would never look into a mirror. There was a large mirror in Ball's living room, and Ball noticed that Daklugie was always careful to sit with his back to it. Nor would he ever look into a mirror under any circumstances. Ball's Apache friend told her, "That man's a witch. He can witch people just by looking at them. No witch will see himself in a mirror."[45]

Asa Daklugie (right) acting as translator for Geronimo (middle) in talking to Steven Melvil (left) c.1906.

Ball took note herself once of how well-behaved Apache children were around Daklugie in particular. She asked him how he kept the children so well-behaved, and he answered simply, "I just tell them what to do and they do it."

Ball wrote, "I was to learn that almost all of the Apaches followed suit when he spoke. I did not know at that time that part of their subservience was owing to their firm conviction that Daklugie was a witch."[46]

UFOs or Witches in Flight?

As times change, so too does folklore. Whereas in the early days people thought of fireballs solely as witches in flight, by the beginning of the space age, they began to think of them as UFOs. In his book *Treasure of the Sangre de Cristos: Tales and Traditions of the Spanish Southwest*, author Arthur L. Campa wrote,

Another natural phenomenon forming the source from which legends grow may be seen in the fireballs of the Sandias. Old-timers who live in the Rio Grande Valley near Albuquerque often speak of the lights they have seen floating down from these mountains east of the city and disappearing over the extinct volcanoes west of the river.[47]

286

Along the Albuquerque region's Rim Road, a motorist claimed to have almost been forced off the road by what he first took to be the headlights of an approaching car. Just as the man came upon a sharp curve, the lights suddenly swerved and bounced into the canyon wall and vanished.

An earlier sighting of a bouncing orb of light was recorded by Mr. Ben Baca of an Albuquerque suburb known at one time as Martinez Town. Baca was out hunting along the mesas near the Sandias when he noticed a ball of light in the distance. At first he assumed it was a camp of sheepherders, but whenever he thought he was approaching it, the camp would be just as far away as it was before. Finally, Baca realized that the fire was moving. Eventually he got close enough to discern that the ball of light was about the size of a large pumpkin. Since witches often rode pumpkins and balls of light, then it must be a witch. Baca fired at the ball of light and it leaped out of the way. Now he knew it was a witch. Baca took out one of his bullets and etched a cross onto it and fired again. But unlike the folktales of the old days, the ball of fire kept dodging the shots.

Suddenly he heard a voice cry out, "Compadre, compadre!" Baca, relieved to hear the voice of another human being, called out to ask where the person was. He heard no response, only footsteps in the dark. Thoroughly frightened, Baca decided to make haste in returning to Martinez Town. As he did, the voice spoke to him again, and he finally recognized it as that of a long-departed friend. "Don't be alarmed, *compadre*. Just promise me to have a Mass said for the repose of my soul," it said.[48] Baca promised to do so and after that the ghostly orb disappeared over the cemetery on the edge of town.

Arthur Campa had a similar experience himself back in 1917 as a youth walking to a basketball game at Menaul School. "We were about half a mile from Menaul Road on what is now North Fourth Street, when we noticed two yellow lights halfway up the mountainside to the east of the highway," Campa remembered in his book.[49]

Campa's friend thought that the lights were the fires of sheepherders camping for the night. However, as the two youths traveled down the road, shifting their view of the mountains, the lights appeared to be moving. As such, their next thought was that they belonged to the headlights of a truck on one of the mountain roads. Finally, they saw the lights ascend into the air, and they floated to meet them over the Santa Fe railroad tracks. Both young men were terrified and Campa's friend fell to his knees and began to pray. Coincidentally or not, the lights changed direction and flew away and the two youths watched them disappear towards the extinct volcanos to the west of them.

Campas never saw the lights again until 1930, when he was conversing with a man who ran a gas station on North Albuquerque Street. As Campa filled his vehicle late one night, he and the man took note of the bright moon, which seemed to be out awfully late. However, the moon eventually shifted positions to where it was now halfway down the mountain, and the man remarked that it was the second time that the "bright light" had fooled him into thinking it was the moon. As the two men discussed what might cause the strange light, the service station manager said, "I'll betcha that's nothing but a witch from that mountain village of San Antonio. They've got plenty of 'em up there."[50]

Campas concluded his chapter on the ghost lights of the Sandias writing, "Meanwhile, the lights, according to the press, still float over the mesas by the Sandia Mountains and leave people to conjecture about witches on a broomstick, and more recently about flying saucers."

In the late 1940s, the phenomena of the "Green Fireballs" became so widespread, particularly in northern New Mexico, that meteor expert Dr. Lincoln La Paz was called in to investigate. The fireballs didn't behave like meteors and often slowed down or changed course, leading him to believe that they might be extraterrestrial in origin. Or, perhaps they were just witches in flight? Painting of Green Fireball by Mrs. Lincoln La Paz, above.

ROSWELL'S LECHUZA

Our next tale is unusual for two reasons. First, it takes place in modern times, comparatively speaking, and second, it happened in Roswell, the town made famous for UFOs and aliens as opposed to witches. Brought to light in an episode of *Monsters and Mysteries of America,* Octavio Ramos related an encounter that his parents had with the owl witch, La Lechuza, while he was a baby. His parents, Juan and Maria Ramos, emigrated to America from Mexico separately in the 1960s, when they were both in their twenties. As the two worked odd jobs in Roswell, they met, fell in love, and got married.

The couple wasn't plagued with the Lechuza until after the birth of their son Octavio. Like the Tlahuelpuchi witches that preyed on babies and ravaged Mexico around the same time, it is thought that the Lechuza was attracted to the home because of baby Octavio. The first major incident occurred in the Autumn of 1964. As Juan went outside to water some trees on the property, he saw an orange fireball float from his neighbor's home toward his own house. He called Maria to come witness it as well. Apparently not superstitious, Juan thought it may have been a strange meteor of some sort. Every night following, the fireball would swarm about the house as the dogs howled madly outside. But Juan still had to go out and water the trees at night, as it was his job.

While in the barn checking on a generator, he heard a strange commotion. He looked up in the rafters to see about a dozen owls gathered there. A feeling of sheer terror crept over him and he ran back to his house, knowing it was more than just a gathering of owls. As he clutched his gun, he and Maria listened in terror as the owls walked across the roof of their house. Among them sounded to be either a human being or one giant owl on the rooftop. The large being made its way down to one of the shudders, which Maria opened in curiosity. Rather than a giant owl, she saw a ghostly shrieking woman not unlike La Llorona.

Things escalated when Juan was struck with appendicitis either the next day or a few days later while working in the field. As Juan deteriorated night after night, the owl witch seemed to be lurking outside to taunt the family. Maria called for a local curandera to come and help, and the woman speculated one of their enemies was using the owl witch to try and drive them away. Just as in the old days, Juan was instructed to take a bullet and engrave a cross on it. Though weak with his illness, Juan had to be the one to kill it, said the curandera. Juan took his rifle outside, carefully loaded with the special bullet, and waited. Suddenly, he heard a high-pitched scream, and the witch, in fireball form, was racing toward him. He hit the fireball dead on and it disappeared. Upon inspection, blood and feathers were found in the vicinity of the fireball, but neither the body of an owl or a woman was found. As such, Juan had to wonder if he only wounded the witch and it got away. Whether it survived or not, the owl witch never returned to torment them again.

Roswell hosted only one other witchcraft tale that I know of, that being the "Witch of Chihuahuita." Chihuahuita was a small Spanish village that eventually fell into the confines of Roswell as the town grew, making it the oldest historic district in the town. Today, the neighborhood is still called Chihuahuita. Years ago, probably around the 1950s, an old woman suspected of being a witch there broke into one of the churches. Her objective was to steal candle wax, as it was said that voodoo dolls could be made of them. She stole the wax and was attacked and killed by neighborhood dogs on the way home. Chihuahuita was notorious for unleashed dogs running around the neighborhoods, but not very many attacked without provocation. In any case, it was said that the usually peaceable dogs tore the witch to pieces.

THE WHITEWATER "WEREWOLF"

Tales of skinwalkers seen on the roadside late at night in Navajo country are quite common, though many lack specific times, dates, and names. An exception is this account, retrieved from the Gallup *Independent* of January 29, 1970. Earlier that month, a witness identified only as Tony Zecca was driving down a secluded road near Whitewater in the area of Gallup. Though he didn't give any real description, he claimed to have seen "a man from a flying saucer" walking around. (It's important to note here that Zecca never claimed to see a flying saucer, he was apparently just likening the being he saw to an alien due to its odd, undisclosed description.)

A few hours later, a group of four youths comprising of Clifford Heronemus, Bob Davis, Carl Martinez, and David Chiaramonte drove along the same road and saw a being that they described as looking like a werewolf, as back then the term skinwalker wasn't prevalent. (As for other specifics, Heronemus was listed as being a high school junior in the article, though the other three's ages weren't given. Also, the paper stated that the sighting occurred about three weeks prior to the article's publication on January 29th.)

The quartet was on their way to Zuni when they spotted a "kinda hairy thing with two legs" keeping pace with their car, which was traveling at 45 miles an hour. "It was about five feet seven, and I was surprised it could go so fast," Heronemus told the paper. "At first I thought my friends were playing a joke on me, but when I found out they weren't, I was scared!"

Heronemus continued,

> We rolled up the windows real fast and locked the doors of the car. I started driving faster, about 60, but it was hard because that highway had a lot of sharp turns. Someone finally got a gun out and shot it. I know it got hit and fell down, but there was no blood. I know it couldn't be a person because people cannot move that fast.

And with that, the frightening encounter ended and the werewolf ran away for parts unknown. The article continued that Heronemus called the creature "the thing" since he really wasn't sure what it was. The article also specified that the creature that Zecca claimed to have seen was not a werewolf, though he still gave no description of it other than comparing it to an alien.[51]

Is it possible that the story amounts to nothing more than a few youths making up a tall tale? Considering the fact that it took place on the night of the full moon, which is associated with werewolves but not necessarily skinwalkers, it's possible that they did. Werewolves would have been popular at the time via TV broadcasts of old movies like *The Wolf Man*, still shown frequently on television, even if there weren't necessarily any big werewolf films out in 1969/ 1970. However, the beast's speed lines up more so with a skinwalker than a typical werewolf. Skinwalkers were noted to be supernaturally quick, while werewolves might be able to run as fast as a normal wolf or canine, but certainly not 60 miles per hour.

For whatever reason, Heronemus is the only witness quoted of the four young men. His sister, Sherry, was also quoted stating that she thought it was possible that her brother saw a werewolf, even though their parents didn't believe their son's claim. Heronemus went on to state that he and his friends had plans to try and find the creature again:

> They want to track it down, and if it tries to hurt them, shoot at it. "If we keep shooting it it'll keep falling down and we can get away."
> "But everyone is getting kind of scared and I'm sure not going to go out there by myself," Heronemus explained.

Or, failing to shoot the creature, Heronemus thought perhaps they might at least take a photo of it. The paper went on to tease him about bringing along "golden stakes" and "silver bullets" on his excursion. Heronemus ended the article by expressing a fear of the "curses and spells they tell about in the movies."

However, I'm forced to wonder if that last line was just the reporter paraphrasing the witness. (I have myself been carelessly paraphrased by reporters in the past in interesting ways.) As it stands, I don't recall any popular horror films where killing the werewolf incited a curse. Perhaps Heronemus was actually speaking of local skinwalker lore?

Unfortunately there aren't any follow-ups to the story that I could find. If the four youths perpetrated a hoax, surely one of them would have admitted it by now. I found mention of the incident on a Facebook group entitled "If you ever grew up or lived in Gallup, NM you remember when...." A post was created devoted to the incident, and the poster claimed to have spoken with one of the original witnesses though she didn't specify which one and implied that they stuck to their story. Comments then followed—not to mock the story—but to relate Grants area residents' own skinwalker stories they heard and believed from the region.

THE BRUJO OF COLUMBUS

When author Antonio R. Garcez set about to create a definitive tome on *New Mexico Ghost Stories*, which he did in the form of two volumes under that name, he came across more than a few stories telling of the ghosts of witches. One of the more interesting ones came from the Columbus region towards the southern border, which is famous for Pancho Villa's 1916 raid.

The tale was told by Manuel Pantoja, who related the discovery of the ruins of an old home near the Tres Hermanas mountains. The house was said to have belonged to a brujo named El Delgado ("the Skinny Man"), who made a living skinning rattlesnakes. A bit like the witches of Abiquiú, a black raven was said to follow him overhead everywhere he went. At night, El Delgado was followed by a white owl.

His spellcasting abilities were revered on both sides of the border. He did this by use of an enchanted clay doll. What would typically happen was that a potential client would be given a single kernel of corn to place in the doll's mouth. If it appeared to swallow the kernel, then El Delgado would commence with the desired spell. If not, he turned the customer away.

The customer that proved to be El Delgado's undoing was a woman seeking a love spell on a certain man. When this news reached the man's ears via town gossip, he set out to confront El Delgado. The man did so, and El Delgado countered with the threat of a death curse. Later that night, the man heard the white owl clawing about on his roof. Enraged, he returned to the brujo's abode. When the witch threatened him again, the man gathered some brush and set fire to the home. Eventually the roof collapsed, and El Delgado was no more.

Later, as residents combed through the ruins of the house, they were shocked that no remains of El Delgado's body were found. What they did find, though, was many carved wooden effigies that greatly resembled people in the nearby areas. The effigies were destroyed, and the old house was eventually forgotten.

Though it has all the trappings of a folktale, the teller of the tale, Manuel Pantoja, provided photographic evidence, both of the remains of the house and of one of the stone dolls. Pantoja bought the property the ruins resided on in recent years and inspected them out of curiosity when neighbors told him of their history. Pantoja noticed at once the place was the home of many rattlesnakes, which was in line with the history he had heard. Searching the ruins, he found a small stone carved in the shape of a head. (The mouth was closed, so it wasn't the one fed the corn kernels.) Pantoja took it home to show his wife and set it on the kitchen window counter. Oddly, it was always turned in the other direction or had moved in some way whenever he left it alone and returned. Ever since, they have kept it outside of the home and stored it in their old shed.

THE WITCH'S GRAVE

You won't find mention of this witch in any of the older history books on New Mexico, and yet, her history would appear to be ancient. In the form of a strange cinderblock tomb in the middle of Mesilla, the former joint capitol of New Mexico and Arizona alike, lies the grave of an unnamed bruja. Her abode is located at the end of a shady unpaved road called Calle de Lupe is San Albino Cemetery.

The Witch's Grave, photo by Donna Blake Birchell.

Though there are many eye-catching sculptures and statues within the cemetery, the "Witch's Grave" catches the eye easily in the form of a six-foot by six-foot concrete tomb topped with a tall black cross of wrought iron.[52] On the cross, someone has scribbled the Mark of the Beast, 666. Notably, no names or inscriptions are present on the

294

grave. To this day, no records have been found as to who is really buried there, but locals whisper it was a powerful witch from the 1800s. They say she was buried with a large rock placed atop her grave, which in turn was further fortified with concrete so that she could not come back from the dead. As time passed, cracks appeared in the tomb, and locals feared the witch's spirit might be about to escape. Others claimed that rather than her spirit, it was her undead body trying to claw through the concrete.[53] As such, a group of families that live near the cemetery, since dubbed 'the Watchers,' were tasked by the church to keep an eye on the grave and repair it whenever cracks appeared. Some also say that the tomb has grown over the years due to the frequent maintenance to repair the cracks. When some visit the spot, they report cold spots associated with ghosts as well as the sounds of a woman crying in the distance.[54]

One of the newer urban legends went that several years ago, a group of teenagers was cavorting around the graveyard late at night as teenagers do. One of the girls was dared to lay atop the witch's tomb. She did so, but the moment she stood up, she was struck by a violent seizure, and an ambulance had to come and take her away. An alteration of the tale stated that the girl was dared to spend the entire night asleep on the witch's grave and was afflicted with a severe case of epilepsy.

Section Notes

[1] Espinosa, "New-Mexican Spanish Folk-Lore," p.399.

[2] Brown, *Hispano Folklife,* p.77.

[3] Ibid.

[4] Ibid, p.78.

[5] Ibid.

[6] However, the cross could represent the four corners of the wind in some cases. Or, perhaps the cross kept the snakes at bay in this instance, who knows.

[7] Hurt, "Witchcraft in New Mexico," p.77.

[8] In *Tales of Witchcraft and the Supernatural in the Pecos Valley* on pages 65-66, Lala Gallegos told the story of a strange old woman in Villanueva always seen sitting atop a crate. One day, when she dismounted the crate, someone looked inside and saw a bunch of lizards that she "used to inflict her evil doings". Pedro V. Gallegos, also of Villanueva, knew the story of the same witch. He said he heard she skinned the lizards and used the skins to make her powders to bewitch people.

[9] García, *Tales of Witchcraft and the Supernatural in the Pecos Valley,* 71.

[10] Presumably, Dobie collected it in the 1920s or thereabouts, as the book it appears in, *Coronado's Children,* was first published in 1930.

[11] Dobie, *Coronado's Children,* p.205.

[12] Ibid.

[13] Ibid, p.206.

[14] Ibid, p.198.

[15] Ibid, p.199.

[16] Ibid.

[17] They could also be filled with lead or silver, and there were notably four holes for each.

[18] Ibid, p.209.

[19] Parsons, *Social Organization of the Tewa of New Mexico,* p. 67.

[20] Batchen, "Felicia the Bruja," 5-5-31 #2. WPA New Mexico Collection, Fray Angélico Chávez History Library, Santa Fe, New Mexico, U.S.A.

[21] Ibid.

[22] Ibid.

[23] García, *Brujerías,* p.26.

[24] One source gave his first name as Evelino instead.

[25] "But Everything's Alright Now—Sorcerer Arrested for Turning into Frog," *Abilene Reporter News,* January 11, 1940.

[26] In *Medicine Women, Curanderas, and Woman Doctors,* the authors stated on page 183 that, "Frogs have entered rooms and tried to attack sick people." This line appeared in a section of the book dedicated to

the methods of witches and wasn't touched upon again. Presumably, they were either referring to this case or others where frogs attacked people.

[27] "But Everything's Alright Now—Sorcerer Arrested for Turning into Frog," *Abilene Reporter News*, January 11, 1940.

[28] "'Frog Man' Witch Story Scares N.M. Mountaineers," *Cedar Rapids Gazette*, January 1, 1940.

[29] Ibid.

[30] "State Probes Story of Man Able to Take Form of Frog, Bewitch People," *Boone News Republican*, January 11, 1940, p.10.

[31] An alternate account from "State Probes Story of Man Able to Take Form of Frog, Bewitch People" (*Boone News Republican*, January 11, 1940) claimed that Espinoza disappeared for about one week after his wife began making the claims, and only resurfaced after she told him she would not press charges which doesn't seem to gel with accounts of the trial.

[32] This was then followed by a brief article on Navajo witchcraft which covered everything from shooting sorcery to the way of the skinwalker.

[33] Not to be confused with the Shoshone sometimes called the Snake Indians.

[34] Actually, it's W.C. Jameson who cited the location as Dog Canyon in *Legend and Lore of the Guadalupe Mountains*. Murray never gave a place name. Furthermore, Jameson had this story taking place in the 1940s, so there's discrepancies between the two versions.

[35] Garcez, *Adobe Angels*, p.23.

[36] Ibid.

[37] Ibid.

[38] Ibid, p.24.

[39] Ibid, p.25.

[40] Ibid, p.21.

[41] http:cryptidz.fandom.com/wiki/User_blog:DeinonychusDinosaur999/Prehistoric_Phantom

[42] Ball, *Indeh*, p.93.

[43] Ibid, p.64.

[44] Eventually, he came to consider Ball his friend and gifted her with his war club before he died.

[45] Ibid, p.87.

[46] Ibid, p.xx.

[47] Campa, *Treasure of the Sangre de Cristos*, p.155.

[48] Ibid, p.156.

[49] Ibid, p.157.

[50] Ibid, p.159.

[51] Details on Zecca are non-existent apart from his name. If he was the same age as the other four youths, perhaps he heard of their sighting first and decided to make fun of them by claiming that he saw an alien. That's just my conjecture, though. It's also possible that they all drove through what paranormal investigators call a "Window Area" where a wide range of phenomena can be experienced.

[52] Others listed the tomb's dimensions as four foot by four foot.

[53] Similar stories exist in Mexico, as in the case of a vampire buried in Guadalajara.

[54] The book *Spirits of the Border* stated that La Llorona is seen in this same cemetery, though the authors don't connect her to the witch's grave.

Special Section
LA LLORONA, THE DITCH WITCH

La Llorona, aka the Ditch Witch, is unquestionably New Mexico's most famous ghost, and tales of her spectral wandering and wailing span from Texas to California and even down into Mexico. Classically speaking, La Llorona is a woman in white who lures children to bodies of water where she drowns them, just as she was said to do to her own children years ago. If the children are lucky enough to escape, they come back with tales of her wailing cries and ghostly visage, and that's the end of it.

Just as Mexico's Montezuma is whispered to have roots in New Mexico to the north, the reverse is true of the Land of Enchantment's most famous ghost, La Llorona, who may have her origin in Mexico. You may also be asking why a ghost is included in this book. That's because some think that La Llorona is an undead witch in addition to being a ghost. Two of New Mexico's more prominent folklorists have cited the belief that La Llorona is a witch, with Aurelio M. Espinosa stating in his piece "New-Mexican Spanish Folklore" in 1910 that "There are also some who state that the llorona is an infernal spirit wandering through the world, and entering the houses of those who are to be visited by great misfortunes, especially death in the family; and a few say that she is nothing more than an old witch (una vieja bruja)."[1] More recently, Jack Kutz called La Llorona "New Mexico's most famous witch" in his 1988 classic *Mysteries & Miracles of New Mexico*. Even Rudolfo Anaya, one of New Mexico's most respected novelists and folklorists, called La Llorona an "old witch" that cried along the river and sought "the blood of boys and men to drink!" in *Bless Me, Ultima*.[2] So, could La Llorona be the most famous witch of the Southwest, or is she a simple ghost story and nothing more?

Let's begin with her ancient origins. Some have likened her to Lillith, Adam's rebellious first wife from Jewish folklore who was mentioned earlier in relation to La Lechuza and doesn't bear repeating. Also like La Lechuza, some link La Llorona to Cihuacoatl, the Aztec goddess of motherhood. Sometimes Cihuacoatl would stalk the Earth, appearing as a woman in all white. With a crib strapped to her back, she would wander the marketplace until she found an unattended child to steal. Eventually she would disappear, leaving only the crib behind, and in it would be found a type of flint knife used in sacrifices in place of the baby.

299

Statue of La Llorona on an island of Xochimilco, Mexico, 2015.
KatyaMSL – CC BY-SA 4.0

While Cihuacoatl was singled out as a candidate for the inspiration for La Llorona due to her association with motherhood, Robert Barakat also proposed Chalchiuhtliycue, the goddess of waterways and storms, as another possibility. In addition to being the goddess of rivers and other waterways, she, too, was associated with motherhood. Not to be trifled with, she was even the goddess who helped destroy the Fourth World via flood according to Aztec legend.

Some think that either Cihuacoatl or Chalchiuhtliycue embodied themselves at one point to warn the Aztecs of the coming Spaniards. For those unfamiliar with the Spanish Conquest, preceding the arrival of the Spaniards were eight omens spanning everything from fire in the sky to strange creatures. The sixth omen occurred around 1509 when a wailing, weeping woman wandered the streets for several nights, crying out, "My children, it is already too late," or "My children, where can I take you?" All who heard the woman were filled with a deep sense of dread and foreboding. Specifically, Book VIII of the Codex recorded that, "In the days of this same Motecuçoma it happened that the demon Cioacoatl walked about weeping at night in the streets of Mexico. Everyone heard it saying: 'My children, woe is me that I must soon leave you.'"

La Llorona is further linked to Mexico in the form of *La Malinche*, or The Tongue. La Malinche's real name was Doña Marina, and she was from the Tehuantepec region of Mexico. Throughout the Conquest, she served as Hernán Cortés's interpreter and eventually became his mistress, bearing him either one son, Martín Cortés, or possibly two children depending on the source. These children were also significant for possibly being the first *mestizos*, or, in other words, the true progenitor of the Mexican people today, being of Spanish and Aztec parentage. As Robert Bitto put it in an article on Mexico Unexplained, "Martín Cortés was the first publicly acknowledged person of mestizo, or mixed-race, heritage in Mexican history. This is the reason why Marina is sometimes referred to as 'The Mother of Mexico.'"3

Naturally, Cortés was not going to marry his Indian mistress, and when it came time to return to Spain, he left her behind. Some legends stated that Cortés desired to take his son with him, but not La Malinche herself. In her grief, further fueled by the anguish of being rejected by her lover, she killed the child and then herself. Some say she did this by drowning him, and others imply she used a sacrificial flint knife. Whatever the case, afterward she committed suicide. "When her spirit left her body, it cried 'Aaaaayy!' Ever since, her ghost has been

La Malinche.

wandering, and people everywhere hear her cry of pain. People call her La Llorona," wrote John Bierhorst in *The Hungry Woman: Myths and Legends of the Aztec*. In truth, just how La Malinche died is unknown, and where facts are absent, folklore will take its place.

LA MALINCHE AND TLAXCALA

If you know your history of the Conquest, La Malinche helped Cortes to barter an alliance with the kingdom of Tlaxcala, which was at odds with the Aztecs. Tlaxcala, you might also recall, was the home of the vampiric Tlahuelpuchi, which came out during the rainy season to kill children similar to Lillith and La Llorona. How interesting then, that Tlaxcala also plays home to a volcano named La Malinche, and which hosts a reptilian monster. Though not related to the Tlahuelpuchi, this reptile monster has the same attributes of coming down from its volcano lair during the rainy season to abduct children. Is it just coincidence? Who knows, but it's interesting to note the similarities just the same.

Since La Malinche, there have been many, many other candidates for La Llorona. Chances are, she lived in your village if you hailed from one of the tiny mountain settlements in northern New Mexico.

As it is, nearly every village will have its own tale of a woman who drowned her children or lost them to the river by accident.

In *Shadows of the Past*, for instance, Cleofas Jaramillo related that "Each village seemed to have a different version of La Llorona." In Jaramillo's case, in Arroyo Hondo, La Llorona was described as a woman who appeared shrouded in a white mist before growing taller and taller until disappearing from sight, after which only her moans and wailing could be heard. Jaramillo was told that La Llorona lived inside a big black rock located in a meadow behind their home.

Detail from "Carved tree in Arteaga, Coahuila, with La Llorona" Photographed by Gabriel Perez Salazar. CC BY-SA 4.0

Valerio García recounted the idea in *Tales of Witchcraft and the Supernatural in the Pecos Valley* that La Llorona actually originated in Spain rather than Mexico. Instead of being a real witch, she was a wrongfully accused witch burned at the stake in Spain. Because she was innocent, the myth went that her descendants, even those that came to the New World, would hear her wailing cries for years to come. As such, García reckoned that since he never heard her wailing cries himself, he wasn't a descendant of the woman.

That is but one of many variations of La Llorona's appearance and attributes. At her core, she's almost always a wandering spirit haunting the rivers—an old wives' tale to keep children from going too close to the water's edge lest she snatch them in an effort to replace her own children. She can also be used to frighten wayward husbands with wandering eyes. More than a few stories had La Llorona causing men to quit drinking and turn to sobriety. In more recent years, she's even strayed from the waterways to the highways.

Classically, La Llorona is dressed in all white and occasionally even rides a white horse, though in many other variations she is draped in all black instead. In at least one, she is also dressed in yellow, which is interesting since the ghosts of Spanish folklore are always either associated with the colors white, black, or yellow. Usually, La Llorona has the shape and form of a normal woman but sometimes she can be short, like a duende, or unusually tall. One sighting placed her at nine feet in height. In addition to La Llorona herself, a few sightings even tell of her lost children. Whatever deviations exist between the sightings, she always wails and cries. While these traits are mostly ghostly, more than a few stories exist that align the Southwest's most famous specter with witches.

A good example of this is exemplified in a story from the early 1930s in Santa Fe. It told of a state penitentiary guard identified only as Tafoya driving down a lonely road. It was late at night, and he was on his way home when an owl flew in front of his headlights, sailing ahead of the car. Tafoya claimed that either he or his car became bewitched by the owl, and the car seemed to follow the owl all the way to Guadalupe Cemetery. Tafoya parked the car and watched the owl soar over the graveyard and then disappear behind one of the headstones. From behind it arose a wailing woman dressed in all black. She walked through Tafoya's headlights, motioning behind her urgently as though she wished for him to do something. Free of the owl's bewitchment, he put the car in reverse and sped away. When he returned to the cemetery in daylight to look at the tombstone, he discovered it was for a deceased infant. This is but one of a few stories linking La Llorona to owls.[4]

The next such tale came from Mora and was submitted by Margarita Olivas to authors Edward Garcia Kraul and Judith Beatty for their comprehensive work *The Weeping Woman: Encounters with La Llorona*. Olivas told the authors, "My father used to tell me that La Llorona dressed like a witch."[5] She then went on to tell how they owned a meeting house in Mora which owls ominously congregated about.[6] Olivas recollected:

> Owls used to gather on the roof, sometimes ten at a time. My dad used to say they were witches. When they came down from the roof, they turned into women dressed in black. You couldn't see their faces. The leader was dressed in white and she was said to be *La Llorona*.[7]

303

Like other New Mexico witch tales, these brujas could be expelled with a simple religious exclamation of *"Jesus, Maria y Jose!"* and so on. At that, the brujas would jump and vanish into thin air.

La Llorona was heralded by owls yet again in Pojoaque in 1946, where Stephen W. Long and other children saw La Llorona walking along a river and up to a cemetery where her twin boys were rumored to be buried. The full story went that a woman named Enriqueta Gomez y Lujan had a twin pair of boys slain by the Ute Indians of Colorado. The boys were killed near a river in Pojoaque and buried in the cemetery there where she often searched for them.[8]

Like other witches, La Llorona was also occasionally linked to fireballs and glowing orbs of light. Sometime in the 1940s, she was seen throwing balls of fire in Santa Fe towards Camino de Las Animas, which not coincidentally means Street of Spirits. On a warm spring night in Santa Fe in 1945, two men were walking down Romero Street at 11 PM on their way home from the pool hall. As they approached the railroad tracks, a ball of fire suddenly rolled in their direction.[9] Almost immediately, the orb of fire turned into "a bundle wrapped in a patchwork quilt."[10] The bundle came to a stop about 20 feet away, and so they trepidly approached it. Soon they could hear the sound of a baby crying. They unwrapped the quilt to find a frightening apparition. Within was what appeared to be a six-month-old baby; only it had fangs and a gruesome face. In an account from one of the men's relatives, it was written that "It opened its mouth as if to cry, but instead it smiled at them and said, *'Mira, Daddy, tengo dientes*—Look, Daddy, I have teeth.'"[11] The two men ran home in terror, and soon after, one of the men's hair turned snow white. When they told their family the tale, they swore it was the child of La Llorona.

That said, the story was still just a variation of a common Spanish folktale where a mysterious baby found along the roadside sprouts fangs and turns into a monster. Another variation of this tale took place at an unknown date in Santa Fe yet again. It concerned a man only identified as Mr. Garcia, who went out drinking on Good Friday despite his wife's warnings that he would be cursed for it. As he stumbled home later that night, he saw an apparition of a woman in white. He ran all the way home, and when he arrived, found a mysterious baby in his driveway wrapped in a white blanket. Unfolding it, he found not a baby, but a miniature La Llorona with dark, black eyes and a bony hand pointing at him. He dropped the demonic baby, ran inside, and never took another drink for the rest of his life.

A witch-like La Llorona was sighted in Santa Fe yet again in 1949 by a man on his way home from a screening of *Frankenstein Meets the Wolf Man*. He described this La Llorona as short, only three to four feet tall,[12] and with a wrinkly face sporting a long nose covered in warts. Like all the others, she wailed in a fearsome manner, hence his belief it had been the Wailing Woman. An earlier Santa Fe sighting from the 1920s had also given La Llorona the glowing, cat-like eyes of a witch out on her nightly prowl.

Speaking of witches and shapeshifting, one tale, appropriately from the vicinity of Puerto de Luna, linked La Llorona to a wolf. A man, Ernest Lucero, walking from Puerto de Luna to Santa Rosa, reported hearing a strange, wailing wolf howl as he approached a bridge over the river. As a feeling of dread overcame him, he said the wolf's howl transformed into that of the Wailing Woman. It's worth noting here that, like a skinwalker, in stories from Mexico, La Llorona was also able to mimic the voices of different women, specifically the girlfriends or wives of her intended victims.

Benjamin Radford touched upon La Llorona's shapeshifting abilities in *Mysterious New Mexico: Miracles, Magic, and Monsters in the Land of Enchantment,* where he wrote:

> In the classic witch tradition of familiars, La Llorona is said to be able to change into animals—most often an owl but sometimes a cat, wolf, raven, or coyote. Sometimes an owl seen by a villager in a tree or loft is thought to be La Llorona, who doesn't turn into her human form until she lands on the ground.[13]

Nasario García created a pastiche of La Lorona in his book *Grandma's Santo on Its Head* taking place south of Santa Clara in the Chaco Canyon region. Though admittedly his own creation, presumably the story was crafted from "true" tales of the old-timers. In García's tale, La Llorona took the form of a dog with a human face. Interestingly, it was both black and white, and thusly claimed it was neither good nor bad.[14] This story also cherrypicked the popular folktale of the baby or ragdoll that grabbed onto a horseman with skeletal hands to hitch a ride. In this case, it was La Llorona in dog form, trying to hitch a ride across the river. When the man tossed the dog-creature into the river it then reiterated to him that it was neither good nor bad, and didn't know if one day it would end up in Heaven or Hell when it was done wandering the earth.

One of the best tales to conjoin La Llorona with witch lore came from the Las Vegas region, specifically nearby Trujillo. There, many years ago, lived a teenage boy who loved horses. He desired to have one of his own, but his father told him he would need to become a good horseman first. One day the young man complained of this to a ranch hand he knew. The man told him that to become an excellent horseman, he could sell his soul to the witch, La Llorona, that lived in a cave three miles away. He would have to arrive there at night, as La Llorona slept all day like a vampire, the ranch hand said. As a bruja, La Llorona would know he was coming and be waiting for him at the cave's entrance at nightfall.

Similar to novices who attended the witches' sabbat to gain power, the boy set off for the cave, which he was familiar with but had never had the courage to enter. On the way there, he wondered what selling his soul would entail. Would he have to lie in a coffin? Would he sign a book of some kind? His worries got the best of him, and as he watched the sun set on the cave just ahead, he decided to ride home as quickly as he could. The story ended with a twist, stating that the boy did eventually become a good horseman and was widely recognized for the fact by the time he was seventeen, and it was all due to the fact that he had overcome his fears and visited La Llorona the next night.

A La Llorona story from Prescott, Arizona, printed in *Brujerías: Stories of Witchcraft and the Supernatural in the American Southwest and Beyond*, also pointed out her witchy attributes. The witness in that instance claimed that La Llorona's shadow resembled a hunchbacked witch that cried tears of blood. Also from *Brujerías*, a woman named Rita Leyba Last from Bernalillo said that her brother drowned in a ditch at the age of three, and later they associated balls of light seen jumping from fencepost to fencepost with La Llorona.

Ray John de Aragón related an interesting new development in the lore in his *La Llorona* book. Aragón stated, "A cult has grown in Teotihuacan, Southern Mexico, and Honduras in a half reverence, half idealism of La Llorona."[15] Perhaps quasi-similar to the Santa Muerte movement, Aragon related how a ritual is performed wherein La Llorona's followers try to bring up her spirit by singing a ceremonial song in her honor. The singer is typically a young man who beseeches her to appear before him in the form of her past, beautiful self. The hope is that in seeing her captivating beauty that the revelers will all be "taken by her to live in what they think would be an eternal bliss."[16]

So, is La Llorona really a witch? Ultimately, I would say no. Just as anglos sometimes conflate the Navajo chindi with witchcraft, in reality, a ghost is a ghost and a witch is a witch. They are not the same thing, though the ghosts of witches certainly do turn up to torment the living from time to time, but La Llorona is most likely not one of them. In *Adobe Angels*, Paul Garcia spoke of a ghostly, wailing woman in black who roams a cemetery at Abiquiu. His comment of the specter summed up New Mexican views of La Llorona pretty well: "For lack of a better word to describe her, we all just refer to her as *La Llorona*."[17]

As such, any boogey-woman or female ghost glimpsed in the Land of Enchantment is liable to be labeled as a "La Llorona."

Section Notes

[1] Espinosa, "New-Mexican Spanish Folk-Lore," p.401.

[2] Anaya, *Bless Me, Ultima*, p.23.

[3] Bitto, "The Mysterious Doña Marina, the Most Important Woman in Mexican History," Mexico Unexplained (June 13, 2016) https://mexicounexplained.com/mysterious-dona-marina-important-woman-mexican-history/

[4] It should be noted that among Apache, owls were thought of as harbingers of ghosts and spirits as opposed to witches in animal form. Perhaps this story correlates more closely to that.

[5] Kraul and Beatty, *The Weeping Woman*, p.17.

[6] Tales of La Llorona are so prevalent in Mora, that some call the Mora River La Llorona's Highway. Interestingly, not only was she blamed for missing children in the region, but even missing livestock. One account had her dressed in sheepskin and entering a barn full of livestock. The next day, several animals were mysteriously missing from the barn.

[7] Kraul and Beatty, *The Weeping Woman*, p.17.

[8] Twins, as they are in witchcraft, are yet another interesting facet of the La Llorona myth. La Malinche was herself said to be a twin, and in many instances the other La Lloronas in Malinche's wake sometimes had twin sons, or if not twins, at least a pair of children.

[9] That a baby was found near the railroad crossing dates back to La Llorona folklore from Mexico that stated Cihuacoatl and her cihuateteo haunted the crossroads. Yet another Cihuacoatl myth stated that she was the mother of the god Mixcoatl, who she abandoned at a crossroads. An interesting coincidence to be certain.

[10] Kraul and Beatty, *The Weeping Woman*, p.3.

[11] Ibid.

[12] *The Journal of American Folklore* printed a letter relating an "Aztec Spectre" in the form of "a small female dwarf, whose apparition-at night was a presage of misfortune or death. This spectre is described as having long, loose hair to its waist, and as waddling along like a duck. It also evaded pursuers, and vanished and reappeared unexpectedly..." Perhaps this iteration of La Llorona was inspired by or linked to that specter in some way? [*Journal of American Folklore*, Vol. 12, No. 47 (Oct. - Dec., 1899), p. 295].

[13] Radford, *Mysterious New Mexico*, p.227.

[14] If you'll recall the myth of the Cadejo, there were black and white varieties which were respectively bad and good. Typically black and white always denoted good and evil in the Southwest from the Spanish to the Native American population.

[15] Aragón, *La Llorona*, p.2.

[16] Ibid.

[17] Garcez, *Adobe Angels*, p.48.

AFTERWORD
DO NEW MEXICAN WITCHES REALLY RIDE FIREBALLS?

"New Mexican witches tend to ride fireballs…their most spectacular means of aviation is simply to pop like a flashbulb and streak off in a fireball."
—*Jack Kutz,* Mysteries and Miracles of New Mexico.[1]

Growing up, I thought witches rode broomsticks just like everyone else. Now, obviously, I know different. I was first introduced to the New Mexico variety of witches in Jack Kutz's *Mysteries and Miracles of New Mexico,* first published in 1988. His chapter "New Mexican Witches Ride Fireballs" gave me my first taste of just how different the witches of the Spanish Southwest were, namely in that they rode the aforementioned fireballs. Initially, I just thought it was silly. But, after compiling this book, I find myself wondering if what I once brushed off as pure folklore might contain a few kernels of truth.

Before you get too concerned for my sanity, I don't believe anyone ever rode a flying goat all the way to Colorado. Or that women sat over fires whilst literally removing their limbs to become turkey vampires. But I do believe it's possible that they turned into "fireballs". Why? Too many people have seen them, for one, and continue to see them to this day. Such reports are always brushed off with no real objectivity by skeptics. Equally frustrating is the fact that many believers in the supernatural don't put forth any real effort in trying to figure out the how's and the why's of these strange accounts. To them it's just magic, plain and simple. There is no rhyme or reason as to how a witch takes the form of an animal or fireball; they just do. If anything, skeptics sometimes seem to put more thought into disproving these matters than believers do in trying to understand them.

One of the few researchers I've come across that intelligently questions how the supernatural works is Nasario García, the author of *Brujerías: Stories of Witchcraft and the Supernatural in the American Southwest and Beyond.* García himself saw a spectral figure in his youth and recollected, "This was something real—not a figment of my imagination."[2]

In particular, I enjoyed García's musings on the power of the name Juan/John and its witch-wrangling abilities. "What can be demonstrated beyond question is how, by invoking the magical name of John, a person can bring to earth streaking lights that traverse the skies in the dead of night," García wrote. He continued, "Is it mind over matter, or is it a manifestation of how the religious force with which the name of John is imbued can countermand the occult..."3

In other words, was it the true faith of the Juans in question that enabled them to confront the power of the witches? The New Testament, for instance, has a story of some faithless men in Acts 19 that fail to drive out demons. Though they say the right words, they do so without true belief or conviction, and the demons don't leave. (Not only that, the possessed proceed to beat the men.) Along the same lines, in *Brujerías*, García went on to mention a tale told by Nasario P. García wherein two Juans caught a pair of witches by turning their shirts inside out and placing them within a circle. Of the shirts and the circle, García speculated that they "may be of secondary importance, but it is an indispensable part of the ritual." In other words, the actions, though possibly meaningless, helped the Juans to believe in what they were doing to boost their faith to perform an act that was tangent in some way to an exorcism.

I would have to agree with García that it's not the name Juan itself, but rather the confidence and faith imbued upon the people with the name of Juan that enabled them to catch witches. But, if we are to take such tales at face value, what were the balls of light and how did they work? Though I might be skeptical of the ball of light turning into a flesh and blood human being, could it be that the balls of light were manifestations of witch spirits in flight?

Along those spiritual lines, there is some implication that when one witnesses the balls of light, they are witnessing something in the spiritual realm rather than the physical plane. In *Brujerías*, Marcos C. Durán spoke of driving with his wife and two sons in the car one night. Durán stated that all three pointed to an area excitedly proclaiming to see sparks of light coming from an old shack. When Durán looked, he could see nothing. Some will simply think that mother and sons were playing a joke on him, but Durán had a different take: "...God hasn't given me the ability to see," he told García. "The Lord has not given me permission to witness any of that stuff."4 Or, in other words, his wife and children were witnessing something in the spiritual realm.

Many psychics believe in something called astral projection wherein the "astral body," or spirit, leaves the physical body. In this practice, the astral body is also sometimes referred to as a body of light. In other words, an out of body experience. Christians and other people of faith have had out of body experiences where their spirit left their body for a brief flight before returning. Even people with no real belief in the spirit realm have reported having out of body experiences after succumbing to some near fatal injury. However, in the case of Christians, the out of body experience is thought to have been done by God and not of the person's own will. In the witches' case, if we're to examine such tales as if they actually occurred, it makes sense that a witch was practicing astral projection. As such, could it be that the balls of light seen floating about at night were indeed the witches' spirits in flight? Perhaps that's too much for some of you, but if you ask around, chances are you will find someone who has seen one. Or, if you keep your eyes and heart open, you might see one for yourself some lonely night...

Ultimately, while taking one's shirt off and turning it inside out to catch a witch might just be a silly folk custom, rest assured, things do "go bump in the night." Since my introduction to the witches of New Mexico was the late Jack Kutz, and because I also began this afterword with a quote from Kutz, I will also leave you with one: "[Witches] give us brief glimpses of a shadowy realm that exists somewhere just beyond the limits of our comprehension about the natural world."[5]

Section Notes

[1] Kutz, *Mysteries and Miracles of New Mexico*, p.97.
[2] García, *Brujerías*, p.8.
[3] Ibid, p.81.
[4] Ibid, p.84.
[5] Kutz, *Mysteries and Miracles of New Mexico*, p.103.

BIBLIOGRAPHY

Books

Anaya, Rudolfo. *Bless Me, Ultima.* Toñatiuh International, 1972.

Applegate, Frank G. *Indian Stories from the Pueblos.* Borodino Books (Kindle Edition).

Aragón, Ray John de. *Enchanted Legends and Lore of New Mexico: Witches, Ghosts & Spirits.* The History Press, 2012.

-------------------------- *New Mexico Book of the Undead: Goblin & Ghoul Folklore.* The History Press, 2014.

-------------------------- *New Mexico Native American Lore: Skinwalkers, Kachinas, Spirits and Dark Omens.* The History Press, 2022.

Ball, Eve with Nora Henn and Lynda A. Sanchez. *Indeh: An Apache Odyssey.* University of Oklahoma Press, 1988 (second edition).

Ball, Eve. *In the Days of Victorio: Recollections of a Warm Springs Apache.* University of Arizona Press, 1970.

------------ *Ma'am Jones of the Pecos.* University of Arizona, 1969.

Bandelier, Adolph. *A Visit to the Aboriginal Ruins in the Valley of the Rio Pecos.* Archaeological Institute of America, 1881.

Barker, Ruth Laughlin. "New Mexico Witch Tales." *Tone the Bell Easy.* J. Frank Dobie (ed.) Southern Methodist University Press, 1965.

Basso, Keith H. *Western Apache Witchcraft.* University of Arizona Press, Kindle Edition.

Blue, Martha. *Indian Trader: The Life and Times of J. L. Hubbell.* Kiva Publishing, Inc., 2000.

----------------------*The Witch Purge of 1878.* Navajo Community College Press, 1988.

Bourke, John G. *The Medicine-Men of the Apache: Illustrated Edition.* Madison & Adams Press, Kindle Edition.

Brown, Lorin W. *Hispano Folklife of New Mexico: The Lorin W. Brown Federal Writers' Project Manuscripts.* University of New Mexico Press, 1978.

Bullock, Alice. *Living Legends Of The Santa Fe Country: A Collection Of Southwestern Stories.* Green Mountain Press, 1970.

Campa, Arthur L. *Treasure of the Sangre de Cristos: Tales and Traditions of the Spanish Southwest.* University of Oklahoma, 1963.

Dobie, Frank J. *Coronado's Children: Tales of Lost Mines and Buried Treasure in the Southwest.* University of Texas Press, 1978.

Ebright, Malcolm & Rick Hendricks. *The Witches of Abiquiu: The Governor, the Priest, the Genizaro Indians, and the Devil.* University of New Mexico Press, 2006.

Espinoza, J. Manuel. *The Pueblo Indian Revolt of 1696 and the Franciscan Missions in New Mexico: Letters of the Missionaries and Related Documents.* (English and Spanish Edition)

García, Nasario. *Brujerías: Stories of Witchcraft and the Supernatural in the American Southwest and Beyond.* Texas Tech University Press; 2007.

-------------------- *Tales of Witchcraft and the Supernatural in the Pecos Valley.* Western Edge Press, 1999.

Garcez, Antonio R. *Adobe Angels: Ghost Stories of O'Keefe Country.* Red Rabbit Press, 1998.

-----------------------*New Mexico Ghost Stories Volume I.* Red Rabbit Press, 2018 (Kindle Edition)

Gregg, Josiah. *Commerce of the Prairies.* University of Oklahoma Press, 1958.

Hackett, Charles W. and Charmion C. Shelby. *Revolt of the Pueblo Indians of New Mexico and Otermin's Attempted Reconquest, 1680-1682.* Albuquerque: University of New Mexico Press, 1970.

Hodge, Frederick Webb & Hammond, George P. & Rey, Agapito. *Fray Alonso de Benavides' Revised Memorial of 1634 With Numerous Supplementary Documents Elaborately Annotated.* University of New Mexico Press, 1945.

Horgan, Paul. *Conquistadors in North American History.* Farrar, Straus & Company, 1963.

------------------ *Great River: The Rio Grande in North American History.* Holt, Rinehart and Winston, 1965.

Jameson, W.C. *Legend and Lore of the Guadalupe Mountains.* University of New Mexico Press, 2007.

Jaramillo, Cleofas M. *Shadows of the Past.* Ancient City Press, 1972.

Kluckhohn, Clyde. *Navaho Witchcraft.* Beacon Press, 1963.

Kraul, Edward Garcia and Judith Beatty. *The Weeping Woman: Encounters with La Llorona.* The Word Process, 1988.

Kutz, Jack. *Mysteries and Miracles of New Mexico.* Rhombus Press, 1988.

Lacey, Ann & Anne Valley-Fox (ed.). *Lost Treasures and Old Mines: A New Mexico Federal Writer's Project* Book. Sunstone Press, 2011.

Lange, Charles H. and Carroll L. Riley (Ed.) *The Southwestern Journals of Adolph F. Bandelier 1883-1884 edited and annotated by Charles H. Lange and Carroll L. Riley.* University of New Mexico Press, 1970.

Lummis, Charles. *A New Mexico David: And Other Stories and Sketches of the Southwest.* Charles Scribner's Sons, 1891.

---------------------- *Some Strange Corners of Our Country: The Wonderland of the Southwest.* The Century Co., 1892.

---------------------- *A Tramp Across the Continent.* Charles Scribner's Sons, 1913.

----------------------*Mesa, Cañon and Pueblo: Our Wonderland of the Southwest, Its Marvels of Nature, Its Pageant of the Earth Building, Its Strange Peoples, Its Centuried Romance.* The Century Co., 1925.

Mayor, Adrienne. *Fossil Legends of the First Americans*. Princeton University Press, 2005.

Opler, Morris E. *Apache Odyssey: A Journey between Two Worlds*. Bison Books, 2002.

Pacheco, Allan. *Ghosts—Murder—Mayhem: A Chronicle of Santa Fe*. Sunstone Press, 2004.

Padilla, Jerry A. "Crypto New Mexico." *Cryptozoology and the Investigation of Lesser-Known Mystery Animals*. (Chad Arment, Ed.) Coachwhip Publications, 2006.

Parsons, Elsie C. *The Social Organization of the Tewa of New Mexico*. Kraus, 1974.

Perrone, Bobette and Victoria Krueger & H. Henrietta Stockel. *Medicine Women, Curanderas, and Women Doctors*. University of Oklahoma, 1989.

Ronstadt Milich, Alicia (translator). *Relaciones by Gerónimo Zarate Salmeron*. Horn and Wallace, 1966.

Simmons, Marc. *Witchcraft in the Southwest: Spanish and Indian Supernaturalism on the Rio Grande*. Bison Books; Kindle Edition.

Stanley, F. *The Abo (New Mexico) Story*. By the Author, 1966.

------------ *The Abiquiú (New Mexico) Story*. By the Author, 1969

------------ *The Zia (New Mexico) Story*. By the Author, 1969.

------------ *The Liberty (New Mexico) Story*. By the author, 1972.

Steiger, Brad and Sherry Hansen-Steiger. *Montezuma's Serpent and Other Supernatural Tales of the Southwest*. Paragon House, 1992.

Usner, Don J. & Benigna Ortega Chavez. *Benigna's Chimayó: Cuentos from the Old Plaza*. Museum of New Mexico Press, 2001.

United States Work Projects Administration. Rebolledo, Tey Diana & Maria Teresa Marquez (Ed.). *Women's Tales from the New Mexico WPA: La Diabla a Pie*. Kindle Edition.

Articles

"Aztec Spectre" *The Journal of American Folklore* (Vol. 12, No. 47 Oct. - Dec., 1899)

Alexander, Kathy. "Navajo Skinwalkers – Witches of the Southwest." Legends of America. https://www.legendsofamerica.com/navajo-skinwalkers/

Allison, A. Lynn. "The Navajo Witch Purge Of 1878." *Arizona State University West Literary Magazine* (May 2001). www.west.asu.edu//paloverde-/Paloverde2ooi/Witch, him.

Bandelier, Adolph. "The "'Montezuma' of the Pueblo Indians." *American Anthropologist* (Vol. 5. October 1892).

Beninato, Stefanie. "Popé, Pose-yemu, and Naranjo: A New Look at Leadership in the Pueblo Revolt of 1680." *New Mexico Historical Review* (Vol. 65, #4, 1990). https://digitalrepository.unm.edu/nmhr/vol65/iss4/2

Birmingham Osburn, Katherine Marie. "The Navajo at the Bosque Redondo: Cooperation, Resistance, and Initiative, 1864–1868." *New Mexico Historical Review* (Vol. 60, #4, 1985). https://digitalrepository.unm.edu/nmhr/vol60/iss4/4

Bitto, Robert. "The Mysterious Doña Marina, the Most Important Woman in Mexican History." Mexico Unexplained (June 13, 2016) https://mexicounexplained.com/mysterious-dona-marina-important-woman-mexican-history/

---------------- "The Vampire Witches of Central Mexico." Mexico Unexplained (July 18, 2016) https://mexicounexplained.com/vampire-witches-central-mexico/

Chavez, Fray Angelico. "Pohé-yemo's Representative and the Pueblo Revolt." *New Mexico Historical Review* (Vol. 42, #2, April 1967).

Espinosa, Aurelio M. "New-Mexican Spanish Folk-Lore" *The Journal of American Folklore* Vol. 23, No. 90 (Oct. - Dec., 1910)

Greenleaf, Richard E. "The Inquisition in Eighteenth-Century New Mexico." *New Mexico Historical Review* (Vol. 60, #1, 1985).
https://digitalrepository.unm.edu/nmhr/vol60/iss1/4

Hurt Jr., Wesley R. "Witchcraft in New Mexico." *El Palacio* #47 (1940).

------------------------- "Spanish American Superstitions." *El Palacio* (Vol. 47, #9 September 1940)

Lofton, Monk. "The Devil Never Sleeps" *Old West* (Winter 1972).

Mason, J. Alden. "The Papago Migration Legend." *Journal of American Folklore* (Vol. 34, No. 133, Jul.-Sep., 1921)

Ortega, Dr. Emmanuel. "The Virgin of the Macana and the Pueblo Revolution of 1680." Smarthistory (October 16, 2020).
https://smarthistory.org/virgin-macana/.

Turzillo, Jane Ann. "The witches of Santa Fe," Dark Hearted Women (October 17, 2018) https://darkheartedwomen.wordpress.com/2018/10/17/the-witches-of-santa-fe/

Zumel, Nina. "The Tlahuelpuchi Epidemic." Multo Ghost. (September 10, 2015) https://multoghost.wordpress.com/2015/09/10/the-tlahuelpuchi-epidemic

Documents

"Witchcraft in San Gabriel: Accusations of Sorcery against María de Zamora San Gabriel, New Mexico, 1607." Archivo General de la Nación, Méxicoramo Inquisición, tomo 467, expediente 78-79, fols. 342r-353r.

Batchen, Mrs. Lou Sage. "The Story of La Curandera." 5-5-31WPA New Mexico Collection, Fray Angélico Chávez History Library, Santa Fe, New Mexico, U.S.A.

---------------------------- "Felicia the Bruja," 5-5-31 #2. WPA New Mexico Collection, Fray Angélico Chávez History Library, Santa Fe, New Mexico, U.S.A.

----------------------------- "Doña Tomasa – The Witch Nurse." 5-5-49 #'s 29 to 33. WPA New Mexico Collection, Fray Angélico Chávez History Library, Santa Fe, New Mexico, U.S.A.

Berg, Manuel. "New Mexico Witchcraft: The Magic Ointment," (Museum of New Mexico, FWP Citation 5-31-6)

------------------. "The Flying Brujas." WPA 5-5-60 #1. New Mexico Collection, Fray Angélico Chávez History Library, Santa Fe, New Mexico, U.S.A.

Bright, Lynn. "La Brujas." (Museum of New Mexico, FWP citation, 5-5-7-44ocr.) New Mexico Collection, Fray Angélico Chávez History Library, Santa Fe, New Mexico, U.S.A.

Harpham, Lois Bartlett. "Witches and Witchcraft in the Hispanic Folklore of New Mexico." (Thesis, 1950).
https://digitalrepository.unm.edu/span_etds/65

Martinez, Reyes. "The Witch of Arroyo Hondo." 5-5-60 #8. WPA New Mexico Collection, Fray Angélico Chávez History Library, Santa Fe, New Mexico, U.S.A.

Smith-Kromer, Janet. "Witchcraft in Ranchos de Albuquerque." WPA 5-5-31. New Mexico Collection, Fray Angélico Chávez History Library, Santa Fe, New Mexico, U.S.A.

Thorp, Annette H. "Fabiana – Witch Story." 5-5-52 #69. WPA New Mexico Collection, Fray Angélico Chávez History Library, Santa Fe, New Mexico, U.S.A.

Online Videos

Martinez, Robert. "Brujeria: A History of Witchcraft in New Mexico." (presentation)

Santenello, Peter. "Inside Secret Areas of the Navajo Nation (with the locals)." (Apr 15, 2023) https://www.youtube.com/watch?v=tdl9Rtz_oeo&t=2133s

INDEX

323

ABOUT THE AUTHOR

John LeMay was born and raised in Roswell, NM, the "UFO Capital of the World." He is the author of over 45 books many of them on the history of the Southwest such as *Tall Tales and Half Truths of Billy the Kid*, and *Roswell USA: Towns That Celebrate UFOs, Lake Monsters, Bigfoot and Other Weirdness*. In addition to non-fiction, he is also the author of the novels *The Noted Desperado Pancho Dumez* and *Once Upon a Time in Fort Sumner*. He is also the editor/publisher of *Strange West Magazine* and has written for magazines such as *True West* and *The Coalition Journal*. He is a Past President of the Board of Directors for the Historical Society for Southeast New Mexico and is the co-host of the podcast Plot Pit.

THE BICEP BOOKS CATALOGUE

The following titles are available for purchase on Amazon.com, and are available to bookstores at a wholesale discount via Ingram Content Group (ISBNs of available editions listed for this purpose)

CRYPTOZOOLOGY/COWBOYS & SAURIANS

Cowboys & Saurians: Prehistoric Beasts as Seen by the Pioneers explores dinosaur sightings from the pioneer period via real newspaper reports from the time. Well-known cases like the Tombstone Thunderbird are covered along with more obscure cases like the Crosswicks Monster and more. Softcover (357 pp/5.06" X 7.8") Suggested Retail: $19.95 ISBN: 978-1-7341546-1-0

Cowboys & Saurians: Ice Age zeroes in on snowbound saurians like the Cerato-saurus of the Arctic Circle and a Tyrannosaurus of the Tundra, as well as sightings of Ice Age megafauna like mammoths, glyptodonts, Sarkastodons and Saber-toothed tigers. Tales of a land that time forgot in the Arctic are also covered. Softcover (264 pp/5.06" X 7.8") Suggested Retail: $14.99 ISBN: 978-1-7341546-7-2

Southerners & Saurians takes the series formula of exploring newspaper accounts of monsters in the pioneer period with an eye to the Old South. In addition to dinosaurs are covered Lizardmen, Frogmen, giant leeches and mosquitoes, and the Dingocroc, which might be an alien rather than a prehistoric survivor. Softcover (202 pp/5.06" X 7.8") Suggested Retail: $13.99 ISBN: 978-1-7344730-4-9

Cowboys & Saurians South of the Border explores the saurians of Central and South America, like the Patagonian Plesiosaurus that was really an Iemisch, plus tales of the Neo-Mylodon, a menacing monster from underground called the Minhocao, Glyptodonts, and even Bolivia's three-headed dinosaur! Softcover (412 pp/5.06"X7.8") Suggested Retail: $17.95 ISBN: 978-1-953221-73-5

UFOLOGY/THE REAL COWBOYS & ALIENS IN CONJUNCTION WITH ROSWELL BOOKS

The Real Cowboys and Aliens: Early American UFOs explores UFO sightings in the USA between the years 1800-1864. Stories of encounters sometimes involved famous figures in U.S. history such as Lewis and Clark, and Thomas Jefferson.Hardcover (242pp/6" X 9") Softcover (262 pp/5.06" X 7.8") Suggested Retail: $24.99 (hc)/$15.95(sc) ISBN: 978-1-7341546-8-9\(hc)/978-1-7344 730-8-7(sc)

The second entry in the series, *Old West UFOs*, covers reports spanning the years 1865-1895. Includes tales of Men in Black, Reptilians, Spring-Heeled Jack, Sasquatch from space, and other alien beings, in addition to the UFOs and airships. Hardcover (276 pp/6" X 9") Softcover (308 pp/5.06" X 7.8") Suggested Retail: $29.95 (hc)/$17.95(sc) ISBN: 978-1-7344730-0-1 (hc)/ 978-1-73447 30-2-5 (sc)

The third entry in the series, *The Coming of the Airships*, encompasses a short time frame with an incredibly high concentration of airship sightings between 1896-1899. The famous Aurora, Texas, UFO crash of 1897 is covered in depth along with many others. Hardcover (196 pp/6" X 9") Softcover (222 pp/5.06" X 7.8") Suggested Retail: $24.99 (hc)/$15.95(sc) ISBN: 978-1-7347816 -1-8 (hc)/978-1-7347816-0-1(sc)

Featuring cases the authors missed, *The Lost Cases* covers things such as the skyquakes recorded by Lewis and Clark, airships and the Spanish American War, Pancho Villa and crystal skulls, lost alien tribe of the Tundra, invisible alien monsters, the Great Moon Hoax of 1835, hellhounds and airships, the Sonora Airship Club and more. Softcover (252 pp/5.06" X 7.8") Suggested Retail: $18.99 ISBN: 978-1-953221-55-1

326

BICEP BOOKS HISTORY

COWBOYS & SAURIANS CONT'D

Cowboys & Saurians: Dinosaurs Down Under takes the series to Australia to explore tales of the cattle devouring Burrunjor, the dreaded Diprotodon, the terrible Tantanoola Tiger, the marsupial Sasquatch known as the Yowie, plus Thylacines, Bunyips, giant rabbits, Megalodons and dinosaurs in nearby New Zealand. Softcover (240 pp/ 5.06" X 7.8") Suggested Retail: $14.95 ISBN: 978-1-953221-34-6

As the title suggest, *Cowboys & Saurians in the Modern Era* takes the series into the 20th Century with tales of the Texas Pterosaur flap of 1976, the Bladenboro Beast of the 1950s, the Busco Turtle Beast of the 1940s, dinosaur sightings in the Great Depression and far out tales of mini-mastodons, dinosaur men, and Snallygasters. Softcover (320 pp/ 5.06" X 7.8") Suggested Retail: $19.95 ISBN: 978-1-953221-22-3

Settlers & Serpents wrangles the best "Snaik Stories" of the Southwest and beyond in a single volume. Whether it's simple giant snakes or lake serpents, they're corralled in the pages within. Also included are entries on the Leviathan in Mesoamerica and the Southwest plus a detailed look at the giant rattlesnake of Pecos Pueblo. Softcover (180 pp/ 5.06" X 7.8") Suggested Retail: $14.99 ISBN: 978-1-953221-21-6

Written for young readers ages 9-12, *Monsters of the Old South* collects the best creature stories of the swamplands including the White River Monster, Green Eyes, the Crocodingo, the Averasboro Gallinipper, the Tennessee Snake Woman, the Arkansas Gowrow, Bigfoot in the Mississippi River and more. Softcover (122 pp/4.25" X 7") Suggested Retail: $12.99 ISBN: 978-17347816-9-4

THE REAL COWBOYS & ALIENS CONT'D

Early 20th Century UFOs kicks off a new series that investigates UFO sightings of the early 1900s. Includes tales of UFOs sighted over the *Titanic* as it sunk, Nikola Tesla receiving messages from the stars, an alien being found encased in ice, and a possible virus from outer space!Hardcover (196 pp/6" X 9") Softcover (222 pp/5.06" X 7.8") Suggested Retail: $27.99 (hc)/$16.95(sc) ISBN: 978-1-7347816-1-8 (hc)/978-1-73478 16-0-1(sc)

UFOs in the Roaring Twenties takes a look at UFO sightings in the 1920s just as the title suggests, along with accounts of Mothman in Nebraska, Lincoln LaPaz's first UFO case, Men in Black investigating an airship crash in Braxton County, West Virginia, Camden's Cosmic Sniper, and much more! Softcover (248 pp/5.06" X 7.8") Suggested Retail: $19.99 ISBN: 978-1-953221-51-3

UFOs of the Turbulent Thirties concludes the authors' investigation of the last unexplored decade of Ufology in the Great Depression with accounts of Mothman, Ghost Fliers, Nazi Bells, the Underground City of the Lizard People, a vanished village on the tundra, and even gangsters and aliens. Softcover (212 pp/5.06" X 7.8") Suggested Retail: $17.95 ISBN: 978-1-953221-35-3

Written for young readers ages 9-12, *Space Monsters of the Old West* collects the best alien sightings of the Wild West including Mummies from Mars, Bigfoot from the Moon, Pascagoula's space ghouls, the Crawfordsville Monster, Spring-Heeled Jack, Blobs from space, and even the dinosaurian alien creatures that invaded Van Meter, Iowa. Softcover (120 pp/4.25" X 7") Suggested Retail: $12.99 ISBN: 978-1-953221-87-2

327

BICEP BOOKS HISTORY

COWBOYS & MONSTERS

Cowboys & Monsters features potentially true stories of real vampires, werewolves, and even mummies unique to America's Wild West period. Examples include the cursed mummy of John Wilkes Booth, New Orleans immortal vampire Jacques St. Germain, precursors to the Beast of Bray Road, and the origins of Skinwalker Ranch. Softcover (316 pp/5.06" X 7.8") Suggested Retail: $19.99 ISBN: 978-1-953221-46-9

The first entry in this trilogy of non-fiction terror sinks its teeth into the lore of the vampire in North America and Mexico, with detailed rundowns on the vampire hunters of Exeter, Rhode Island, a tribe of Bat People, the nocturnal shape-shifting vampire witches of Tlaxcala, the immortal ways of Comte St. Germain in New Orleans and more. Softcover (200 pp/ 5.06" X 7.8") Suggested Retail: $12.99 ISBN: 978-1-953221-38-4

Mummies of the Americas explores Death Valley's city of the Dead, King Tut's Tomb along the Arkansas, the Egyptian City of the Grand Canyon plus the famous mummies of John Wilkes Boothe, Elmer McCurdy, the Cardiff Giant, the Mummy of Helldorado, and even Billy the Kid's pickled trigger finger! Softcover (200 pp/5.06" X 7.8") Suggested Retail: $12.99 ISBN: 978-1-953221-37-7

Cowboys & Dogmen is devoted to tales of werewolves of the Wild West including the dreaded Navajo skinwalker, the Watrous Werewolf, the Beast of the Land Between Lakes, the Hellhounds of El Dorado Canyon, the dreaded Dog Eater, the Wahhoo, the Wolf Man of Versailles, the Michigan Dog-Man and more! Softcover (212 pp/5.06" X 7.8") Suggested Retail: $12.99 ISBN: 978-1-953221-36-0

FICTION/ MISC. HISTORY

The first novel from historian John LeMay weaves a fantastic web of fiction via real life mysteries and legends of New Mexico, namely the puzzling theft and return of Billy the Kid's tombstone in 1976, the legend of the Lost Adams Diggings, the villainous Santa Fe Ring, and the enigmatic Acoma Mesa. Softcover (250 pp/5.5" X 7.5") Suggested Retail: $14.95 ISBN: 978-1-953221-42-1

The year is 1950, and old timers connected to the long-dead outlaw Billy the Kid are turning up murdered in New Mexico. Some blame the killings on the avenging witch of the Navajo nation, the skinwalker, while others think it's no coincidence that a man claiming to be a surviving Billy the Kid is set to meet with the governor soon... Softcover (260 pp/5.5" X 7.5") Suggested Retail: $16.95 ISBN: 978-1-953221-32-2

Roswell, USA, the long-forgotten debut work of John LeMay, is available again and covers the minutia of the infamous Roswell UFO Crash of 1947. Notable chapters include tales of an alien ghost haunting the old airbase, monsters in the nearby Bottomless Lakes, and even a dinosaur sighting outside of town. Softcover (248 pp/6" X 9") Suggested Retail: $14.95 ISBN: 978-0-9817597-5-3

This biography, for the first time ever, tells the history of western journalist Ash Upson, who ghostwrote Pat Garrett's The Authentic Life of Billy the Kid in 1882 and also reproduces many of Upson's letters that detailed the harsh realities of frontier life in New Mexico during the turbulent Lincoln County War. Softcover (318 pp/5.5" X 8.5") Suggested Retail: $16.99 ISBN: 978-1953221919

328

STRANGE WEST Magazine

322

OFFICIAL SUPPLEMENT TO THE
21 GUNS SERIES
ISSUE #1 FALL 2022

The Tombstone Thunderbird: New Evidence?

PUCK

THIS ISSUE:
Ambrose Bierce Disappears into Devil's Cave in Ojinaga!

PLUS: Albert J. Fountain's Lost Gold ...and the Bones of a Monster?

Fantastic Weird FWP: Jack the Ripper Goes West?

The Mummy of Helldorado!

Twenty-six years ago, outlaw Billy the Kid's tombstone was stolen from Fort Sumner, New Mexico. Now it has mysteriously been returned. When teenage brothers Pancho and Dorado Dumez steal it themselves, they get more than they bargained for. Encased inside the tombstone is a map that leads to the Southwest's greatest treasure: The Lost Adams Diggings—a canyon comprised of solid gold. But the brothers aren't the only ones on the treasure's trail. So is bounty hunter Seven McCaw, and along with him comes a modern-day incarnation of the Santa Fe Ring—a secretive organization that once ruled the West. Forced onto the open roads of New Mexico, the brothers must solve the mystery of Billy the Kid's death and find the lost canyon before the Ring does...

330

JOHN LEMAY

(II)
ONCE UPON A TIME AT FORT SUMNER
1950

The year is 1950, and old timers connected to the outlaw Billy the Kid are popping up dead in the sleepy town of Fort Sumner, New Mexico. It's up to the local sheriff, Hondo Dumez, to figure out why. Matters become complicated upon the news that a man claiming to be a surviving Billy the Kid is about to meet with the current governor of New Mexico. Added to the mystery are whispers of a secretive organization known as the Santa Fe Ring and rumors of something called a Skinwalker haunting the area. As the case twists and turns its way from the haunted halls of Dorsey Mansion to the ice caves of the Malpais, Dumez won't just need all the help he can get to solve the greatest mystery of the Southwest, he'll be lucky to survive the investigation at all.

331

332